BRITISH LITERATURE THE NINETEENTH CENTURY

CONTENTS

I. **THE ROMANTIC ERA** 1

   INTRODUCTION 1
   - William Blake 5
   - William Wordsworth 9
   - Samuel Taylor Coleridge 14
   - Sir Walter Scott 26

II. **THE LATE ROMANTIC ERA** 40
   - Jane Austen 40
   - Charles Lamb 47
   - George Gordon–Lord Byron 52
   - Percy Bysshe Shelley 58
   - John Keats 63

III. **THE VICTORIAN ERA** 71

   INTRODUCTION 71
   - Thomas Carlyle 75
   - John Henry Cardinal Newman 80
   - Alfred, Lord Tennyson 84
   - Charles John Huffman Dickens 90
   - Robert Browning 100
   - George Eliot (Mary Ann Evans) 103
   - Oscar Wilde 109
   - Lewis Carroll (Charles Lutwidge Dodgson) 118

Author: Krista L. White, B.S.
Editor: Alan Christopherson, M.S.
Graphic Design: Alpha Omega Staff

804 N. 2nd Ave. E., Rock Rapids, IA 51246-1759
© MM by Alpha Omega Publications, Inc. All rights reserved.
LIFEPAC is a registered trademark of Alpha Omega Publications, Inc.

BRITISH LITERATURE LIFEPAC 4
THE NINETEENTH CENTURY (1798–1900)

OBJECTIVES:

When you have completed this LIFEPAC®, you should be able to:

1. Gain an overview of the events of the French Revolution in relation to England.
2. Discern the roots of rebellion against traditional religion and politics.
3. Understand the religious beliefs of the Romantic and Victorian writers in relation to Christianity.
4. Identify the effects of industrialism, evolution, higher criticism, and traditionalism on Victorian culture.
5. Discern England's need for political and economic reform in the nineteenth century.
6. Gain an appreciation for the works of Romantic and Victorian writers.

VOCABULARY:

aestheticism - nineteenth-century literary movement that taught that art was useful for teaching morality
higher criticism - a method of studying the Bible that seeks to determine the historical authenticity of the text
manifesto - a written public declaration of motives, intentions, and beliefs
mysticism - the belief that knowledge of God is gained by means of visions and/or intuition
nostalgia - a desire for the things and events of the past
notoriety - the state of being well known, usually unfavorably
sordid - morally debased or corrupt
transcendentalism - a philosophy that emphasizes the spiritual as the ultimate reality
upheaval - radical change; disorder

I. THE ROMANTIC ERA
INTRODUCTION

The Romantic Period (1798–1832). The "liberalism in literature" that distinguished the Romantic period was a natural result of the political and economic revolutions of the time. Inspired by the radical individualism and nationalism of the American and French revolutions, writers and artists reacted, in some cases violently, to the religious, social, and political restraints of the Neoclassic Age. The economic and social upheavals caused by the Industrial Revolution also affected shifts in concerns and modes of expression.

Jean-Jaques Rosseau

A Time of Dereliction and Dismay. England has always been influenced by trends in European thought and culture. During the Neoclassical Period, this influence was manifested in the glorification of man's intellectual and moral abilities during an era known as the Enlightenment. The Enlightenment was founded on the philosophical assertions of several men, prominent among whom was the French philosopher Rene Descartes (1596–1650). With his famous axiom, "*Cogito ergo sum* (I think, therefore I am)," Descartes offered the world a new foundation for truth: human reason. The Englishman John Locke (1632–1704) advanced the notion by advocating that government and society should be established on the natural law as interpreted by reason. Locke's theories were extremely influential in the forming of the U.S. Constitution. In his political treatise *The Social Contract*, the French philosopher Jean-Jacques Rousseau (1712–1778) took the Enlightenment's concept of the supremacy of human reason to its logical end. In political circles, he argued that the authority of the state must be based upon the will of the people and not upon divine appointment. Rousseau believed that people were born innocent and free. Misery and bondage were a result of oppressive institutions. This notion of society's problems naturally led to a standard of morality based solely on the will of the people. The basis of society, therefore, should be a social pact between men. God was no longer acknowledged as the ultimate lawgiver. Enlightenment thinkers placed man at the center of both state and religion.

Rousseau's radical ideas about the basis of church and state were profoundly influential during the French Revolution. His work encouraged individualism and nationalism. Desiring to rid France of its class-bound society, he pointed the people to the ancient Roman model of a republic. Strong leaders in government were the keys to a society free of corruption. However, the political turmoil, wars, and economic depressions that followed the French Revolution were less than ideal. Indeed, the time was, as William Wordsworth deemed it, a period of "dereliction and dismay."

The revolution in France began as an intellectual revolt against the French monarchy. Rationalist thinkers such as Voltaire, Montesquieu, and Quesnay objected to the absolute authority of the crown. Its incompetence and extravagance had laden France with debt. The feudal system, still in effect, prevented the country from further economic progress.

In 1788 Louis XVI was forced to call a session of the Estates General. The Estates General, originally a legislative body of feudal lords, changed its role and presented the king with a constitution that was based on the revolutionary slogan "liberty, equality, fraternity." The constitution called for a reduction of the king's authority and power and an eradication of the state church. At first, Louis complied with the revolutionaries but then refused. The attempt to establish a constitutional monarchy failed, and a group of revolutionaries took control of the country. The king and his family were executed, and a republic was established.

Influenced by the romanticism of Rousseau, many liberal Englishmen supported the revolution enthusiastically. However, the Reign of Terror effected by the revolutionary French government that followed confused many sympathizers. Rousseau's ideas were used to violently enforce compliance with the Revolution's ideas and principles. With the consent of France's National Convention, Robespierre dragged to the guillotine thousands of people who would not worship at the cult of the Supreme Being and wholeheartedly espouse the overthrow of all monarchal systems. As one historian has observed, the French Revolution had run the cycle of rebellion, radicalism, and reaction and eventually ended in the dictatorship of Napoleon Bonaparte.

As "child and champion of the French Revolution," Napoleon carried out the ambitions of previous leaders to spread French power and influence with renewed vigor. His military campaigns to conquer Italy and the Netherlands, as well as those to recover lost regions in the New World, were met with fierce opposition. As France's most hated enemy, England proved to be its greatest rival on land and sea. After failing to conquer Moscow in 1812, all of Europe opposed Napoleon. In 1815 he was finally defeated at the Battle of Waterloo.

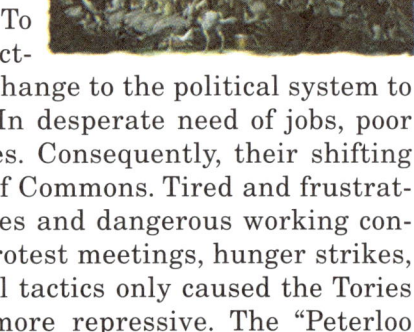

After the end of the Napoleonic wars, many of the English expected to enjoy a period of peace. The threat of atheism and moral anarchy had been defeated. However, with the return of many soldiers to the work force and an overabundance of supplies, economic depression set in. To aggravate the problem further, political restraints enacted during the French Revolution prevented necessary change to the political system to accommodate the rapidly changing social conditions. In desperate need of jobs, poor families moved into the cities to work in the factories. Consequently, their shifting numbers were not properly represented in the House of Commons. Tired and frustrated with lack of governmental protection from low wages and dangerous working conditions, workers sought to effect reform by means of protest meetings, hunger strikes, signed petitions, and even riots. However, their radical tactics only caused the Tories in government to enact measures that were even more repressive. The "Peterloo Massacre," in which an assembly of workers was violently suppressed by British troops at St. Peter's Fields, inspired many writers to support the plight of the working poor.

Religion in Revolutionary Times. Although the writings of the Romantics did much to fan the flames of revolution in England, a violent **upheaval*** never took place there. Many people believe that the spread of Methodism quelled the spirit of revolution in England. The revival meetings of John Wesley and George Whitefield took place mainly among the lower classes, those who were most affected by the economic depression that followed the Napoleonic wars. Transformed by the power of the Word, they were unwilling to enact a "systematic rebellion against the God of revelation" as their French counterparts had. They understood that the basis of society rested ultimately upon the Law of the Old Testament. Although doubts about the inspiration of Scripture began to arise among the intellectual elite in the form of **higher criticism**,* the lower classes generally trusted the Bible as God's Word to them. They believed in the miracles of Jesus and, most importantly, in His resurrection. The natural religion of Coleridge and Wordsworth was not popular among such people.

Although the doctrines of the French Revolution did not effect an overthrow of the British government, a revolution of heart and mind did begin to occur in the late eighteenth and early nineteenth centuries. Unlike the French, the British did not call into question the center of religion and state: God. Instead, they questioned their own sensibilities. Did the way they viewed life need to be changed? One of the most important changes in English society was the abolition of the slave trade in 1807. Evangelicals were largely responsible for not only this feat, but also other humane reform measures passed by Parliament. As one prominent historian has noted, "the liberty of England and of America is permeated with the breath of the Puritans," quite dissimilar to the liberty of France, which was *anti-Christian* to the core.

"The Revolution is a unique event," Groen Van Prinsterer once wrote. "It is a revolution of beliefs; it is the emergence of a new sect, of a new religion; of a religion which is nothing but irreligion itself, atheism, the hatred of Christianity raised into a system." Those in England who were attracted to the tenets of the "new religion" rejected traditional Christianity and embraced **transcendentalism**,* a mystical religion that focused on the human spirit's relationship to Nature. God was everywhere and in everything. Like those who rejected the teachings of Scripture, the transcendentalists believed that a true knowledge of God came in the form of visions. Although charged with enthusiasm for the "spiritual," the transcendentalists lacked any kind of moral structure. The feelings of the Romantics often led them to live morally corrupt lives.

Rebellion and Reaction in Literature. As a literary movement, Romanticism began in France and Germany and moved westward to England and North America. In England, Romanticism was inaugurated by the publication of William Wordsworth and Samuel Taylor Coleridge's *Lyrical Ballads* in 1798 and ended with the Reform Bill in 1832. Wordsworth's *The Preface,* added to the second edition of *Lyrical Ballads* (1800), is considered the **manifesto*** of English Romanticism. In the *The Preface,* Wordsworth affirmed the importance of the emotions and the imagination to the creative process, disclaiming the need for order and precision. The literature of the Romantic period in England is characterized by individualism, **mysticism**,* emotionalism, love of nature, **nostalgia**,* and a fascination with the medieval past.

Intellectually, the Romantic Movement was grounded in the Enlightenment. The writings of French philosopher Rousseau inspired not only a revolution of state but also a revolution of literary style. The German writer Johann Wolfgang von Goethe added to Rousseau's concept of the freedom of the human spirit by exalting personal sentiment. This emphasis on the emotions and individual experience expressed a violent turn from the strict social and religious conventions of the Neoclassical Age.

The first generation of English romantic poets includes Wordsworth, Coleridge, and William Blake. Their works are influenced by transcendental thought, showing a concern for nature and its mystical relationship to man. Their works also demonstrate a radical break with traditional forms and styles. Emphasizing content over form, they asserted the self, wrote in blank verse, and used rural language and characters. Their sympathies for the Revolution caused them to focus on the life of the "common man." Many poets saw themselves as prophets during a time of crisis who were able to bring about a golden age of peace by reforming society by means of the imagination.

The second generation of English romantic poets includes Percy Shelley, Lord Byron, and John Keats. As one critic has noted, they "wrote swiftly, traveled widely (Greece, Switzerland, and Italy), and died prematurely; their life-stories and letters became almost as important for Romanticism as their poetry." Their revolutionary ideals were manifested in heroes who were flawed yet functioned outside of reality. Exiled for their aberrant behavior and radical political beliefs, their works demonstrate an increased interest in exotic cultures and religions of the medieval and oriental past. Disillusioned with the results of freedom from "oppressive" structures of morality, their mood is often melancholy.

Although poetry demonstrated most profoundly the revolutionary shift in style and content, the prose of the day was no less remarkable. Mary Shelley's *Frankenstein* reflects the development of the Gothic novel and the fascination with strange and unnatural events. Another female novelist, Jane Austen, wrote in a progressively conversational style but did not follow the romantic vein in matters of content. Nevertheless, her novels about the manners and customs of her society are considered to be some of the greatest in English literature. The novels of Sir Walter Scott are also less concerned with the economic and political revolutions of the time. Consistent with the romantic fascination with the medieval past, Scott wrote highly imaginative novels based loosely on the history of Scotland, France, and England.

The familiar essay, with its easy-to-read style and nostalgic content, became increasingly popular during the nineteenth century. To accommodate the tastes of the reading public, many reviews and magazines were founded, including the *Edinburgh Review* (1802), the *Quarterly Review* (1809), and the *London Magazine* (1820).

With the increase in readership, talented writers such as William Hazlitt were able to make a living solely from their essays. Others, like Lamb, worked a normal job and used the earnings from their writing to supplement their income.

⇒ **Answer *true* or *false* for each of the following statements.**

1.1 __T__ The Enlightenment glorified the intellectual and moral abilities of man.

1.2 __F__ Rousseau's Enlightenment philosophy of the basis of church and state was profoundly influential during the English Reformation.

1.3 __T__ The revolutionary constitution of the Estates General sought to reduce the king's authority and power and eradicate the state church.

1.4 _____ Robespierre's Reign of Terror violently enforced compliance with the Revolution's ideas and principles.

1.5 __T__ Despite the Reign of Terror, liberal-minded Englishmen continued to support the Revolutionary government.

1.6 _____ The French Revolution resulted in a free democracy.

1.7 _____ After the Napoleonic wars, England experienced an economic boom and social tranquility.

1.8 _____ The spread of transcendentalism quelled the spirit of revolution in England.

1.9 _____ Evangelicals were largely responsible for the abolition of the slave trade in 1807.

1.10 _____ Evangelicalism is a mystical religion that focuses on the human spirit's relationship to Nature.

1.11 _____ The Romantic period in England was inaugurated by the publication of Wordsworth and Coleridge's *Lyrical Ballads* in 1798.

1.12 _____ The literature of the Romantic period in England is characterized by individualism, mysticism, emotionalism, love of nature, nostalgia, and a fascination with the medieval past.

1.13 _____ Intellectually, the Romantic Movement was grounded in the Renaissance.

1.14 _____ Many Romantic poets believed that a golden age of peace could be brought about by reforming society by means of the imagination.

1.15 _____ In his *The Preface* to *Lyrical Ballads*, Wordsworth affirmed the importance of reason, precision, and order.

1.16 _____ The first generation of Romantic poets exalted the cause of the "common man" by writing in blank verse and rural language.

1.17 _____ The second generation of Romantic poets demonstrated an increased interest in exotic cultures and religions of the medieval and oriental past.

1.18 _____ The increasing popularity of the novel led to the founding of many magazines and reviews.

THE ROMANTIC ERA

William Blake (1757–1827). William Blake was a mystical visionary. His art and literature imbued the revolutionary spirit of the age, rebelling against neoclassical styles and modes of thought by emphasizing imagination over reason.

Born the son of a London hosier, Blake was apprenticed for seven years (1730–1802) to James Basire, a well-known engraver. Blake read widely but received no formal education, except for his studies in art at the Royal Academy of the Arts. In 1782 at the age of twenty-four, Blake married Catherine Boucher who was illiterate. Blake taught her to read and to assist him in his print shop. The couple remained childless.

Blake began writing poetry at the age of twelve. His first volume of poetry, *Poetical Sketches*, was printed in 1783. The early poems were traditional in style and content. In 1789 Blake self-published and illustrated *Songs of Innocence* followed by its companion volume, *Songs of Experience,* in 1794. The poems revealed Blake's growing mysticism. He believed that there were "two contrary states of the human soul," Innocence and Experience. Representative poems from each volume, such as "The Lamb" and "The Tyger," demonstrate Blake's contrast.

Although Blake claimed that "all he knew was in the Bible," his understanding of the fall of man, the mode of redemption, the apocalypse, and the cause of societal problems was far from biblical. As a young man, he had come to embrace the teachings of the Swedish mystic Emanuel Swedenborg (1688–1772), whose writings were becoming popular among an obscure number of Englishmen. Blake believed that the Scriptures should be interpreted symbolically, thus allowing for great liberality with the text but leading to gross errors in theology. Blake believed that the Fall was not caused by man's rebellion against a holy God but was a result of spiritual disintegration, which could be redeemed only through a process of imaginative or spiritual understanding of the world. The poet acted as a prophet, revealing a secret knowledge of reality not readily perceived in Scripture or Nature. Blake's claims to possessing a hidden knowledge of God were similar to the false teachers at Ephesus whom Paul criticized in 1 Timothy 6:20.

Blake's development of his personal mythology and its prophetic vision of the momentous world events of the period can be seen in his series of Prophetic Books: *The Book of Thel* (1789), *The French Revolution* (1791), *America, a Prophecy* (1793), *Visions of the Daughters of Albion* (1793), *The Book of Unrizen* (1794), and *Europe: a Prophecy* (1794).

In 1800 Blake was forced to shut down his printing business and move to the seacoast of Felpham, where he was offered the patronage of William Hayley. But, Hayley was not sympathetic to Blake's radical moral and **aesthetic*** ideas. Rejecting Hayley's designs to shape him into a conventional illustrator, Blake exclaimed, he "is the Enemy of my Spiritual Life while he pretends to be the Friend of my Corporeal."

Nurturing his mystical beliefs, Blake went on to record more of his "spiritual insights." In 1800 he rewrote and published *The Four Zoas*, in which he claimed that "an improvement of sensual enjoyment" would effect our redemption. Blake completed *Milton* and *Jerusalem* in 1808 and 1820, respectively. The series—which also included the satirical prose work, *The Marriage of Heaven and Hell* (1790–93)—was Blake's conscious decision to "Create a System or be enslaved by another man's." Blake rejoiced in the revolutions of the time, hoping that the violent upheavals of state and church would bring about a period of peace and tranquility similar to that prophesied in the Bible.

In 1803 Blake and his wife returned to London. Using his artistic skills, he eked out a meager living as an illustrator of such works as the book of Job, John Milton's *Paradise Lost,* and John Bunyan's *Pilgrim's Progress.* Until his death, Blake continued to write but received little appreciation for his work. Although he was a talented and original poet, his contemporaries generally considered him to be mad, and they disregarded him for years. However, in the morally rebellious age of the 1920s, Blake's work was enthusiastically rediscovered by scholars and poets.

Underline the correct answer in each of the following statements.

1.19 As a young man, Blake was apprenticed to a(n) (hosier, engraver, clergyman).

1.20 Blake's first poems were (revolutionary, traditional, radical) in style and content.

1.21 The companion volumes *Songs of Innocence* and *Songs of Experience* reveal Blake's growing (mysticism, rationalism, traditionalism).

1.22 As a follower of the Swedish mystic Emanuel Swedenborg, Blake believed that the Scriptures should be interpreted (literally, in context, symbolically).

1.23 Believing himself to be a prophet, Blake wrote a series of prophetic (books, sermons, tracts) explaining his interpretative visions of the momentous world events of the period.

1.24 Blake believed that the upheavals of state and church would bring about a period of peace and tranquility similar to that prophesied in (Scripture, Greek mythology, Celtic religion).

1.25 A skilled artist, Blake made a living as a(n) (sculptor, illustrator, poet).

1.26 During his lifetime, Blake was generally considered to be (a genius, insane, underappreciated).

What to Look For:

Mystical religions emphasize the soul's need for a direct, intimate union with God. This union is achieved through visions and feelings of love. Consequently, Scripture is not looked to as God's complete and final revelation to man. It is interpreted symbolically as to allow for hidden meanings known only to a few.

As you read the following selected poems, consider the results of Blake's mystically guided thought. Are his visions of reality in line with Scripture? Are there "two contrary states of the human soul?" When someone chooses to interpret the Bible symbolically, who ends up being the ultimate authority—God or man? According to 2 Timothy 3:16, why is it important to test our belief and behavior by the Word of God?

From: *Songs of Innocence* and *Songs of Experience*

In 1795, Blake added to his *Songs of Innocence* a contrary set of poems. The combination was published under the title *Songs of Innocence and Experience: Shewing the Contrary States of the Human Soul.* The poems of "innocence" are written from a child's perspective; the poems of "experience" grant the reader a vision of the same reality as colored by adult experience.

Introduction to Songs of Innocence

Piping down the valleys wild,
Piping songs of pleasant glee,
On a cloud I saw a child,
And he laughing said to me,

'Pipe a song about a Lamb!'
So I piped with merry cheer.
'Piper, pipe that song again!'
So I piped. He wept to hear.

'Drop thy pipe, thy happy pipe;
Sing thy songs of happy cheer.'
So I sung the same again
While he wept with joy to hear.

'Piper, sit thee down and write
In a book that all may read.'
So he vanished from my sight,
And I plucked a hollow reed,

And I made a rural pen,
And I stained the water clear,
And I wrote my happy songs
Every child may joy to hear.

The Lamb

  Little Lamb, who made thee?
  Dost thou know who made thee?
Gave thee life and bid thee feed,
By the stream and o'er the mead;
Gave thee clothing of delight,
Softest clothing, wooly, bright;
Gave thee such a tender voice,
Making all the vales rejoice!
  Little Lamb, who made thee?
  Dost thou know who made thee?

  Little Lamb, I'll tell thee,
  Little Lamb, I'll tell thee!
He is called by thy name,
For he calls himself a Lamb;
He is meek and he is mild;
He became a little child.
I a child and thou a lamb;
We are called by his name.
  Little Lamb, God bless thee
  Little Lamb, God bless thee

Introduction to Songs of Experience

Hear the voice of the Bard! [1]
Who Present, Past, and Future sees;
Whose ears have heard
The Holy Word
That walk'd among the ancient trees; [2]

Calling the lapsed Soul
And weeping in the evening dew,
That might control
The starry pole,
And fallen, fallen light renew!

"O Earth, O Earth, return!
Arise from out the dewy grass;
Night is worn,
And the morn
Rises from the slumberous mass.

"Turn away no more;
Why wilt thou turn away?
The starry floor
The watry shore
Is giv'n thee till the break of day."

[1] *Bard - a poet-prophet who is endowed with mystical powers*
[2] *an allusion to the garden of Eden*

The Tyger

Tyger! Tyger! burning bright
In the forests of the night,
What immortal hand or eye
Could frame thy fearful symmetry?

In what distant deeps or skies
Burnt the fire of thine eyes?
On what wings dare he aspire?
What the hand dare seize the fire?

And what shoulder, and what art,
Could twist the sinews of thy heart?
And when thy heart began to beat,
What dread hand? and what dread feet?

What the hammer? what the chain?
In what furnace was thy brain?
What the anvil? what dread grasp
Dare its deadly terrors clasp?

When the stars threw down their spears
And water'd heaven with their tears,
Did he smile his work to see?
Did he who made the Lamb make thee?

Tyger! Tyger! burning bright
In the forests of the night,
What immortal hand or eye
Dare frame thy fearful symmetry?

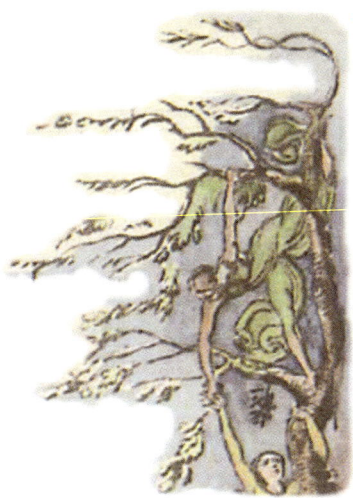

The Garden of Love

I went to the Garden of Love,
And saw what I never had seen:
A chapel was built in the midst,
Where I used to play on the green.

And the gates of this chapel were shut,
And "Thou shalt not" writ over the door;
So I turn'd to the Garden of Love,
That so many sweet flowers bore;

And I saw it was filled with graves,
And tombstones where flowers should be;
And Priests in black gowns were walking their rounds,
And binding with briars my joys and desires.

Fill in each of the following blanks with the correct explanation or answer.

1.27 Describe the "two contrary states of the human soul" as understood by Blake.
The two contrary states as understood by Blake are innocence and experience

1.28 In the introduction to *Songs of Innocence*, Blake states that he is writing what kind of songs?
Songs of pleasant glee.

1.29 In *Songs of Innocence*, about whom is Blake "piping" a song?
About a Lamb.

1.30 Who is the stated writer of "The Lamb?"
_____

1.31 Who and what does the Lamb symbolize?
Jesus Christ.

1.32 In the introduction to *Songs of Experience*, to whom is the reader told to listen for spiritual guidance?
The Bard.

1.33 What does the Tyger symbolize?
Man.

1.34 What question is asked of the Tyger that is also asked of the Lamb?
Who made thee?

1.35 In the companion poems "The Lamb" and "The Tyger," how does Blake answer the age-old question, "If God is good and all powerful, then why does evil exist?"
_____

1.36 In "The Garden of Love," what has been built that prohibits his "play?"
A chapel.

1.37 What institution of society does the chapel symbolize?
Christianity.

1.38 Who is binding the poet's "joys and desires?"
Priests.

1.39 In light of "The Garden of Love," what do you think Blake thought about codified morality and religion?

~~~~~ That it prevented true happiness.

William Wordsworth (1770–1850). The greatest of the Romantic poets, William Wordsworth inaugurated a tradition of poetry that was inspired by the political, religious, and social tenets of the French Revolution.

Wordsworth was born in Cockermouth in Cumbria. As a boy, he attended Hawkeshead Grammar School and later St. John's College, Cambridge. During the summer of 1790, just before taking his degree, Wordsworth and a friend traveled on foot through France and over the Alps. The French at that time were celebrating the first anniversary of the storming of the Bastille. Wordsworth at once became interested in the revolution of ideas. After graduating from Cambridge, he returned to France in 1791 and embraced wholeheartedly the ideals of the French Revolution. Unfortunately, Wordsworth, like many others, abused the new freedoms. No longer legally compelled to follow the doctrines of a state-sanctioned church, Wordsworth had an affair with Annette Vallon. When Annette gave birth to their daughter, Wordsworth abandoned her. He returned to England unable to support himself or a family.

In 1793 England entered into war with France. The atrocities of the Reign of Terror and the aggressive military campaigns could not be ignored. Disillusioned by the war and the results of the Revolution, Wordsworth became "sick, wearied out with contraries." In the same year, Wordsworth published two poems, *An Evening Walk* and *Descriptive Sketches*. The works were written in the orderly style of the past age and yielded Wordsworth little worldly advancement.

After a friend died in 1795, Wordsworth received a legacy of £900 a year. He moved with his sister Dorothy to Racedown in Dorset and began to pursue a career as a poet. Dorothy's involvement in Wordsworth's life was integral to his success as a poet. She served as a confidant and an encourager. Two years later, Wordsworth moved to Alfoxden in Somerset to be near Samuel Taylor Coleridge. The two men met and worked together almost every day. In 1798 they published the monumental volume *Lyrical Ballads, with a Few Other Poems*. Anticipating the negative reaction that their new style of poetry would cause, they published the work anonymously. Although critics derided it as a work of the revolution, subversive to Christian morals and traditional social standards, *Lyrical Ballads* sold out in two years. In 1800, Wordsworth republished the work, adding to it a second volume of poems and *The Preface*, which has served as the manifesto of Romanticism.

In 1798 Wordsworth and his sister followed Coleridge to Germany but soon returned to England and to the region of their childhood, the Lake District of England. Coleridge rejoined his friends, moving to Keswick, just thirteen miles from the Grasmere, where Wordsworth lived. In 1802 Wordsworth received his father's inheritance and traveled to France to settle his financial obligations to Annette Vallon. He married Mary Hutchinson, a childhood friend, soon after he returned.

Wordsworth's appointment as Stamp Distributor for Westmoreland in 1813 marked a change in his status and reputation. A middle-aged man with the experience of many of life's sufferings, he had become increasingly conservative in politics and religion. His broken relationship with Coleridge and his sister's declining health were particularly sobering.

The year 1807 saw the last of Wordsworth's great works, *Poems in Two Volumes*. He continued to write until his death, publishing *The Excursion* (1814), *The White Doe of*

Rylestone (1815), *Miscellaneous Poems* (1815), and *The Waggoner* (1819), but the "sponteousness overflow of emotion" that had marked his earlier works was gone.

In 1843 Wordsworth was appointed poet laureate. The event marked a softened attitude among the English toward unorthodox religious beliefs and liberal politics. Wordsworth's autobiographical poem, *The Prelude,* was published posthumously in 1850. Considered his greatest work, it demonstrates his lasting affect on the direction of English poetry. As one critic has noted, the concept of the human soul's dependence upon nature for harmony and peace emphasized within Victorian and modern literature is partially a result of Wordsworth's revolutionary work and ideals.

Fill in each of the following blanks with the correct answer.

1.40 After graduating from _Cambridge_, Wordsworth returned to France and embraced the ideals of the _French_ Revolution.

1.41 In 1797 Wordsworth moved with his _sister_ to Alfoxden in Somerset to be near _Samuel Taylor Coleridge_.

1.42 Wordsworth collaborated with Coleridge on _Lyrical Ballads_.

1.43 Wordsworth's Preface to *Lyrical Ballads* is considered the manifesto of _Romanticism_.

1.44 In 1799 William and Dorothy moved to the _Lake District_ of England.

1.45 Published in 1807, _Poems in Two Volumes_ was the last of Wordsworth's great works.

1.46 In 1843 Wordsworth was appointed _poet laureate_.

1.47 Published posthumously in 1850, _The Prelude_ demonstrates Wordsworth's lasting affect on the direction of English poetry.

1.48 The concept of the human soul's dependence upon _nature_ for harmony and peace emphasized within _Victorian_ and modern literature is partially a result of Wordsworth's revolutionary work and ideals.

What to Look For:

Wordsworth viewed himself as a poet-prophet. With his poetry, he intended to overturn traditional concepts of religion and literary practice. As you read, notice his revolutionary thought. Why does Wordsworth point to Nature as *the* moral guide? How does this concept relate to his idea that the emotions and the imagination are superior to reason in the creative process?

From The Preface to *Lyrical Ballads*, 1802

The principal object, then, which I proposed to myself in these poems
was to choose incidents and situations from common life, and to relate
or describe them, throughout, as far as was possible, in a selection of
language really used by men; and, at the same time, to throw over them
5 a certain colouring of imagination, whereby ordinary things should be
presented to the mind in an unusual way; 'and, further, and above all,
to make these incidents and situations interesting by tracing in them,
truly though not ostentatiously, the primary laws of our nature: chiefly,
as far as regards the manner in which we associate ideas in a state of
10 excitement. Low and rustic life was generally chosen, because in that
condition, the essential passions of the heart find a better soil in which

they can attain their maturity, are less under restraint, and speak a plainer and more emphatic language; because in that condition of life our elementary feelings coexist in a state of greater simplicity, and, consequently, may be more accurately contemplated, and more forcibly communicated; because the manners of rural life germinates from those elementary feelings; and, from the necessary character of rural occupations, are more easily comprehended; and are more durable; and lastly, because in that condition the passions of men are incorporated with the beautiful and permanent forms of nature. The language, too, of these men is adopted (purified indeed from what appear to be its real defects, from all lasting and rational causes of dislike or disgust) because such men hourly communicate with the best objects from which the best part of language is originally derived; and because, from their rank in society and the sameness and narrow circle of their intercourse, being less under the influence of social vanity they convey their feelings and notions in simple and unelaborated expressions. Accordingly, such a language, arising out of repeated experience and regular feelings, is a more permanent and a far more philosophical language, than that which is frequently substituted for it by poets, who think that they are conferring honour upon themselves and their art, in proportion as they separate themselves from the sympathies of men, and indulge in arbitrary and capricious habits of expression, in order to furnish food for fickle tastes, and fickle appetites, of their own creation.

    I cannot, however, be insensible of the present outcry against the triviality and meanness both of thought and language, which some of my contemporaries have occasionally introduced into their metrical compositions; and I acknowledge that this defect, where it exists, is more dishonourable to the writer's own character than false refinement or arbitrary innovation, though I should contend at the same time that it is far less pernicious in the sum of its consequences. From such verses the poems in these volumes will be found distinguished at least by one mark of difference, that each of them has a worthy *purpose*. Not that I mean to say, that I always began to write with a distinct purpose formally conceived; but I believe that my habits of meditation have so formed my feelings, as that my descriptions of such objects as strongly excite those feelings, will be found to carry along with them a *purpose*. If in this opinion I am mistaken, I can have little right to the name of a poet. For all good poetry is the spontaneous overflow of powerful feelings: but though this be true, poems to which any value can be attached, were never produced on any variety of subjects but by a man, who being possessed of more than usual organic, sensibility, had also thought long and deeply. For our continued influxes of feelings are modified and directed by our thoughts, which are indeed the representatives of all our past feelings; and, as by contemplating the relation of these general representatives to each other we discover what is really important to men, so, by the repetition and continuance of this act, our feelings will be connected with important subjects, till at length, if we be originally possessed by much sensibility, such habits of mind will be produced, that, by obeying blindly and mechanically the impulses of those habits, we shall describe objects, and utter sentiments, of such a nature and in such connection with each other, that the understanding of the being to whom we address ourselves, if he be in a healthful state of association, must necessarily be in some degree enlightened, and his affections ameliorated.

 I have said that poetry is the spontaneous overflow of powerful feelings: it takes its origin from emotion recollected in tranquillity: the emotion is contemplated till by a species of reaction the tranquillity gradually disappears, and an emotion, kindred to that which was before the subject of contemplation, is gradually produced, and does itself actually exist in the mind. In this mood successful composition generally begins, and in a mood similar to this it is carried on; but the emotion, of whatever kind and in whatever degree, from various causes is qualified by various pleasures, so that in describing any passions whatsoever, which are voluntarily described, the mind will upon the whole be in a state of enjoyment. Now, if nature be thus cautious in preserving in a state of enjoyment a being thus employed, the poet ought to profit by the lesson thus held forth to him, and ought especially to take care, that whatever passions he communicates to his reader, those passions, if his reader's mind be sound and vigorous, should always be accompanied with an overbalance of pleasure. Now the music of harmonious metrical language, the sense of difficulty overcome, and the blind association of pleasure which has been previously received from works of rhyme or metre of the same or similar construction, an indistinct perception perpetually renewed of language closely resembling that of real life, and yet, in the circumstance of metre, differing from it so widely, all these imperceptibly make up a complex feeling of delight, which is of the most important use in tempering the painful feeling which will always be found intermingled with powerful descriptions of the deeper passions. This effect is always produced in pathetic and impassioned poetry; while, in lighter compositions, the ease and gracefulness with which the poet manages his numbers are themselves confessedly a principal source of the gratification of the reader. I might perhaps include all which it is *necessary* to say upon this subject by affirming, what few persons will deny, that, of two descriptions, either of passions, manners, or characters, each of them equally well executed, the one in prose and the other in verse, the verse will be read a hundred times where the prose is read once.

From Lyrical Ballads, 1798
The Tables Turned

Up! up! my Friend, and quit your books,* *allusion to traditional forms of education*
Or surely you'll grow double.
Up! up! my Friend, and clear your looks;
Why all this toil and trouble?

The sun, above the mountain's head,
A freshening luster mellow
Through all the long green fields has spread,
His first sweet evening yellow.

Books! 'tis a dull and endless strife.
Come, hear the woodland linnet,*
How sweet his music! on my life,
There's more of wisdom in it.

linnet-finch

throstle-thrush

And hark! how blithe the throstle* sings!
He, too, is no mean preacher.
Come forth into the light of things;
Let Nature be your teacher.

She has a world of ready wealth,
Our minds and hearts to bless—
Spontaneous wisdom breathed by health,
Truth breathed by cheerfulness.

One impulse from a vernal wood
May teach you more of man,
Of moral evil and of good,
Than all the sages* can.

teachers, both religious and secular

Sweet is the lore which Nature brings;
Our meddling intellect
Misshapes the beauteous forms of things:—
We murder to dissect.

Enough of science and of art;
Close up those barren leaves;
Come forth, and bring with you a heart
That watches and receives.

My Heart Leaps Up

The rainbow was traditionally regarded as a sign of God's covenant of redemption. In this poem, Wordsworth offers an alternate view of the rainbow. He sees it as simply a natural phenomenon. Wordsworth does not glorify God as its Creator or as the Covenant maker. Instead, he finds religious meaning in the "emotion recollected in tranquillity."

My Heart Leaps Up

My heart leaps up when I behold
    A rainbow in the sky;
So was it when my life began,
So is it now I am a man,
So be it when I shall grow old
    Or let me die!
The child is father of the man;
And I could wish my days to be
Bound each to each by natural piety.

Fill in each of the following blanks with the correct explanation or answer.

1.49 According to the Preface to *Lyrical Ballads,* how should the Romantic poet present ordinary things?

___

1.50 Why is the "low and rustic life" chosen to relate the poet's ideas and feelings?

___

1.51 How does Wordsworth describe "good poetry?"

___

1.52 According to Wordsworth, what is the origin of good poetry?

___

1.53 How are books, or rather traditional forms of education, described in "The Tables Turned?"

___

1.54 In "The Tables Turned," what does the poet claim is man's best moral teacher?

___

1.55 According to the last two stanzas of "The Tables Turned," describe what the intellect or reason do to "things."

___

1.56 In" My Heart Leaps Up," what is the poet's emotional response to the rainbow?

___

1.57 How does the poet's religious idea of the rainbow contradict Scripture?

___

Samuel Taylor Coleridge (1772–1834). Poet, literary critic, philosopher, and friend of Wordsworth, Samuel Taylor Coleridge was one of the most influential leaders of English Romanticism.

The youngest son of an Anglican clergyman, Coleridge was a precocious child who proved to be a successful student at Christ's Hospital, a charitable grammar school in London. Coleridge's dreamy yet eloquent talk drew many supporters to his side even as a child. Among the life-long friends that he made at Christ's Hospital were Charles Lamb and Leigh Hunt.

In 1791 Coleridge entered Jesus College, Cambridge. But his attention to his studies soon waned. The momentous political events of the French Revolution and their social and religious implications redirected his interests and passions. After succumbing to the temptations of drink and enduring a failed love affair, he left Cambridge and, using an assumed name enlisted in the Light Dragoons. Coleridge's brothers eventually retrieved him from his desperate attempt to make it as a cavalryman and brought him back to Cambridge. Although Coleridge left college in 1794 without taking a degree, he became knowledgeable in the radical religious and political ideas of the day. He rejected the hierarchical systems of Anglicanism and the monarchy for the more democratic Unitarianism and the republican state.

After leaving Cambridge, Coleridge met Robert Southey, an Oxford student and poet. The two men formulated a plan to start a settlement in America based on the social and political ideals of the French Revolution. Coleridge named the democratic experiment a pantisocracy, signifying that it would be ruled by equals. To secure the venture's success for posterity, the twelve men involved needed to take wives. As part of the plan, Coleridge agreed to marry the sister of Southey's fiancée, Sara Fricker. Although the pantisocracy never came to fruition, Coleridge, at Southey's insistence, went ahead with the marriage. After only a few years, Coleridge left the care and responsibility of his wife and children with Southey.

By 1796 Coleridge, burdened with physical and mental illness, was addicted to opium. Despite his various afflictions, Coleridge preached in the Unitarian Church and wrote poetry. Not long after publishing *Poems on Various Subjects* (1796), he met Wordsworth and his sister, Dorothy, at Racedown. So impressed was he with the now recognized Wordsworth that he proclaimed him to be "the best poet of the age," encouraging Wordsworth to espouse the tenets of transcendentalism in his poetry. The two men enjoyed an enduring friendship that was manifested in the publication of the revolutionary work *Lyrical Ballads* in 1798. Blessed with Wordsworth's intimate friendship and the benevolence of the Wedgwood heirs, Coleridge produced some of his greatest works from 1797–1798, among those being *The Rime of the Ancient Mariner* and *Kubla Khan*.

Fearful of being accused as French sympathizers, Coleridge and Wordsworth traveled to Germany in 1798. Coleridge pursued his mystical beliefs, which first became evident in his unfinished poem "Christabel." He studied the idealism of the German philosopher Immanuel Kant and the mystical writings of Jakob Boehme at the University of Göttingen. It was the beginning of a life-long study of German Romanticism. Coleridge is generally credited with the importation of transcendentalism into England.

In the spring of 1799, Coleridge, Wordsworth, and Dorothy returned to the Lake District. Coleridge moved into Greta Hall, Keswick, not far from Wordsworth. Unwilling to reconcile his relationship with his wife, Coleridge fell in love with Sara Hutchinson, sister to Wordsworth's future wife, Mary. In 1808 Coleridge was legally separated from his wife.

Disillusioned with his transcendental beliefs, Coleridge turned increasingly to opium to alleviate his guilt and pain. But the drug's euphoric effects only secured his destruction. He began to record daily his dreams, writing, and life in his *Notebooks*. In 1802 he lamented his failing creative abilities in "Dejection: an Ode." Hoping to renew his health, Coleridge moved to the Mediterranean island of Malta and served as the Secretary to the Governor. However, he returned to England in worse health, crippled by his opium addiction.

After giving a series of lectures on literature and philosophy in London, Coleridge began writing for newspapers and, with Sara Hutchinson, founded a weekly journal, *The Friend*. In 1808 he published *Shakespearian Criticism*. Later, he traveled to Vienna to give another series of lectures on Shakespeare. Coleridge's writing and lectures encouraged a renewed interest in the Elizabethan playwright.

In 1810 Coleridge discovered that Wordsworth had some reservations about him residing in his home. An argument ensued, and the two friends remained unreconciled for several decades. The loss threw Coleridge into a deep depression for many years. At times, he contemplated suicide. Not until he totally abandoned his aberrant religious beliefs and returned to Anglicanism did he find emotional relief. However, Coleridge continued to read and study the works of Kant. Hoping to synthesize modern philosophy with Christianity, he interpreted the Scriptures symbolically. In 1816 Dr. James Gillman and his wife took Coleridge into their home in Highgate. The couple helped him to control his addiction to opium and heal his relationship with Wordsworth.

In 1817 he published his major prose work, *Biographia Literaria*. The work outlines the purposes of romantic poetry and establishes Coleridge as the father of a new tradition of literary criticism. As a modern thinker, Coleridge reverses the traditional emphasis of poetry, which is first to teach and then to delight, by focusing on its ability to evoke pleasure in the reader. Truth and reason, he taught, are secondary to emotion and imagination.

Before the end of his life in 1834, Coleridge published many other notable works, among which were a collection of poems titled *Sibylline Leaves* (1817, 1828, 1834); a religious and philosophical treaty, *Aids to Reflection* (1825); and a cultural essay, *On the Constitution of Church and State* (1830).

When Coleridge died of heart failure, many of his fellows sorely lamented the loss. Wordsworth declared that Coleridge was "the most *wonderful* man that I have ever known." A record of his "inspired conversations" was published posthumously in 1836 with the title *Table Talk* (1836).

Circle the letter of the line that best answers each of the following questions.

1.58 While at Cambridge, Coleridge embraced which religious and political ideals?

    a. American Revolution

    b. English Reformation

    c. Tory party

    d. French Revolution

1.59 After meeting Wordsworth at Racedown, Coleridge encouraged him to espouse which religion in his poetry?

    a. Transcendentalism

    b. Unitarianism

    c. Christianity

    d. Anglicanism

1.60 Coleridge's friendship with Wordsworth was manifested in the publication of which revolutionary collection of poems?

    a. *Kubla Khan*

    b. *The Rime of the Ancient Mariner*

    c. *Lyrical Ballads*

    d. *Biographia Literaria*

1.61 In 1798 Coleridge traveled with William and Dorothy Wordsworth to Germany where he studied which subject?

    a. the extra biblical writings of Paul and Timothy

    b. the mystical writings of Jakob Boehme and the idealism of Immanuel Kant

    c. the mystical writings of William Blake and the Christianity of Martin Luther

    d. the Trinitarian writings of the ancient Christian philosopher St. Athanasius

1.62 Coleridge's literary criticism and lectures in London and Vienna encouraged a renewed interest in which playwright?

    a. John Milton

    b. Christopher Marlowe

    c. William Shakespeare

    d. Ben Jonson

1.63 Coleridge's argument with whom threw him into a severe depression for many years?

    a. his sister

    b. his wife

    c. Robert Southey

    d. Wordsworth

1.64   In 1816 Dr. James Gillman and his wife took Coleridge into their home to help him cope with his addiction to which drug?

a. cocaine
b. alcohol
c. opium
d. sleeping pills

1.65   The publication of *Biographia Literaria* in 1817 established Coleridge's reputation as what?

a. the father of the modern novel
b. the father of a new tradition of literary criticism
c. England's poet laureate
d. the father of a new tradition of poetry

1.66   How did Coleridge's literary criticism reverse the traditional emphasis of poetry?

a. It focused on poetry's ability to evoke pleasure in the reader.
b. It placed emotion and imagination second to truth and reason.
c. It emphasized poetry's ability to teach truth and morals.
d. It de-emphasized the imagination.

1.67   After abandoning transcendentalism, Coleridge returned to the faith of his father, which was what?

a. Roman Catholicism
b. Anglicanism
c. Dutch Reformed
d. Baptist

What to Look For:

St. Augustine once wrote, "Thou has made us for Thyself, and our hearts are restless until they find their rest in Thee." Coleridge sought rest in many things. But his addiction to opium, adulterous affairs, transcendental beliefs, and mystical visions could not give him peace. The guilt and pain that he incurred from his sin haunted him. As you read the following selection, notice the effects of guilt that are evident in *The Rime of the Ancient Mariner*. As a transcendentalist, how does Coleridge attempt to solve these problems?

The Rime of the Ancient Mariner

This poem is a tale of a sailor who kills a friendly albatross for no reason. The sailor, now old, insists on telling his story to a passer-by who is enroute to a wedding. The sailor tells him the circumstances and results of the senseless act. Conceived with the help of Wordsworth, the poem contains both transcendental and Christian elements. The transcendental belief in the journey from disunity to unity is joined with the Christian steps toward restoration: sin, guilt, and repentance. However, because no mention is made of Christ's effective work on the cross, the poem cannot be read as a testimony to the Christian faith. Coleridge is acknowledging, if anything, the temporary emotional benefits of confession. The lasting spiritual need for repentance and faith in Christ is not addressed.

ARGUMENT

How a Ship having passed the Line was driven by storms to the cold Country towards the South Pole, and how from thence she made her course to the tropical Latitude of the Great Pacific Ocean, and of the strange things that befell; and in what manner the Ancient Mariner came back to his own Country.

PART ONE

[An ancient Mariner meeteth three gallants bidden to a wedding-feast, and detaineth one.]

    It is an ancient Mariner,
    And he stoppeth one of three.

    "By thy long grey beard and glittering eye,
    Now wherefore stopp'st thou me?

    "The bridegroom's doors are opened wide,
    And I am next of kin;
    The guests are met, the feast is set:
    May'st hear the merry din.'

    He holds him with his skinny hand,
10 "There was a ship," quoth he.
    "Hold off! unhand me, grey-beard loon!"
    Eftsoons his hand dropt he.

[The Wedding-Guest is spell-bound by the eye of the old seafaring man and constrained to hear his tale.]

    He holds him with his glittering eye—
    The Wedding-Guest stood still,
    And listens like a three years' child.
    The Mariner hath his will.

    The Wedding-Guest sat on a stone:
    He cannot choose but hear;
    And thus spake on that ancient man,
20 The bright-eyed Mariner.
    "The ship was cheered, the harbour cleared,
    Merrily did we drop
    Below the kirk, below the hill,
    Below the lighthouse top.

[The Mariner tells how the ship sailed southward with a good wind and fair weather, till it reached the Line.]

    "The Sun came up upon the left,
    Out of the sea came he!
    And he shone bright, and on the right
    Went down into the sea.

    "Higher and higher every day,
30 Till over the mast at noon—"
    The Wedding-Guest here beat his breast,
    For he heard the loud bassoon.

[The Wedding-Guest heareth the bridal music; but the Mariner continueth his tale.]

    The bride hath paced into the hall,
    Red as a rose is she;
    Nodding their heads before her goes
    The merry minstrelsy.

    The Wedding-Guest he beat his breast,
    Yet he cannot choose but hear;
    And thus spake on that ancient man,
40 The bright-eyed Mariner.

    "And now the storm-blast came, and he
    Was tyrannous and strong:
    He struck with his o'ertaking wings,
    And chased us south along.

    "With sloping masts and dipping prow,
    As who pursued with yell and blow
    Still treads the shadow of his foe,
    And forward bends his head,
    The ship drove fast, loud roared the blast,
50 And southward aye we fled.

    "And now there came both mist and snow,
    And it grew wondrous cold:
    And ice, mast-high, came floating by,
    As green as emerald.

[The land of ice, and of fearful sounds where no living thing was to be seen.]

    "And through the drifts the snowy clifts
    Did send a dismal sheen:
    Nor shapes of men nor beasts we ken—
    The ice was all between.

    "The ice was here, the ice was there,
60 The ice was all around:
    It cracked and growled, and roared and howled,
    Like noises in a swound!

[Till a great sea-bird, called the albatross, came through the snow-fog, and was received with great joy and hospitality.]

    "At length did cross an albatross,
    Through the fog it came;
    As if it had been a Christian soul,
    We hailed it in God's name.

    "It ate the food it ne'er had eat,
    And round and round it flew.
    The ice did split with a thunder-fit;
70 The helmsman steered us through!

[And lo ! the albatross proveth a bird of good omen, and followeth the ship as it returned northward through fog and floating ice.]

    "And a good south wind sprung up behind;
    The albatross did follow,
    And every day, for food or play,
    Came to the mariners' hollo!

"In mist or cloud, on mast or shroud,
It perched for vespers nine;
Whiles all the night, through fog-smoke white,
Glimmered the white moon-shine."

[The ancient Mariner inhospitably killeth the pious bird of good omen.]

"God save thee, ancient Mariner!
80 From the fiends, that plague thee thus!—
Why look'st thou so?"— "With my cross-bow
I shot the albatross."

PART TWO

"The Sun now rose upon the right:
Out of the sea came he,
Still hid in mist, and on the left
Went down into the sea.

"And the good south wind still blew behind,
But no sweet bird did follow,
Nor any day for food or play
90 Came to the mariners' hollo!

[His shipmates cry out against the ancient Mariner, for killing the bird of good luck.]

"And I had done a hellish thing,
And it would work 'em woe:
For all averred, I had killed the bird
That made the breeze to blow.
Ah, wretch! said they, the bird to slay,
That made the breeze to blow!

[But when the fog cleared off, they justify the same, and thus make themselves accomplices in the crime.]

"Nor dim nor red, like God's own head,
The glorious Sun uprist:
Then all averred, I had killed the bird
100 That brought the fog and mist.
'Twas right, said they, such birds to slay,
That bring the fog and mist.

"The fair breeze blew, the white foam flew,
The furrow followed free;
We were the first that ever burst
Into that silent sea.

[The ship hath been suddenly becalmed.]

"Down dropt the breeze, the sails dropt down,
'Twas sad as sad could be;
And we did speak only to break
101 The silence of the sea!

"All in a hot and copper sky,
The bloody sun, at noon,
Right up above the mast did stand,
No bigger than the moon.

"Day after day, day after day,
We stuck, nor breath nor motion;
As idle as a painted ship
Upon a painted ocean.

[And the albatross begins to be avenged.]

110 "Water, water, everywhere,
And all the boards did shrink;
Water, water, every where,
Nor any drop to drink.

"The very deep did rot: O Christ!*
That ever this should be!
Yea, slimy things did crawl with legs
Upon the slimy sea.

"About, about, in reel and rout
The death-fires danced at night;
120 The water, like a witch's oils,
Burnt green, and blue and white.

[A Spirit had followed them; one of the invisible inhabitants of this planet, neither departed souls nor angels; concerning whom the learned Jew, Josephus, and the Platonic Constantinopolitan, Michael Psellus, may be consulted. They are very numerous, and there is no climate or element without one or more.]

"And some in dreams assurèd were
Of the Spirit that plagued us so;
Nine fathom deep he had followed us
From the land of mist and snow.

"And every tongue, through utter drought,
Was withered at the root;
We could not speak, no more than if
We had been choked with soot.

[The shipmates, in their sore distress, would fain throw the whole guilt on the ancient Mariner: in sign whereof they hang the dead sea bird round his neck.]

130 "Ah! well-a-day! what evil looks
Had I from old and young!
Instead of the cross, the albatross*
About my neck was hung."

(*a cry to God, not an expression of vanity)

PART THREE

"There passed a weary time. Each throat
Was parched, and glazed each eye.
A weary time! a weary time!
How glazed each weary eye,
When looking westward, I beheld
A something in the sky.

[The ancient Mariner beholdeth a sign in the element afar off.]

140 "At first it seemed a little speck,
   And then it seemed a mist;
   It moved and moved, and took at last
   A certain shape, I wist.*

   "A speck, a mist, a shape, I wist!
   And still it neared and neared:
   As if it dodged a water-sprite,
   It plunged and tacked and veered.

[At its nearer approach, it seemeth him to be a ship; and at a dear ransom he freeth his speech from the bonds of thirst.]

   "With throats unslaked, with black lips baked,
   We could nor laugh nor wail;
150 Through utter drought all dumb we stood!
   I bit my arm, I sucked the blood,
   And cried, A sail! a sail!

[A flash of joy;]

   "With throats unslaked, with black lips baked,
   Agape they heard me call:
   Gramercy!* they for joy did grin,
   And all at once their breath drew in,
   As they were drinking all.

[And horror follows. For can it be a ship that comes onward without wind or tide?]

   "See! see! (I cried) she tacks no more!
   Hither to work us weal—
160 Without a breeze, without a tide,
   She steadies with upright keel!

   "The western wave was all aflame,
   The day was well nigh done!
   Almost upon the western wave
   Rested the broad bright sun;
   When that strange shape drove suddenly
   Betwixt us and the sun.

[It seemeth him but the skeleton of a ship.]

   "And straight the sun was flecked with bars,
   (Heaven's Mother send us grace!)
170 As if through a dungeon-grate he peered
   With broad and burning face.

   "Alas! (thought I, and my heart beat loud)
   How fast she nears and nears!
   Are those her sails that glance in the sun,
   Like restless gossameres?

[And its ribs are seen as bars on the face of the setting Sun. The spectre-woman and her death-mate, and no other on board the skeleton ship.]

(*wist-knew)

(*gramercy-great mercy)

   "Are those her ribs through which the sun
   Did peer, as through a grate?
   And is that woman all her crew?
   Is that a Death? and are there two?
180 Is Death that woman's mate?

[Like vessel, like crew!]

   "Her lips were red, her looks were free,
   Her locks were yellow as gold:
   Her skin was as white as leprosy,
   The night-mare Life-in-Death was she,
   Who thicks man's blood with cold.

[Death and Life-in-Death have diced for the ship's crew, and she (the latter) winneth the ancient Mariner]

   "The naked hulk alongside came,
   And the twain were casting dice;
   'The game is done! I've won! I've won!'
   Quoth she, and whistles thrice.

[No twilight within the courts of the sun.]

190 "The sun's rim dips; the stars rush out:
   At one stride comes the dark;
   With far-heard whisper, o'er the sea,
   Off shot the spectre-bark.

[At the rising of the moon,]

   "We listened and looked sideways up!
   Fear at my heart, as at a cup,
   My life-blood seemed to sip!
   The stars were dim, and thick the night,
   The steersman's face by his lamp gleamed white;
   From the sails the dew did drip—
200 Till clomb above the eastern bar
   The hornéd Moon, with one bright star
   Within the nether tip.

[One after another,]

   "One after one, by the star-dogged moon,
   Too quick for groan or sigh,
   Each turned his face with a ghastly pang,
   And cursed me with his eye.

[His shipmates drop down dead.]

   "Four times fifty living men,
   (And I heard nor sigh nor groan)
   With heavy thump, a lifeless lump,
210 They dropped down one by one.

[But Life-in-Death begins her work on the ancient Mariner.]

   "The souls did from their bodies fly—
   They fled to bliss or woe!
   And every soul, it passed me by,
   Like the whizz of my cross-bow!"

PART FOUR

[The Wedding-Guest feareth that a Spirit is talking to him;]

>"I fear thee, ancient Mariner!
>I fear thy skinny hand!
>And thou art long, and lank, and brown,
>As is the ribbed sea-sand.

>"I fear thee and thy glittering eye,
220 And thy skinny hand, so brown."—
>Fear not, fear not, thou Wedding-Guest!
>This body dropt not down.

[But the ancient Mariner assureth him of his bodily life, and proceedeth to relate his horrible penance.]

>"Alone, alone, all, all alone,
>Alone on a wide, wide sea!
>And never a saint took pity on
>My soul in agony.

[He despiseth the creatures of the calm.]

>"The many men, so beautiful!
>And they all dead did lie:
>And a thousand thousand slimy things
230 Lived on; and so did I.

[And envieth that they should live, and so many lie dead.]

>"I looked upon the rotting sea,
>And drew my eyes away
>I looked upon the rotting deck,
>And there the dead men lay

>"I looked to Heaven, and tried to pray;
>But or ever a prayer had gusht,
>A wicked whisper came, and made
>My heart as dry as dust.

>"I closed my lids, and kept them close,
240 And the balls like pulses beat;
>For the sky and the sea, and the sea and the sky
>Lay like a load on my weary eye,
>And the dead were at my feet.

[But the curse liveth for him in the eye of the dead men.]

>"The cold sweat melted from their limbs,
>Nor rot nor reek did they:
>The look with which they looked on me
>Had never passed away.

>"An orphan's curse would drag to hell
>A spirit from on high;
250 But oh! more horrible than that
>Is the curse in a dead man's eye!
>Seven days, seven nights, I saw that curse,
>And yet I could not die.

[In his loneliness and fixedness he yearneth towards the journeying moon, and the stars that still sojourn, yet still move onward; and everywhere the blue sky belongs to them, and is their appointed rest, and their native country and their own natural homes, which they enter unannounced, as lords that are certainly expected, and yet there is a silent joy at their arrival.]

>"The moving moon went up the sky,
>And nowhere did abide:
>Softly she was going up,
>And a star or two beside—

>"Her beams bemocked the sultry main,
>Like April hoar-frost spread;
>But where the ship's huge shadow lay,
>The charméd water burnt alway
>A still and awful red.

[By the light of the moon he beholdeth God's creatures of the great calm.]

260 "Beyond the shadow of the ship,
>I watched the water-snakes:
>They moved in tracks of shining white,
>And when they reared, the elfish light
>Fell off in hoary flakes.

>"Within the shadow of the ship
>I watched their rich attire:
>Blue, glossy green, and velvet black,
>Then coiled and swam; and every track
>Was a flash of golden fire.

[Their beauty and their happiness.]

[He blesseth them in his heart.]

270 "O happy living things! no tongue
>Their beauty might declare:
>A spring of love gushed from my heart,
>And I blessed them unaware;
>Sure my kind saint took pity on me,
>And I blessed them unaware.

[The spell begins to break.]

>"The self-same moment I could pray;
>And from my neck so free
>The albatross fell off, and sank
>Like lead into the sea."

PART FIVE

280 "O sleep! it is a gentle thing,
　　Beloved from pole to pole!
　　To Mary Queen the praise be given!
　　She sent the gentle sleep from heaven,
　　That slid into my soul.

[By grace of the holy Mother, the ancient Mariner is refreshed with rain.]

　　"The silly buckets on the deck,
　　That had so long remained,
　　I dreamt that they were filled with dew;
　　And when I awoke, it rained.

　　"My lips were wet, my throat was cold,
290 My garments all were dank;
　　Sure I had drunken in my dreams,
　　And still my body drank.

　　"I moved, and could not feel my limbs:
　　I was so light—almost
　　I thought that I had died in sleep,
　　And was a blessèd ghost.

[He heareth sounds and seeth strange sights and commotions in the sky and the element.]

　　"And soon I heard a roaring wind:
　　It did not come anear;
　　But with its sound it shook the sails,
300 That were so thin and sere.

　　"The upper air burst into life!
　　And a hundred fire-flags sheen,
　　To and fro they were hurried about!
　　And to and fro, and in and out,
　　The wan stars danced between.

　　"And the coming wind did roar more loud,
　　And the sails did sigh like sedge;
　　And the rain poured down from one black cloud;
　　The moon was at its edge.

310 "The thick black cloud was cleft, and still
　　The moon was at its side:
　　Like waters shot from some high crag,
　　The lightning fell with never a jag,
　　A river steep and wide.

[The bodies of the ship's crew are inspirited, and the ship moves on;]

　　"The loud wind never reached the ship,
　　Yet now the ship moved on!
　　Beneath the lightning and the moon
　　The dead men gave a groan.

　　"They groaned, they stirred, they all uprose,
320 Nor spake, nor moved their eyes;
　　It had been strange, even in a dream,
　　To have seen those dead men rise.

　　"The helmsman steered, the ship moved on;
　　Yet never a breeze up blew;
　　The mariners all 'gan work the ropes,
　　Where they were wont to do;
　　They raised their limbs like lifeless tools—
　　We were a ghastly crew.

　　"The body of my brother's son
330 Stood by me, knee to knee:
　　The body and I pulled at one rope,
　　But he said nought to me."

[But not by the souls of the men, nor by demons of earth or middle air, but by a blessed troop of angelic spirits, sent down by the invocation of the guardian saint.]

　　"I fear thee, ancient Mariner!"
　　"Be calm, thou Wedding-Guest!
　　'Twas not those souls that fled in pain,
　　Which to their corses came again,
　　But a troop of spirits blest:

　　"For when it dawned—they dropped their arms,
　　And clustered round the mast;
340 Sweet sounds rose slowly through their mouths,
　　And from their bodies passed.

　　"Around, around, flew each sweet sound,
　　Then darted to the sun;
　　Slowly the sounds came back again,
　　Now mixed, now one by one.

　　"Sometimes a-dropping from the sky
　　I heard the sky-lark sing;
　　Sometimes all little birds that are,
　　How they seemed to fill the sea and air
350 With their sweet jargoning!

　　"And now 'twas like all instruments,
　　Now like a lonely flute;
　　And now it is an angel's song,
　　That makes the heavens be mute.

　　"It ceased; yet still the sails made on
　　A pleasant noise till noon,
　　A noise like of a hidden brook
　　In the leafy month of June,
　　That to the sleeping woods all night
360 Singeth a quiet tune.

"Till noon we quietly sailed on,
Yet never a breeze did breathe:
Slowly and smoothly went the ship,
Moved onward from beneath.

[The lonesome spirit from the South Pole carries on the ship as far as the Line, in obedience to the angelic troop, but still requireth vengeance.]

"Under the keel nine fathom deep,
From the land of mist and snow,
The spirit slid: and it was he
That made the ship to go.
The sails at noon left off their tune,
370 And the ship stood still also.

"The sun, right up above the mast,
Had fixed her to the ocean:
But in a minute she 'gan stir,
With a short uneasy motion—
Backwards and forwards half her length
With a short uneasy motion.

"Then like a pawing horse let go,
She made a sudden bound:
It flung the blood into my head,
380 And I fell down in a swound.

[The polar spirit's fellow-demons, the invisible inhabitants of the element, take part in his wrong; and two of them relate, one to the other, that penance long and heavy for the ancient Mariner hath been accorded to the polar spirit, who returneth southward.]

"How long in that same fit I lay,
I have not to declare;
But ere my living life returned,
I heard, and in my soul discerned,
Two voices in the air.

" 'Is it he?' quoth one, 'Is this the man?
By Him who died on cross,
With his cruel bow he laid full low
The harmless albatross.

390 " 'The spirit who bideth by himself
In the land of mist and snow,
He loved the bird that loved the man
Who shot him with his bow.'

"The other was a softer voice,
As soft as honey-dew:
Quoth he, 'The man hath penance done,
And penance more will do.'

PART SIX

FIRST VOICE

" 'But tell me, tell me! speak again,
They soft response renewing—
400 What makes that ship drive on so fast?
What is the ocean doing?'

SECOND VOICE

" 'Still as a slave before his lord,
The ocean hath no blast;
His great bright eye most silently
Up to the moon is cast—

" 'If he may know which way to go;
For she guides him smooth or grim.
See, brother, see! how graciously
She looketh down on him.'

[The Mariner hath been cast into a trance; for the angelic power causeth the vessel to drive northward faster than human life could endure.]

FIRST VOICE

410 " 'But why drives on that ship so fast,
Without or wave or wind?'

SECOND VOICE

" 'The air is cut away before,
And closes from behind.'

" 'Fly, brother, fly! more high, more high!
Or we shall be belated:
For slow and slow that ship will go,
When the Mariner's trance is abated.'

[The supernatural motion is retarded; the Mariner awakes, and his penance begins anew.]

"I woke, and we were sailing on
As in a gentle weather:
420 'Twas night, calm night, the moon was high;
The dead men stood together.

"All stood together on the deck,
For a charnel-dungeon fitter:
All fixed on me their stony eyes,
That in the moon did glitter.

"The pang, the curse, with which they died,
Had never passed away:
I could not draw my eyes from theirs,
Nor turn them up to pray.

[The curse is finally expiated.]

430 "And now this spell was snapt: once more
I viewed the ocean green,
And looked far forth, yet little saw
Of what had else been seen—

"Like one, that on a lonesome road
Doth walk in fear and dread,
And having once turned round, walks on,
And turns no more his head;
Because he knows, a frightful fiend
Doth close behind him tread.

440 "But soon there breathed a wind on me,
Nor sound nor motion made:
Its path was not upon the sea,
In ripple or in shade.

"It raised my hair, it fanned my cheek
Like a meadow-gale of spring—
It mingled strangely with my fears,
Yet it felt like a welcoming.

"Swiftly, swiftly flew the ship,
Yet she sailed softly too:
450 Sweetly, sweetly blew the breeze—
On me alone it blew.

[And the ancient Mariner beholdeth his native country.]

"Oh! dream of joy! is this indeed
The light-house top I see?
Is this the hill? is this the kirk?
Is this mine own countree?

"We drifted o'er the harbour-bar,
And I with sobs did pray—
O let me be awake, my God!
Or let me sleep alway.

460 "The harbour-bay was clear as glass,
So smoothly it was strewn!
And on the bay the moonlight lay,
And the shadow of the Moon.

"The rock shone bright, the kirk no less,
That stands above the rock:
The moonlight steeped in silentness
The steady, weathercock.

[The angelic spirits leave the dead bodies,]

"And the bay was white with silent light
Till, rising from the same,
470 Full many shapes, that shadows were,
In crimson colours came.

[And appear in their own forms of light.]

"A little distance from the prow
Those crimson shadows were:
I turned my eyes upon the deck—
Oh, Christ! what saw I there!

"Each corse lay flat, lifeless and flat,
And, by the holy rood!
A man all light, a seraph-man,
On every corse there stood.

480 "This seraph-band, each waved his hand:
It was a heavenly, sight!
They stood as signals to the land,
Each one a lovely light;

"This seraph-band, each waved his hand,
No voice did they impart—
No voice; but oh! the silence sank
Like music on my heart.

"But soon I heard the dash of oars,
I heard the pilot's cheer;
490 My head was turned perforce away,
And I saw a boat appear.

"The pilot and the pilot's boy,
I heard them coming fast:
Dear Lord in Heaven! it was a joy
The dead men could not blast.

"I saw a third—I heard his voice:
It is the Hermit good!
He singeth loud his godly hymns
That he makes in the wood.
500 He'll shrieve my soul, he'll wash away
The albatross's blood."

PART SEVEN

[The hermit of the wood,]

"This hermit good lives in that wood
Which slopes down to the sea.
How loudly his sweet voice he rears!
He loves to talk with marineres
That come from a far countree.

"He kneels at morn, and noon, and eve—
He hath a cushion plump:
It is the moss that wholly hides
510 The rotted old oak-stump.

"The skiff-boat neared: I heard them talk,
'Why, this is strange, I trow!
Where are those lights so many and fair,
That signal made but now?'

[Approacheth the ship with wonder.]

" 'Strange, by my faith!' the hermit said—
'And they answered not our cheer!
The planks looked warped! and see those sails,
How thin they are and sere!
I never saw aught like to them,
520 Unless perchance it were

" 'Brown skeletons of leaves that lag
My forest-brook along;
When the ivy-tod is heavy with snow,
And the owlet whoops to the wolf below,
That eats the she-wolf's young.'

" 'Dear Lord! it hath a fiendish look—
(The pilot made reply)
I am a-feared'— 'Push on, push on!'
Said the hermit cheerily.

530 "The boat came closer to the ship,
But I nor spake nor stirred;
The boat came close beneath the ship,
And straight a sound was heard.

[*The ship suddenly sinketh.*]

"Under the water it rumbled on,
Still louder and more dead:
It reached the ship, it split the bay;
The ship went down like lead.

[*The ancient Mariner is saved in the pilot's boat.*]

"Stunned by that loud and dreadful sound,
Which sky and ocean smote,
540 Like one that hath been seven days drowned
My body lay afloat;
But swift as dreams, myself I found
Within the pilot's boat.

"Upon the whirl, where sank the ship,
The boat spun round and round;
And all was still, save that the hill
Was telling of the sound.

"I moved my lips—the pilot shrieked
And fell down in a fit;
550 The holy hermit raised his eyes,
And prayed where he did sit.

"I took the oars: the pilot's boy,
Who now doth crazy go,
Laughed loud and long, and all the while
His eyes went to and fro.
'Ha! ha!' quoth he, 'full plain I see,
The devil knows how to row.'

"And now, all in my own countree,
I stood on the firm land!
560 The hermit stepped forth from the boat,
And scarcely he could stand.

[*The ancient Mariner earnestly entreateth the Hermit to shrieve him; and the penance of life falls on him.*]

" 'O shrieve me, shrieve me, holy man!'
The hermit crossed his brow.
'Say quick,' quoth he, 'I bid thee say—
What manner of man art thou?'

"Forthwith this frame of mine was wrenched
With a woful agony,
Which forced me to begin my tale;
And then it left me free.

[*And ever and anon throughout his future life an agony constraineth him to travel from land to land;*]

570 "Since then, at an uncertain hour,
That agony returns:
And till my ghastly tale is told,
This heart within me burns.

"I pass, like night, from land to land;
I have strange power of speech;
That moment that his face I see,
I know the man that must hear me:
To him my tale I teach.

"What loud uproar bursts from that door!
580 The wedding-guests are there:
But in the garden-bower the bride
And bride-maids singing are:
And hark the little vesper bell,
Which biddeth me to prayer!

"O Wedding-Guest! this soul hath been
Alone on a wide, wide sea:
So lonely 'twas, that God himself
Scarce seemèd there to be.

"Oh sweeter than the marriage-feast,
590 'Tis sweeter far to me,
To walk together to the kirk
With a goodly company!—

"To walk together to the kirk,
And all together pray,
While each to his great Father bends,
Old men, and babes, and loving friends
And youths and maidens gay!

[*And to teach, by his own example, love and reverence to all things that God made and loveth.*]

"Farewell, farewell! but this I tell
To thee, thou Wedding-Guest!
600 He prayeth well, who loveth well
Both man and bird and beast.

"He prayeth best, who loveth best
All things both great and small;
For the dear God who loveth us,
He made and loveth all."

> The Mariner, whose eye is bright,
> Whose beard with age is hoar,
> Is gone: and now the Wedding-Guest
> Turned from the bridegroom's door.
>
> 610 He went like one that hath been stunned,
> And is of sense forlorn:
> A sadder and a wiser man,
> He rose the morrow morn.

 Fill in each of the following blanks with the correct explanation or answer.

1.68 To whom does the Mariner tell his tale, and why? (See Parts I and VII.)
___

1.69 What great offense does the Mariner commit, and why?
___

1.70 What happens to the crew because of the Mariner's offense?
___

1.71 What does the Mariner see in the crew's faces for seven days and seven nights?
___

1.72 What does the dead albatross hanging from the Mariner's neck symbolize?
___

1.73 What caused the albatross to fall from the Mariner's neck?
___

1.74 Describe the state of the crew members in Part V.
___

1.75 To whom does the Mariner look to wash away his guilt? (See Part VI.)
___

1.76 Why is "goodly company" sweet to the Mariner after his experiences on the sea?
___

1.77 What is the moral of the Mariner's tale?
___

Sir Walter Scott (1771–1832). Deemed by a contemporary critic to be "the noblest of all poets in our own day," Sir Walter Scott turned his energies to the novel after Byron superseded him in popularity and skill. Although he was a great poet of the Romantic Period, Scott is known to us as the originator of the modern historical novel.

Born the son of a Calvinist lawyer, Scott was educated in the city of his birth. He studied law at the university in Edinburgh and was apprenticed to his father. Scott had a voracious mind. While in school, he read historical documents, travel journals, medieval romances, and histories. From the time when he was a boy, Scott was particularly interested in the songs, legends, and folklore of the Scottish Border and Highlands, all of which would be the sources from which he would later draw for his novels.

After being called to the bar in 1792, Scott settled down to an unassuming life of a legal official with an interest in literature. In 1796 he published translations of

German romances. He married Catherine Carpenter of Lyon in 1797 and was appointed Sheriff-depute of Selkirkshire in 1799. In 1806 Scott was appointed Clerk of the Court of the Session in Edinburgh, a position he kept until just before his death.

Scott's publication in 1802-03 of *The Minstrelsy of the Scottish Border*, a three-volume edition of ballads, first gained him fame as a serious poet. He followed that work with the romantic poem *The Lay of the Last Minstrel* in 1805. As his first original work, it brought him an unexpected amount of popularity. After becoming a partner at James Ballantyne's printing firm, he published a series of romantic narrative poems, including *Marmion* (1808), *The Lady of the Lake* (1810), *Rokeby* and *The Bridal of Triermain* (1813), and *The Lord of the Isles* (1815). In 1809 he became a partner in the bookselling business John Ballantyne & Co. and helped found the Tory *Quarterly Review*. With the combined success of his medieval-based poetry and the business endeavors, Scott purchased Abbottsford on the Tweed. He built a large estate there, living the life of a medieval lord. The image was completed in 1820 when he was made a baron.

In 1813 Scott was offered the laureateship, but he declined. He recommended Southley and shortly afterward began writing novels. The rising popularity of Byron's romantic verse threatened Scott's decline. In 1814 Scott published anonymously the first of many novels. His historically based novels were a triumphant success, bringing him more (secret) fame than his poems ever would. Included in the rapid succession of novels were *Waverly* (1814), *Old Mortality* (1816), *The Heart of Midlothian* (1818), *Rob Roy* (1818), *Ivanhoe* (1820), *Kenilworth* (1821), *Quentin Durward* (1823), *The Talisman* (1825), *Chronicles of Canongate* (1827), and *The Fair Maid of Perth* (1828).

In 1826 the printing firm of James Ballantyne suffered from the economic crisis of that year. Its business relations with the publishing house of Constable & Co. plunged the partners into debt. Scott was burdened by no fault of his own with a debt of £114,000. A man of honor, he did not claim bankruptcy; instead, he tried to pay his creditors. He acknowledged his authorship and worked furiously, writing new novels, dramas, and essays. He completed the *Life of Napoleon Bonoparte* and contributed to the *Encyclopaedia Britannica* in 1827. In 1830 he wrote *Auchindrane or the Ayrshire Tragedy*, a drama. In 1832 Scott suffered a series of strokes and died in his home at Abbottsford. His debts were repaid in full by the sale of his copyrights.

Scott's influence as the first major historical novelist affected the work of such great writers as Charles Dickens, the Brontë sisters, William Makepeace Thackeray, and George Eliot. As critics have observed, his treatment of rural themes, regional speech, contemporary peasant life, and the interplay between social trends and individual character have shaped the work of many writers who followed him. Another critic has noted that his interest in medieval and Tudor history helped to perpetuate the romantic fascination with the Middle Ages. Many people credit him as one of the originators of the short story genre. The popularity of Scott's work in an age racked by social and political upheaval demonstrates the survival of English conservatism.

Underline the correct answer in each of the following statements.

1.78 From the time when he was a boy, Scott was particularly interested in the songs, legends, and folklore of his native (Germany, England, Scotland).

1.79 Scott is credited as the originator of the modern (romance, historical, adventure) novel.

1.80 While at the university in Edinburgh, Scott studied (law, literature, history) in preparation to become a (poet, lawyer, businessman).

1.81 Scott maintained a position as a (legal official, sailor, history professor) throughout most of his life.

1.82 Scott's first literary success came as a writer of (romantic, historical, religious) narrative poems.

1.83   Scott's success as a (lawyer and a poet, businessman and a poet, novelist and a poet) allowed him to purchase Abbottsford on the Tweed.

1.84   In 1813 Scott declined the laureateship because of the rising popularity of the romantic verse of (Byron, Keats, Coleridge).

1.85   Scott's first (novels, poems, essays) were published anonymously.

1.86   Scott's debts, initially incurred by his business partners, were paid in full after his death by the sale of his (estate, copyrights, clothes).

What to Look For:

Sir Walter Scott's combination of history and romance produced a new form of prose fiction. In a historical novel, both the heroes and the story line are fictional, but the setting and the historical events are real. As you read the following selection, notice Scott's enthusiasm for the past. How does he use romance to make history interesting?

From: ***Ivanhoe***

Returning from the Crusades, King Richard the Lion-Hearted (1157–1199) is believed to be captured by the Duke of Austria and imprisoned. In his absence, his brother, Prince John, has taken the throne. Hoping to prolong his rule, John gains the support of the Norman nobility and instigates several attempts to kill Arthur, who is next in line to the throne. John is opposed by not only the supporters of King Richard but also those who wish to see a Saxon on the throne. The conflict between the Normans and the Saxons serves as the basis of the story.

Also returning from the Crusades is Richard's loyal soldier, Wilfred of Ivanhoe. Ivanhoe is in love with his father's ward, Lady Rowena, who is intended for Athelstane, and intends to make her his bride. However, Ivanhoe's father, Cedric, has other plans. The marriage of Athelstane and Rowena, both of Saxon royal blood, would provide a chance for the reestablishment of Saxon rule, to which Cedric is passionately committed. Angered by his son's loyalty to King Richard and his love for Rowena, Cedric banishes Ivanhoe. Ivanhoe enters the tournament at Ashby-de-la-Zouche disguised as the Disinherited Knight. The tournament is one of two main events in the story.

Chapter 12
Ivanhoe by Sir Walter Scott

The heralds left their pricking up and down,
Now ringen trumpets loud and clarion.
There is no more to say, but east and west,
In go the speares sadly in the rest,
In goth the sharp spur into the side,
There see men who can just and who can ride;
There shiver shaftes upon shieldes thick,
He feeleth through the heart-spone the prick;
Up springen speares, twenty feet in height,
Out go the swordes to the silver bright;
The helms they to-hewn and to-shred;
Out bursts the blood with stern streames red.
                                                Chaucer.

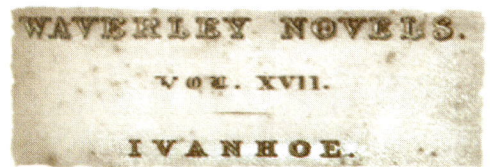

Chapter XII

Morning arose in unclouded splendour, and ere the sun was much above the horizon, the idlest or the most eager of the spectators appeared on the common, moving to the lists as to a general centre, in order to secure a favourable situation for viewing the continuation of the expected games. The marshals and their attendants appeared next on the field, together with the heralds, for the purpose of receiving the names of the knights who intended to joust, with the side which each chose to espouse. This was a necessary precaution, in order to secure equality betwixt the two bodies who should be opposed to each other.

According to due formality, the Disinherited Knight was to be considered as leader of the one body, while Brian de Bois-Guilbert, who had been rated as having done second-best in the preceding day, was named first champion of the other band. Those who had concurred in the challenge adhered to his party of course, excepting only Ralph de Vipont, whom his fall had rendered unfit so soon to put on his armour. There was no want of distinguished and noble candidates to fill up the ranks on either side.

In fact, although the general tournament, in which all knights fought at once, was more dangerous than single encounters, they were, nevertheless, more frequented and practised by the chivalry of the age. Many knights, who had not sufficient confidence in their own skill to defy a single adversary of high reputation, were, nevertheless, desirous of displaying their valour in the general combat, where they might meet others with whom they were more upon an equality. On the present occasion, about fifty knights were inscribed as desirous of combating upon each side, when the marshals declared that no more could be admitted, to the disappointment of several who were too late in preferring their claim to be included.

About the hour of ten o'clock, the whole plain was crowded with horsemen, horsewomen, and foot-passengers, hastening to the tournament; and shortly after, a grand flourish of trumpets announced Prince John and his retinue, attended by many of those knights who meant to take share in the game, as well as others who had no such intention.

About the same time arrived Cedric the Saxon, with the Lady Rowena, unattended, however, by Athelstane. This Saxon lord had arrayed his tall and strong person in armour, in order to take his place among the combatants; and, considerably to the surprise of Cedric, had chosen to enlist himself on the part of the Knight Templar. The Saxon, indeed, had remonstrated strongly with his friend upon the injudicious choice he had made of his party; but he had only received that sort of answer usually given by those who are more obstinate in following their own course, than strong in justifying it.

His best, if not his only reason, for adhering to the party of Brian de Bois-Guilbert, Athelstane had the prudence to keep to himself. Though his apathy of disposition prevented his taking any means to recommend himself to the Lady Rowena, he was, nevertheless, by no means insensible to her charms, and considered his union with her as a matter already fixed beyond doubt, by the assent of Cedric and her other friends. It had therefore been with smothered displeasure that the proud though indolent Lord of Coningsburgh beheld the victor of the preceding day select Rowena as the object of that honour which it became his privilege to confer. In order to punish him for a preference which seemed to interfere with his own suit, Athelstane, confident of his strength, and to whom his flatterers, at least, ascribed great skill in arms, had determined not only to deprive the Disinherited Knight of his powerful succour, but, if an opportunity should occur, to make him feel the weight of his battle-axe.

De Bracy, and other knights attached to Prince John, in obedience to a hint from him, had joined the party of the challengers, John being desirous to secure, if possible, the victory to that side. On the other hand, many other knights, both English and Norman, natives and strangers, took part against the challengers, the more readily that the opposite band was to be led by so distinguished a champion as the Disinherited Knight had approved himself.

As soon as Prince John observed that the destined Queen of the day had arrived upon the field, assuming that air of courtesy which sat well upon him when he was pleased to exhibit it, he rode forward to meet her, doffed his bonnet, and, alighting from his horse, assisted the Lady Rowena from her saddle, while his followers uncovered at the same time, and one of the most distinguished dismounted to hold her palfrey.

"It is thus," said Prince John, "that we set the dutiful example of loyalty to the Queen of Love and Beauty, and are ourselves her guide to the throne which she must this day occupy.—Ladies," he said, "attend your Queen, as you wish in your turn to be distinguished by like honours."

So saying, the Prince marshalled Rowena to the seat of honour opposite his own, while the fairest and most distinguished ladies present crowded after her to obtain places as near as possible to their temporary sovereign.

No sooner was Rowena seated, than a burst of music, half-drowned by the shouts of the multitude, greeted her new dignity. Meantime, the sun shone fierce and bright upon the polished arms of the knights of either side, who crowded the opposite extremities of the lists, and held eager conference together concerning the best mode of arranging their line of battle, and supporting the conflict.

The heralds then proclaimed silence until the laws of the tourney should be rehearsed. These were calculated in some degree to abate the dangers of the day; a precaution the more necessary, as the conflict was to be maintained with sharp swords and pointed lances.

The champions were therefore prohibited to thrust with the sword, and were confined to striking. A knight, it was announced, might use a mace or battle-axe at pleasure, but the dagger was a prohibited weapon. A knight unhorsed might renew the fight on foot with any other on the opposite side in the same predicament; but mounted horsemen were in that case forbidden to assail him. When any knight could force his antagonist to the extremity of the lists, so as to touch the palisade with his person or arms, such opponent was obliged to yield himself vanquished, and his armour and

horse were placed at the disposal of the conqueror. A knight thus overcome was not permitted to take farther share in the combat. If any combatant was struck down, and unable to recover his feet, his squire or page might enter the lists, and drag his master out of the press; but in that case the knight was adjudged vanquished, and his arms and horse declared forfeited. The combat was to cease as soon as Prince John should throw down his leading staff, or truncheon; another precaution usually taken to prevent the unnecessary effusion of blood by the too long endurance of a sport so desperate. Any knight breaking the rules of the tournament, or otherwise transgressing the rules of honourable chivalry, was liable to be stript of his arms, and, having his shield reversed to be placed in that posture astride upon the bars of the palisade, and exposed to public derision, in punishment of his unknightly conduct. Having announced these precautions, the heralds concluded with an exhortation to each good knight to do his duty, and to merit favour from the Queen of Beauty and of Love.

This proclamation having been made, the heralds withdrew to their stations. The knights, entering at either end of the lists in long procession, arranged themselves in a double file, precisely opposite to each other, the leader of each party being in the centre of the foremost rank, a post which he did not occupy until each had carefully marshalled the ranks of his party, and stationed every one in his place.

It was a goodly, and at the same time an anxious, sight, to behold so many gallant champions, mounted bravely, and armed richly, stand ready prepared for an encounter so formidable, seated on their war-saddles like so many pillars of iron, and awaiting the signal of encounter with the same ardour as their generous steeds, which, by neighing and pawing the ground, gave signal of their impatience.

As yet the knights held their long lances upright, their bright points glancing to the sun, and the streamers with which they were decorated fluttering over the plumage of the helmets. Thus they remained while the marshals of the field surveyed their ranks with the utmost exactness, lest either party had more or fewer than the appointed number. The tale was found exactly complete. The marshals then withdrew from the lists, and William de Wyvil, with a voice of thunder, pronounced the signal words— "Laissez aller!" The trumpets sounded as he spoke—the spears of the champions were at once lowered and placed in the rests—the spurs were dashed into the flanks of the horses, and the two foremost ranks of either party rushed upon each other in full gallop, and met in the middle of the lists with a shock, the sound of which was heard at a mile's distance. The rear rank of each party advanced at a slower pace to sustain the defeated, and follow up the success of the victors of their party.

The consequences of the encounter were not instantly seen, for the dust raised by the trampling of so many steeds darkened the air, and it was a minute ere the anxious spectator could see the fate of the encounter. When the fight became visible, half the knights on each side were dismounted, some by the dexterity of their adversary's lance,—some by the superior weight and strength of opponents, which had borne down both horse and man,—some lay stretched on earth as if never more to rise,—some had already gained their feet, and were closing hand to hand with those of their antagonists who were in the same predicament,—and several on both sides, who had received wounds by which they were disabled, were stopping their blood by their scarfs, and endeavouring to extricate themselves from the tumult. The mounted knights, whose lances had been almost all broken by the fury of the encounter, were now closely engaged with their swords, shouting their war-cries, and exchanging buffets, as if honour and life depended on the issue of the combat.

The tumult was presently increased by the advance of the second rank on either side, which, acting as a reserve, now rushed on to aid their companions. The followers of Brian de Bois-Guilbert shouted— "Ha! Beau-seant! Beau-seant!*—For the Temple—For the Temple!" The opposite party shouted in answer— "Desdichado! Desdichado!" —which watch-word they took from the motto upon their leader's shield.

The champions thus encountering each other with the utmost fury, and with alternate success, the tide of battle seemed to flow now toward the southern, now toward the northern extremity of the lists, as the one or the other party prevailed. Meantime the clang of the blows, and the shouts of the combatants, mixed fearfully with the sound of the trumpets, and drowned the groans of those who fell, and lay rolling defenceless beneath the feet of the horses.

*Beau-seant was the name of the Templars' banner, which was half black, half white, to intimate, it is said, that they were candid and fair towards Christians, but black and terrible towards infidels.

The splendid armour of the combatants was now defaced with dust and blood, and gave way at every stroke of the sword and battle-axe. The gay plumage, shorn from the crests, drifted upon the breeze like snow-flakes. All that was beautiful and graceful in the martial array had disappeared, and what was now visible was only calculated to awake terror or compassion.

Yet such is the force of habit, that not only the vulgar spectators, who are naturally attracted by sights of horror, but even the ladies of distinction

who crowded the galleries, saw the conflict with a thrilling interest certainly, but without a wish to withdraw their eyes from a sight so terrible. Here and there, indeed, a fair cheek might turn pale, or a faint scream might be heard, as a lover, a brother, or a husband, was struck from his horse. But, in general, the ladies around encouraged the combatants, not only by clapping their hands and waving their veils and kerchiefs, but even by exclaiming, "Brave lance! Good sword!" when any successful thrust or blow took place under their observation.

Such being the interest taken by the fair sex in this bloody game, that of the men is the more easily understood. It showed itself in loud acclamations upon every change of fortune, while all eyes were so riveted on the lists, that the spectators seemed as if they themselves had dealt and received the blows which were there so freely bestowed. And between every pause was heard the voice of the heralds, exclaiming, "Fight on, brave knights! Man dies, but glory lives!—Fight on—death is better than defeat!—Fight on, brave knights!—for bright eyes behold your deeds!"

Amid the varied fortunes of the combat, the eyes of all endeavoured to discover the leaders of each band, who, mingling in the thick of the fight, encouraged their companions both by voice and example. Both displayed great feats of gallantry, nor did either Bois-Guilbert or the Disinherited Knight find in the ranks opposed to them a champion who could be termed their unquestioned match. They repeatedly endeavoured to single out each other, spurred by mutual animosity, and aware that the fall of either leader might be considered as decisive of victory. Such, however, was the crowd and confusion, that, during the earlier part of the conflict, their efforts to meet were unavailing, and they were repeatedly separated by the eagerness of their followers, each of whom was anxious to win honour, by measuring his strength against the leader of the opposite party.

But when the field became thin by the numbers on either side who had yielded themselves vanquished, had been compelled to the extremity of the lists, or been otherwise rendered incapable of continuing the strife, the Templar and the Disinherited Knight at length encountered hand to hand, with all the fury that mortal animosity, joined to rivalry of honour, could inspire. Such was the address of each in parrying and striking, that the spectators broke forth into a unanimous and involuntary shout, expressive of their delight and admiration.

But at this moment the party of the Disinherited Knight had the worst; the gigantic arm of Front-de-Bœuf on the one flank, and the ponderous strength of Athelstane on the other, bearing down and dispersing those immediately exposed to them. Finding themselves freed from their immediate antagonists, it seems to have occurred to both these knights at the same instant, that they would render the most decisive advantage to their party, by aiding the Templar in his contest with his rival. Turning their horses, therefore, at the same moment, the Norman spurred against the Disinherited Knight on the one side, and the Saxon on the other. It was utterly impossible that the object of this unequal and unexpected assault could have sustained it, had he not been warned by a general cry from the spectators, who could not but take interest in one exposed to such disadvantage.

"Beware! beware! Sir Disinherited!" was shouted so universally, that the knight became aware of his danger; and, striking a full blow at the Templar, he reined back his steed in the same moment, so as to escape the charge of Athelstane and Front-de-Bœuf. These knights, therefore, their aim being thus eluded, rushed from opposite sides betwixt the object of their attack and the Templar, almost running their horses against each other ere they could stop their career. Recovering their horses however, and wheeling them round, the whole three pursued their united purpose of bearing to the earth the Disinherited Knight.

Nothing could have saved him, except the remarkable strength and activity of the noble horse which he had won on the preceding day.

This stood him in the more stead, as the horse of Bois-Guilbert was wounded, and those of Front-de-Bœuf and Athelstane were both tired with the weight of their gigantic masters, clad in complete armour, and with the preceding exertions of the day. The masterly horsemanship of the Disinherited Knight, and the activity of the noble animal which he mounted, enabled him for a few minutes to keep at sword's point his three antagonists, turning and wheeling with the agility of a hawk upon the wing, keeping his enemies as far separate as he could, and rushing now against the one, now against the other, dealing sweeping blows with his sword, without waiting to receive those which were aimed at him in return.

But although the lists rang with the applauses of his dexterity, it was evident that he must at last be overpowered; and the nobles around Prince John implored him with one voice to throw down his warder, and to save so brave a knight from the disgrace of being overcome by odds.

"Not I, by the light of Heaven!" answered Prince John; "this same springal, who conceals his name, and despises our proffered hospitality, hath already gained one prize, and may now afford to let others have their turn." As he spoke thus, an unexpected incident changed the fortune of the day.

There was among the ranks of the Disinherited Knight a champion in black armour, mounted on a black horse, large of size, tall, and to all appearance powerful and strong, like the rider by whom he was mounted, This knight, who bore on his shield no device of any kind, had hitherto evinced very little interest in the event of the fight, beating off with seeming ease those combatants who attacked him, but neither pursuing his advantages, nor himself assailing any one. In short, he had hitherto acted the part rather of a spectator than of a party in the tournament, a circumstance which procured him among the spectators the name of —Le Noir Faineant—, or the Black Sluggard.

At once this knight seemed to throw aside his apathy, when he discovered the leader of his party so hard bestead; for, setting spurs to his horse, which was quite fresh, he came to his assistance like a thunderbolt, exclaiming, in a voice like a trumpet-call, "—Desdichado—, to the rescue!" It was high time; for, while the Disinherited Knight was pressing upon the Templar, Front-de-Bœuf had got nigh to him with his uplifted sword; but ere the blow could descend, the Sable Knight dealt a stroke on his head, which, glancing from the polished helmet, lighted with violence scarcely abated on the —chamfron— of the steed, and Front-de-Bœuf rolled on the ground, both horse and man equally stunned by the fury of the blow. —Le Noir Faineant— then turned his horse upon Athelstane of Coningsburgh; and his own sword having been broken in his encounter with Front-de-Bœuf, he wrenched from the hand of the bulky Saxon the battle-axe which he wielded, and, like one familiar with the use of the weapon, bestowed him such a blow upon the crest, that Athelstane also lay senseless on the field. Having achieved this double feat, for which he was the more highly applauded that it was totally unexpected from him, the knight seemed to resume the sluggishness of his character, returning calmly to the northern extremity of the lists, leaving his leader to cope as he best could with Brian de Bois-Guilbert. This was no longer matter of so much difficulty as formerly. The Templars horse had bled much, and gave way under the shock of the Disinherited Knight's charge. Brian de Bois-Guilbert rolled on the field, encumbered with the stirrup, from which he was unable to draw his foot. His antagonist sprung from horseback, waved his fatal sword over the head of his adversary, and commanded him to yield himself; when Prince John, more moved by the Templars dangerous situation than he had been by that of his rival, saved him the mortification of confessing himself vanquished, by casting down his warder, and putting an end to the conflict.

It was, indeed, only the relics and embers of the fight which continued to burn; for of the few knights who still continued in the lists, the greater part had, by tacit consent, forborne the conflict for some time, leaving it to be determined by the strife of the leaders.

The squires, who had found it a matter of danger and difficulty to attend their masters during the engagement, now thronged into the lists to pay their dutiful attendance to the wounded, who were removed with the utmost care and attention to the neighbouring pavilions, or to the quarters prepared for them in the adjoining village.

Thus ended the memorable field of Ashby-de-la-Zouche, one of the most gallantly contested tournaments of that age; for although only four knights, including one who was smothered by the heat of his armour, had died upon the field, yet upwards of thirty were desperately wounded, four or five of whom never recovered. Several more were disabled for life; and those who escaped best carried the marks of the conflict to the grave with them. Hence it is always mentioned in the old records, as the Gentle and Joyous Passage of Arms of Ashby.

It being now the duty of Prince John to name the knight who had done best, he determined that the honour of the day remained with the knight whom the popular voice had termed —Le Noir Faineant—. It was pointed out to the Prince, in impeachment of this decree, that the victory had been in fact won by the Disinherited Knight, who, in the course of the day, had overcome six champions with his own hand, and who had finally unhorsed and struck down the leader of the opposite party. But Prince John adhered to his own opinion, on the ground that the Disinherited Knight and his party had lost the day, but for the powerful assistance of the Knight of the Black Armour, to whom, therefore, he persisted in awarding the prize.

To the surprise of all present, however, the knight thus preferred was nowhere to be found. He had left the lists immediately when the conflict ceased, and had been observed by some spectators to move down one of the forest glades with the same slow pace and listless and indifferent manner which had procured him the epithet of the Black Sluggard. After he had been summoned twice by sound of trumpet, and proclamation of the heralds, it became necessary to name another to receive the honours which had been assigned to him. Prince John had now no further excuse for resisting the claim of the Disinherited Knight, whom, therefore, he named the champion of the day.

Through a field slippery with blood, and encumbered with broken armour and the bodies of slain and wounded horses, the marshals of the lists again conducted the victor to the foot of Prince John's throne.

"Disinherited Knight," said Prince John, "since by that title only you will consent to be known to us, we a second time award to you the honours of this tournament, and announce to you your right to claim and receive from the hands of the Queen of Love and Beauty, the Chaplet of Honour which your valour has justly deserved."

The Knight bowed low and gracefully, but returned no answer.

While the trumpets sounded, while the heralds strained their voices in proclaiming honour to the brave and glory to the victor—while ladies waved their silken kerchiefs and embroidered veils, and while all ranks joined in a clamorous shout of exultation, the marshals conducted the Disinherited Knight across the lists to the foot of that throne of honour which was occupied by the Lady Rowena.

On the lower step of this throne the champion was made to kneel down. Indeed his whole action since the fight had ended, seemed rather to have been upon the impulse of those around him than from his own free will; and it was observed that he tottered as they guided him the second time across the lists. Rowena, descending from her station with a graceful and dignified step, was about to place the chaplet which she held in her hand upon the helmet of the champion, when the marshals exclaimed with one voice, "It must not be thus—his head must be bare." The knight muttered faintly a few words, which were lost in the hollow of his helmet, but their purport seemed to be a desire that his casque might not be removed.

Whether from love of form, or from curiosity, the marshals paid no attention to his expressions of reluctance, but unhelmed him by cutting the laces of his casque, and undoing the fastening of his gorget. When the helmet was removed, the well-formed, yet sun-burnt features of a young man of twenty-five were seen, amidst a profusion of short fair hair. His countenance was as pale as death, and marked in one or two places with streaks of blood.

Rowena had no sooner beheld him than she uttered a faint shriek; but at once summoning up the energy of her disposition, and compelling herself, as it were, to proceed, while her frame yet trembled with the violence of sudden emotion, she placed upon the drooping head of the victor the splendid chaplet which was the destined reward of the day, and pronounced, in a clear and distinct tone, these words: "I bestow on thee this chaplet, Sir Knight, as the meed of valour assigned to this day's victor." Here she paused a moment, and then firmly added, "And upon brows more worthy could a wreath of chivalry never be placed!"

The knight stooped his head, and kissed the hand of the lovely Sovereign by whom his valour had been rewarded; and then, sinking yet farther forward, lay prostrate at her feet.

There was a general consternation. Cedric, who had been struck mute by the sudden appearance of his banished son, now rushed forward, as if to separate him from Rowena. But this had been already accomplished by the marshals of the field, who, guessing the cause of Ivanhoe's swoon, had hastened to undo his armour, and found that the head of a lance had penetrated his breastplate, and inflicted a wound in his side.

Fill in each of the following blanks with the correct explanation or answer.

1.87 Name the opposing champions in the tournament.
_____

1.88 Who is named the "Queen of Love and Beauty?"
_____

1.89 Why does Prince John refuse to stop the tournament when the odds are against the Disinherited Knight?
_____

1.90 Who saves the Disinherited Knight from defeat?
_____

1.91 How and why is Ivanhoe's identity revealed?
_____

1.92 Why does Ivanhoe collapse at Rowena's feet?
_____

1.93 What interesting facts about life in the Middle Ages are included in this chapter?
_____

1.94 To whom did Prince John want to award the victory?
_____

1.95 What historical conflict for the throne of England serves as the basis for Ivanhoe?
_____

Review the material in this section in preparation for the Self Test, which will check your mastery of this particular section. The items missed on this Self Test will indicate specific areas where restudy is necessary for mastery.

SELF TEST 1

Answer *true* or *false* for each of the following statements (each answer, 2 points).

1.01 _____ The Enlightenment glorified the intellectual and moral abilities of man.

1.02 _____ Rousseau's Enlightenment philosophy of the basis of church and state was profoundly influential during the English Reformation.

1.03 _____ Despite the Reign of Terror, liberal-minded Englishmen continued to support the Revolutionary government.

1.04 _____ After the Napoleonic wars, England experienced an economic boom and social tranquility.

1.05 _____ The spread of transcendentalism quelled the spirit of revolution in England.

1.06 _____ The Romantic period in England was inaugurated by the publication of Wordsworth's and Coleridge's *Lyrical Ballads* in 1798.

1.07 _____ The literature of the Romantic period in England is characterized by individualism, mysticism, emotionalism, love of nature, nostalgia, and a fascination with the medieval past.

1.08 _____ Intellectually, the Romantic Movement was grounded in the Renaissance.

1.09 _____ Many Romantic poets believed that a golden age of peace could be brought about by reforming society by means of the imagination.

1.010 _____ In the Preface to *Lyrical Ballads*, Wordsworth affirmed the importance of reason, precision, and order.

Underline the correct answer in each of the following statements (each answer, 2 points).

1.011 The companion volumes *Songs of Innocence* and *Songs of Experience* reveal William Blake's (mysticism, rationalism, traditionalism).

1.012 As a follower of the Swedish mystic Emanuel Swedenborg, Blake believed that the Scriptures should be interpreted (literally, in context, symbolically).

1.013 Believing himself to be a prophet, Blake wrote a series of prophetic (books, sermons, tracts) explaining his interpretative visions of the momentous world events of the period.

1.014 Sir Walter Scott is credited as the originator of the modern (romance, historical, adventure) novel.

1.015 Scott maintained a position as a (legal official, sailor, history professor) throughout most of his life.

1.016 Scott's first literary success came as a writer of romantic (novels, poems, essays).

Circle the letter of the line that best answer each of the following questions (each answer, 2 points).

1.017 William Blake's "two contrary states of the human soul" may be described as

　　a. a child-like vision of reality and an adult vision of reality.

　　b. an insane vision of reality and a sane vision of reality.

　　c. a spiritual vision of reality and a worldly vision of reality.

　　d. a Christian view of the world and a mystical vision of reality.

1.018   In the *Introduction* to *Songs of Innocence*, Blake states that he is writing what kind of songs?

   a. experience
   b. happiness
   c. evil
   d. God

1.019   In "The Lamb," who does the Lamb symbolize?

   a. Blake as a child
   b. Satan
   c. Jesus Christ
   d. Blake's son

1.020   In the *Introduction to Songs of Experience*, to whom is the reader told to listen for spiritual guidance?

   a. the preacher of the Word
   b. the poet-prophet
   c. Jesus Christ
   d. the Experienced One

1.021   In "The Tyger," what question is asked of the Tyger that is also asked of the Lamb?

   a. "Who is Jesus Christ?"
   b. "What is truth?"
   c. "Who made thee?"
   d. "When will the end of the world come?"

1.022   In *The Garden of Love*, who is binding the poet's "joys & desires?"

   a. ministers of organized religion
   b. mystical poets
   c. Jesus Christ
   d. prophets of the Old Testament

1.023   According to the Preface to *Lyrical Ballads*, how does Wordsworth describe "good poetry?"

   a. the ordered conveyance of common place things
   b. the precise description of powerful feelings
   c. the spontaneous overflow of powerful feelings
   d. the careful description of feelings

1.024   According to Wordsworth, what is the origin of good poetry?

   a. emotion recollected in tranquility
   b. violent emotional outbursts
   c. ordered thoughts on ordinary things
   d. religious doctrine

1.025   In "The Tables Turned," what does the poet claim is man's best moral teacher?

   a. books
   b. mystical visions
   c. experience
   d. Nature

1.026 In "My Heart Leaps Up," how does the poet's religious idea of the rainbow contradict Scripture?

    a. He acknowledges God as the Creator of the universe.

    b. He does not acknowledge God as the Creator of the universe.

    c. He does not find meaning in the emotion brought about by the memory of the rainbow.

    d. He seek immortality in Nature's wisdom.

1.027 In *The Rime of the Ancient Mariner*, what great offense does the Mariner commit?

    a. kills a walrus

    b. harpoons a whale

    c. kills an albatross

    d. disobeys his commanding officer

1.028 What does the dead albatross hanging from the Mariner's neck symbolize?

    a. the restoration that comes after repentance

    b. the burden of his guilt

    c. the blessings of his deeds

    d. his rank as the captain's first mate

1.029 What is the moral of the Mariner's tale?

    a. Whether great or small, God's creatures are ours to misuse and destroy.

    b. There are great spiritual blessings for those who love God's creation.

    c. Physical deeds do not have spiritual consequences.

    d. Taking care of God's creation does not yield spiritual blessings.

1.030 In *Invanhoe*, why does Prince John refuse to stop the tournament when the odds are against the Disinherited Knight?

    a. The Disinherited Knight lost the previous tournament.

    b. The Disinherited Knight refused to reveal his identity and won the previous tournament.

    c. The Disinherited Knight wore all black.

    d. The Disinherited Knight treated the King with disrespect.

1.031 Who saves the Disinherited Knight from defeat?

    a. The White Knight

    b. Cedric

    c. Prince John

    d. The Black Knight

1.032 The historical conflict between which two groups for the throne of England serves as the basis for *Ivanhoe*?

    a. The Normans and the French

    b. The Scots and the Irish

    c. The Normans and the Saxons

    d. The Dutch and the Saxons

Fill in each of the blanks using items from the following word list (each answer, 3 points).

Biographia Literaria *Poems in Two Volumes* transcendental
idealism Poet Laureate *Lyrical Ballads*
Lake District pleasure *The Prelude*
literary criticism mystical

1.033 Coleridge encouraged Wordsworth to espouse _____ beliefs in his poetry.

1.034 Coleridge's friendship with Wordsworth was manifested in the publication in 1798 of the revolutionary collection of poems titled _____.

1.035 In 1798 Coleridge traveled with William and Dorothy Wordsworth to Germany, where he studied the _____ writings of Jakob Boehme and the _____ of Immanuel Kant.

1.036 The publication of _____ in 1817 established Coleridge's reputation as the father of a new tradition of _____.

1.037 Coleridge's literary criticism reversed the traditional emphasis of poetry by focusing on poetry's ability to evoke _____ rather than to teach wisdom.

1.038 In 1799 William and Dorothy Wordsworth moved to the _____ of England.

1.039 Published in 1807, _____ was the last of Wordsworth's great works.

1.040 In 1843 Wordsworth was appointed _____.

1.041 Published posthumously in 1850, _____ demonstrates Wordsworth's lasting affect on the direction of English poetry.

For Thought and Discussion:

Explain to a parent or teacher the story line of *The Rime of the Ancient Mariner* and the moral lesson Coleridge is trying to teach. Be sure to mention the Mariner's sin, curse, and method of restoration. Discuss Coleridge's understanding of sin and his answers to the problem of guilt in reference to Psalm 51. Does he understand sin to be an act of rebellion against a holy God? How is the burden of guilt removed?

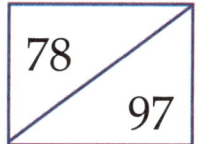

Score _____
Adult Check _____
Initial   Date

II. THE LATE ROMANTIC ERA

Jane Austen (1775–1817). Jane Austen is considered to be one of the greatest novelists in the English language, if not in any language. Born in Steventon, Hampshire, the sixth child of a clergyman, Austen was brought up in a cultured and comfortable environment. She was educated at home but never lacked for intellectual stimulation. Austen's father encouraged her to read a wide variety of authors. The exposure most probably encouraged the young writer's pursuits. By the time she was twenty, she had already written and begun a number of works. She completed *Love and Friendship* when she was fourteen; she wrote *A History of England* at fifteen; and she began *Elinor and Marianne* (later *Sense and Sensibility*) in 1795.

Attractive and witty, Austen was approached by many suitors; however, she never married. Instead, she remained with her family, living and vacationing in such places as London, Bath, Southampton, and Chawton. In an age when the only means of social advancement for a woman was to marry a man of significant wealth and status, it is not surprising that Austen made the subject of romantic entanglements the focus of her eloquent and subtle satire. Like herself, her heroines are intelligent and strong willed.

Austen's reputation as an observant analyst of human nature is based upon six novels, the first three of which were written between 1796–98. However, the first of her novels, *Sense and Sensibility*, was not published until 1811. *First Impressions,* renamed *Pride and Prejudice* before publication, was published in 1813. In 1803 Austen sold the copyright to *Northanger Abbey,* a satire on the Gothic novels of the day, for £10, but it was not published until 1817.

The death of Austen's father in 1805 seemed to stop her productivity. In 1811 some time after she abandoned her efforts on the novel *The Watsons,* she began work on the first of her major works, *Mansfield Park.* It was published in 1813, followed by *Emma* in 1815 and *Persuasion* in 1817.

Austen's works enjoyed increasing popularity during the twentieth century, but despite their focus on a narrow portion of upper-class society, they were well received during the Romantic period. Her meticulous yet witty presentation of daily life caused Sir Walter Scott to write of her "exquisite touch which renders ordinary commonplace things and characters interesting." Her attention to ordinary things more than any other trait identifies Austen with her Romantic contemporaries.

Circle the letter of the line that best answers each of the following questions.

2.1 Born the sixth child of a clergyman and educated at home, Austen was encouraged to read:

a. a wide variety of authors.

b. only the Bible.

c. only books written by Christians.

d. only her school books.

2.2 What was the main target of Austen's satire?

a. the unsanitary living conditions of the poor

b. the romantic entanglements of the upper class

c. the religious controversies of the day

d. the romantic entanglements of the lower class

2.3 An attractive and witty woman, Austen
- a. was married three times.
- b. never married and remained with her family.
- c. married a wealthy gentleman and was the mother of three children.
- d. never married and lived in London alone.

2.4 Austen's reputation as one of the world's greatest novelists is based on the publication of
- a. *Sense and Sensibility, Pride and Prejudice, Northanger Abbey, Mansfield Park, Emma,* and *Persuasion.*
- b. *Sense and Sensibility, A History of England, Northanger Abbey, Mansfield Park, Emma,* and *Persuasion.*
- c. *Love and Friendship, Northanger Abbey, Mansfield Park, Emma,* and *Persuasion.*
- d. *A History of England, Love and Friendship,* and *Elinor and Marianne.*

2.5 In 1805 Austen's productivity probably stopped because of what event in her life?
- a. the death of her husband
- b. the death of her father
- c. the initial lack of popularity of her books
- d. a tragic boating accident

2.6 What is the most pronounced trait that identifies Austen with her Romantic contemporaries?
- a. her mystical undertones
- b. her fascination with the Middle Ages
- c. her focus on the life and circumstances of the lower classes
- d. her attention to ordinary things

What to Look For:

Opposed to her Romantic contemporaries, Jane Austen supported traditional beliefs and social norms. Her polished and eloquent prose demonstrates her Neoclassical frame of thought. As you read, notice Austen's style. In what ways does it differ from the style of her contemporaries? How does she emphasize the powers of reason over the emotions and the teaching of truth over delighting?

From: *Pride and Prejudice*—CHAPTER I

IT is a truth universally acknowledged, that a single man in possession of a good fortune must be in want of a wife.

However little known the feelings or views of such a man may be on his first entering a neighborhood, this truth is so well fixed in the minds of the surrounding families, that he is considered as the rightful property of some one or other of their daughters.

"My dear Mr. Bennet," said his lady to him one day, "have you heard that Netherfield Park is let at last?" Mr. Bennet replied that he had not.

"But it is," returned she; "for Mrs. Long has just been here, and she told me all about it." Mr. Bennet made no answer.

"Do not you want to know who has taken it?" cried his wife impatiently.

"You want to tell me, and I have no objection to hearing it." This was invitation enough.

"Why, my dear, you must know. Mrs. Long says that Netherfield is taken by a young man of large fortune from the north of England; that he came down on Monday in a chaise and four to see the place, and was so much delighted with it, that he agreed with Mr. Morris immediately; that he is to take possession before Michaelmas, and some of his servants are to be in the house by the end of next week." "What is his name?" "Bingley." "Is he married or single?" "Oh! single, my dear, to be sure! A single man of large fortune; four or five thousand a-year. What a fine thing for our girls!" "How so? how can it affect them?" "My dear Mr. Bennet," replied his wife, "how can you be so tiresome! you must know that I am thinking of his marrying one of them." "Is that his design in settling here?" "Design! nonsense, how can you talk so! But it is very likely that he may fall in love with one of them, and therefore you must visit him as soon as he comes." "I see no occasion for that. You and the girls may go, or you may send them by themselves, which perhaps will be still better, for as you are as handsome as any of them, Mr. Bingley might like you the best of the party." "My dear, you flatter me. I certainly have had my share of beauty, but I do not pretend to be anything extraordinary now. When a woman has five grown-up daughters, she ought to give over thinking of her own beauty."

"In such cases, a woman has not often much beauty to think of." "But, my dear, you must indeed go and see Mr. Bingley when he comes into the neighborhood." "It is more than I engage for, I assure you." "But consider your daughters. Only think what an establishment it would be for one of them. Sir William and Lady Lucas are determined to go, merely on that account, for in general, you know, they visit no new-comers. Indeed you must go, for it will be impossible for us to visit him if you do not." "You are over-scrupulous, surely. I dare say Mr. Bingley will be very glad to see you; and I will send a few lines by you to assure him of my hearty consent to his marrying whichever he chooses of the girls: though I must throw in a good word for my little Lizzy." "I desire you will do no such thing. Lizzy is not a bit better than the others; and I am sure she is not half so handsome as Jane, nor half so good-humored as Lydia. But you are always giving her the preference." "They have none of them much to recommend them," replied he; "they are all silly and ignorant, like other girls: but Lizzy has something more of quickness than her sisters." "Mr. Bennet, how can you abuse your own children in such a way! You take delight in vexing me. You have no compassion on my poor nerves."

"You mistake me, my dear. I have a high respect for your nerves. They are my old friends. I have heard you mention them with consideration these twenty years at least." "Ah! you do not know what I suffer." "But I hope you will get over it, and live to see many young men of four thousand a-year come into the neighborhood." "It will be no use to us, if twenty such should come, since you will not visit them." "Depend upon it, my dear, that when there are twenty, I will visit them all." Mr. Bennet was so odd a mixture of quick parts, sarcastic humor, reserve, and caprice, that the experience of three-and-twenty years had been insufficient to make his wife understand his character. Her mind was less difficult to develop.

She was a woman of mean understanding, little information, and uncertain temper. When she was discontented, she fancied herself nervous. The business of her life was to get her daughters married; its solace was visiting and news.

CHAPTER II

MR. BENNET was among the earliest of those who waited on Mr. Bingley.

He had always intended to visit him, though to the last always assuring his wife that he should not go; and till the evening after the visit was paid she had no knowledge of it. It was then disclosed in the following manner:—Observing his second daughter employed in trimming a hat, he suddenly addressed her with, "I hope Mr. Bingley will like it, Lizzy." "We are not in a way to know what Mr. Bingley likes," said her mother resentfully, "since we are not to visit." "But you forget, mamma," said Elizabeth, "that we shall meet him at the assemblies, and that Mrs. Long has promised to introduce him." "I do not believe Mrs. Long will do any such thing. She has two nieces of her own. She is a selfish, hypocritical woman, and I have no opinion of her." "No more have I," said Mr. Bennet; "and I am glad to find that you do not depend on her serving you." Mrs. Bennet deigned not to make any reply, but, unable to contain herself, began scolding one of her daughters.

"Don't keep coughing so, Kitty, for Heaven's sake! Have a little compassion on my nerves. You tear them to pieces." "Kitty has no discretion in her coughs," said her father; "she times them ill."

"I do not cough for my own amusement," replied Kitty fretfully. "When is your next ball to be, Lizzy?" "To-morrow fortnight." "Aye, so it is," cried her mother, "and Mrs. Long does not come back till the day before; so it will be impossible for her to introduce him, for she will not know him herself." "Then, my dear, you may have the advantage of your friend, and introduce Mr. Bingley to her." "Impossible, Mr. Bennet, impossible, when I am not acquainted with him myself; how can you be so teasing?" "I honor your circumspection. A fortnight's acquaintance is certainly very little. One cannot know what a man really is by the end of a fortnight. But if we do not venture somebody else will; and after all, Mrs. Long and her nieces must stand their chance; and, therefore, as she will think it an act of kindness, if you decline the office, I will take it on myself." The girls stared at their father. Mrs. Bennet said only, "Nonsense, nonsense!" "What can be the meaning of that emphatic exclamation?" cried he. "Do you consider the forms of introduction, and the stress that is laid on them, as nonsense? I cannot quite agree with you there. What say you, Mary? for you are a young lady of deep reflection, I know, and read great books and make extracts." Mary wished to say something very sensible, but knew not how.

"While Mary is adjusting her ideas," he continued, "let us return to Mr. Bingley." "I am sick of Mr. Bingley," cried his wife.

"I am sorry to hear that; but why did not you tell me so before? If I had known as much this morning I certainly would not have called on him. It is very unlucky; but as I have actually paid the visit, we cannot escape the acquaintance now." The astonishment of the ladies was just what he wished; that of Mrs. Bennet perhaps surpassing the rest; though, when the first tumult of joy was over, she began to declare that it was what she had expected all the while.

"How good it was in you, my dear Mr. Bennet! But I knew I should persuade you at last. I was sure you loved your girls too well to neglect such an acquaintance. Well, how pleased I am! and it is such a good joke, too, that you should have gone this morning and never said a word about it till now." "Now, Kitty, you may cough as much as you choose," said Mr. Bennet; and, as he spoke, he left the room, fatigued with the raptures of his wife.

"What an excellent father you have, girls!" said she, when the door was shut.

"I do not know how you will ever make him amends for his kindness; or me either, for that matter. At our time of life it is not so pleasant, I can tell you, to be making new acquaintance every day; but for your sakes, we would do anything.

Lydia, my love, though you are the youngest, I dare say Mr. Bingley will dance with you at the next ball." "Oh!" said Lydia stoutly, "I am not afraid; for though I am the youngest, I'm the tallest." The rest of the evening was spent in conjecturing how soon he would return Mr. Bennet's visit, and determining when they should ask him to dinner.

CHAPTER III

NOT all that Mrs. Bennet, however, with the assistance of her five daughters, could ask on the subject, was sufficient to draw from her husband any satisfactory description of Mr. Bingley. They attacked him in various ways—with barefaced questions, ingenious suppositions, and distant surmises; but he eluded the skill of them all, and they were at last obliged to accept the second-hand intelligence of their neighbor, Lady Lucas. Her report was highly favorable. Sir William had been delighted with him. He was quite young, wonderfully handsome, extremely agreeable, and, to crown the whole, he meant to be at the next assembly with a large party. Nothing could be more delightful! To be fond of dancing was a certain step towards falling in love; and very lively hopes of Mr. Bingley's heart were entertained.

"If I can but see one of my daughters happily settled at Netherfield," said Mrs. Bennet to her husband, "and all the others equally well married, I shall have nothing to wish for." In a few days Mr. Bingley returned Mr. Bennet's visit, and sat about ten minutes with him in his library. He had entertained hopes of being admitted to a sight of the young ladies, of whose beauty he had heard much; but he saw only the father. The ladies were somewhat more fortunate, for they had the advantage of ascertaining from an upper window that he wore a blue coat, and rode a black horse.

An invitation to dinner was soon afterwards dispatched; and already had Mrs. Bennet planned the courses that were to do credit to her housekeeping, when an answer arrived which deferred it all. Mr. Bingley was obliged to be in town the following day, and, consequently, unable to accept the honor of their invitation, &c. Mrs. Bennet was quite disconcerted. She could not imagine what business he could have in town so soon after his arrival in Hertfordshire; and she began to fear that he might be always flying about from one place to another, and never settled at Netherfield as he ought to be. Lady Lucas quieted her fears a little by starting the idea of his being gone to London only to get a large party for the ball; and a report soon followed, that Mr. Bingley was to bring twelve ladies and seven gentlemen with him to the assembly. The girls grieved over such a number of ladies, but were comforted the day before the ball by hearing, that instead of twelve he had brought only six with him from London, —his five sisters and a cousin. And when the party entered the assembly room it consisted only of five all together, Mr. Bingley, his two sisters, the husband of the eldest, and another young man.

Mr. Bingley was good-looking and gentlemanlike; he had a pleasant countenance, and easy, unaffected manners. His sisters were fine women, with an air of decided fashion. His brother-in-law, Mr. Hurst, merely looked the gentleman; but his friend Mr. Darcy soon drew the attention of the room by his fine, tall person, handsome features, noble mien, and the report which was in general circulation within five minutes after his entrance, of his having ten thousand a-year. The gentlemen pronounced him to be a fine figure of a man, the ladies declared he was much handsomer than Mr. Bingley, and he was looked at with great admiration for about half the evening, till his manners gave a disgust which turned the tide of his popularity; for he was discovered to be proud; to be above his company, and above being pleased; and not all his large estate in Derbyshire could then save him from having a most forbidding, disagreeable countenance, and being unworthy to be compared with his friend.

Mr. Bingley had soon made himself acquainted with all the principal people in the room; he was lively and unreserved, danced every dance, was angry that the ball closed so early, and talked of giving one himself at Netherfield. Such amiable qualities must speak for themselves. What a contrast between him and his friend! Mr. Darcy danced only once with Mrs. Hurst and once with Miss Bingley, declined being introduced to any other lady, and spent the rest of the evening in walking about the room, speaking occasionally to one of his own party. His character was decided. He was the proudest, most disagreeable man in the world, and everybody hoped that he would never come there again. Amongst the most violent against him was Mrs. Bennet, whose dislike of his general behavior was sharpened into particular resentment by his having slighted one of her daughters.

Elizabeth Bennet had been obliged, by the scarcity of gentlemen, to sit down for two dances; and during part of that time, Mr. Darcy had been standing near enough for her to overhear a conversation between him and Mr. Bingley, who came from the dance for a few minutes, to press his friend to join it.

"Come, Darcy," said he, "I must have you dance. I hate to see you standing about by yourself in this stupid manner. You had much better dance." "I certainly shall not. You know how I detest it, unless I am particularly acquainted with my partner. At such an assembly as this it would be insupportable.

Your sisters are engaged, and there is not another woman in the room whom it would not be a punishment to me to stand up with." "I would not be so fastidious as you are," cried Bingley, "for a kingdom! Upon my honor, I never met with so many pleasant girls in my life as I have this evening; and there are several of them you see uncommonly pretty." "You are dancing with the only handsome girl in the room," said Mr. Darcy, looking at the eldest Miss Bennet.

"Oh! she is the most beautiful creature I ever beheld! But there is one of her sisters sitting down just behind you, who is very pretty, and I dare say very agreeable. Do let me ask my partner to introduce you." "Which do you mean?" and turning round he looked for a moment at Elizabeth, till catching her eye, he withdrew his own and coldly said, "She is tolerable, but not handsome enough to tempt me; and I am in no humor at present to give consequence to young ladies who are slighted by other men. You had better return to your partner and enjoy her smiles, for you are wasting your time with me." Mr. Bingley followed his advice. Mr. Darcy walked off; and Elizabeth remained with no very cordial feelings towards him. She told the story, however, with great spirit among her friends; for she had a lively, playful disposition, which delighted in anything ridiculous.

The evening altogether passed off pleasantly to the whole family. Mrs. Bennet had seen her eldest daughter much admired by the Netherfield party. Mr. Bingley had danced with her twice, and she had been distinguished by his sisters. Jane was as much gratified by this as her mother could be, though in a quieter way.

Elizabeth felt Jane's pleasure. Mary had heard herself mentioned to Miss Bingley as the most accomplished girl in the neighborhood; and Catherine and Lydia had been fortunate enough to be never without partners, which was all that they had yet learnt to care for at a ball. They returned, therefore, in good spirits to Longbourn, the village where they lived, and of which they were the principal inhabitants. They found Mr. Bennet still up. With a book he was regardless of time; and on the present occasion he had a good deal of curiosity as to the event of an evening which had raised such splendid expectations. He had rather hoped that all his wife's views on the stranger would be disappointed; but he soon found that he had a very different story to hear.

"Oh, my dear Mr. Bennet," as she entered the room, "we have had a most delightful evening, a most excellent ball. I wish you had been there. Jane was so admired, nothing could be like it. Everybody said how well she looked; and Mr. Bingley thought her quite beautiful, and danced with her twice! Only think of that, my dear; he actually danced with her twice! and she was the only creature in the room that he asked a second time. First of all, he asked Miss Lucas. I was so vexed to see him stand up with her! but, however, he did not admire her at all; indeed, nobody can, you know; and he seemed quite struck with Jane as she was going down the dance. So he inquired who she was, and got introduced, and asked her for the two next. Then the two third he danced with Miss King, and the two fourth with Maria Lucas, and the two fifth with Jane again, and the two sixth with Lizzie and the Boulanger." "If he had had any compassion for me," cried her husband impatiently, "he would not have danced half so much! For God's sake, say no more of his partners. O that he had sprained his ankle in the first dance!" "Oh! my dear," continued Mrs. Bennet, "I am quite delighted with him. He is so excessively handsome! and his sisters are charming women. I never in my life saw anything more elegant than their dresses. I dare say the lace upon Mrs. Hurst's gown—" Here she was interrupted again. Mr. Bennet protested against any description of finery. She was therefore obliged to seek another branch of the subject, and related, with much bitterness of spirit and some exaggeration, the shocking rudeness of Mr. Darcy.

"But I can assure you," she added, "that Lizzie does not lose much by not suiting his fancy; for he is a most disagreeable, horrid man, not at all worth pleasing.

So high and so conceited that there was no enduring him! He walked here, and he walked there, fancying himself so very great! Not handsome enough to dance with! I wish you had been there, my dear, to have given him one of your setdowns. I quite detest the man."

Give the best answer or explanation for each of the following questions.

2.7 What is ironic about the opening line of the novel ("It is a truth universally acknowledged, that a single man in possession of a good fortune, must be in want of a wife")?

2.8 Contrast briefly the personalities of the two parents.

2.9 Why is Mrs. Bennet so annoyed with Mr. Bennet in Chapter 2?

2.10 Why do you think Austen does not give much attention to the deep inner life of her characters?

2.11 Contrast briefly the actions and manners of Mr. Darcy and Mr. Bingley at the ball.

2.12 Why does Mr. Darcy refuse to dance with Elizabeth Bennet?

2.13 What is different about the initial meeting of Elizabeth Bennet, the heroine, and Mr. Darcy, her future husband, from other romance stories?

Charles Lamb (1775–1834). Considered the prince of English essayists, Charles Lamb wrote in a polished, conversational style with romantic sensibility for the commonplace.

Born in London the son of a clerk, Lamb attended Christ's Hospital, where he met Coleridge, with whom he remained a life-long friend. At the age of seventeen, Lamb began work at the East India House, where he worked in the accounting department until his retirement in 1825. Like Wordsworth, Lamb lived with his sister. Mary was susceptible to fits of insanity and had to be watched for symptoms of attack. Lamb also suffered from the threat of mental illness. From 1795–1796, he endured an attack but recovered to live a normal life.

Although he was plagued by the return of mental illness, Lamb and his sister maintained an active social life. Lamb's home was a regular meeting place for the most talented artists and writers of that time. Among those who attended the Wednesday night gatherings were Wordsworth, Coleridge, DeQuincy, Southley, and Hazlitt. Lamb's person and writings were much admired by his contemporaries. Wordsworth wrote, "Lamb, my friend, writes prose exquisitely." Coleridge included four of Lamb's sonnets in a collection of poems that he published in 1796.

However, much of Lamb's early works met with little success. So bad was the production of one of his plays that Lamb himself even hissed at its performance. In 1807 he collaborated with Mary on *Tales of Shakespeare*. It was intended to introduce Shakespeare's plays to children. In 1808 Lamb published a piece on literary criticism, *Specimens of English Dramatic Poets,* about poets who lived about the time of Shakespeare.

From 1810–1820, Lamb wrote many of his rambling, witty essays on ordinary life for which he is now famous. Many of his works were published in journals and magazines, namely the *Examiner*, the *Quarterly Review,* and the *London Magazine*. From 1821–23, Lamb contributed regularly to the *London Magazine*, publishing essays under the name "Elia." Written in a subjective voice, the essays show most clearly his romantic tendencies. They were published as a collection, *Essays of Elia,* in 1823. A second volume of the essays was published in 1833.

Considered one of the most unromantic of the Romantics, Lamb cared nothing for the exalted view of nature held by both Coleridge and Wordsworth. He loved London and its people. Lamb's essays demonstrate his romantic view of the past and commonplace things. In his unique style, he uses both humor and pathos to "recollect emotion in tranquillity."

Circle the letter of the lines that best answer each of the following questions.

2.14   While attending Christ's Hospital, Lamb first met his life-long friend:

   a. William Wordsworth.
   b. George Gordon, Lord Byron.
   c. Samuel Taylor Coleridge.
   d. William Shakespeare.

2.15   Lamb and his sister both suffered from the threat of:

   a. mental illness.
   b. poverty.
   c. obesity.
   d. physical harm.

2.16 Lamb's home served as the Wednesday night meeting place of:

a. the most renowned ministers and evangelists of the time.
b. the most talented artists and writers of the time.
c. a secret club to overthrow the established government.
d. writers and artists who struggled with mental illness.

2.17 From 1821–1823, Lamb published his most famous essays in the *London Magazine*, which were later published as a collection titled:

a. *Essays of Moses.*
b. *Essays of Elia.*
c. *The Posthumous Papers of Elia.*
d. *Essays of London and Its People.*

2.18 Known as the prince of English essayists, Lamb's style is:

a. spontaneous with a romantic sensibility for nature's powers to stir the emotions.
b. polished with a Neoclassical attention to the powers of reason.
c. polished and conversational with a Romantic sensibility for the commonplace things and activities of London.
d. spontaneous and disorderly.

What to Look For:

Lamb's essays color the past and the ordinary in a Romantic hue. As you read, pay attention to the discussion between the speaker (Elia) and his cousin Bridget. In what ways do the imagination and feelings take precedent over fact and reason? Why does Elia like old china? Why does Bridget prefer the past?

"Old China"

"Old China" was published as part of the collection Essays of Elia *in 1823. As the speaker (Elia) Lamb would often figure his friends and his sister in his essays. Bridget is the name that Lamb uses for his sister.*

Essays of Elia
OLD CHINA

I have an almost feminine partiality for old china. When I go to see any great house, I inquire for the china-closet, and next for the picture gallery. I cannot defend the order of preference, but by saying, that we have all some taste or other, of too ancient a date to admit of our remembering distinctly that it was an acquired one. I can call to mind the first play, and the first exhibition, that I was taken to; but I am not conscious of a time when china jars and saucers were introduced into my imagination.

I had no repugnance then — why should I now have? — to those little, lawless, azure-tinctured grotesques, that under the notion of men and women, float about, uncircumscribed by any element, in that world before perspectives — a china tea-cup.

I like to see my old friends — whom distance cannot diminish — figuring up in the air (so they appear to our optics) yet on terra firma still — so we must in courtesy interpret that speck of deeper blue, which the decorous artist, to prevent absurdity, has made to spring up beneath their sandals.

I love the men with women's faces, and the women, if possible, with still more womanish expressions.

Here is a young and courtly Mandarin, handing tea to a lady from a salver — two miles off. See how distance seems to set off respect! And here the same lady, or another — for likeness is identity on teacups — is stepping into a little fairy boat, moored on the hither side of this calm garden river, with a dainty mincing foot, which in a right angle of incidence (as angles go in our world) must infallibly land her in the midst of a flowery mead — a furlong off on the other side of the same strange stream!

Farther on — if far or near can he predicated of their world — see horses, trees, pagodas, dancing the hays.

Here — a cow and rabbit couchant, and co-extensive — so objects show, seen through the lucid atmosphere of fine Cathay.

I was pointing out to my cousin last evening, over our Hyson (which we are old fashioned enough to drink unmixed still of an afternoon) some of these speciosa miracula upon a set of extra-ordinary old blue china (a recent purchase) which we were now for the first time using; and could not help remarking, how favourable circumstances had been to us of late years, that we could afford to please the eye sometimes with trifles of this sort — when a passing sentiment seemed to over-shade the brows of my companion. I am quick at detecting these summer clouds in Bridget.

"I wish the good old times would come again," she said, "when we were not quite so rich. I do not mean, that I want to be poor; but there was a middle state " — so she was pleased to ramble on, — "in which I am sure we were a great deal happier. A purchase is but a purchase, now that you have money enough and to spare. Formerly it used to be a triumph. When we coveted a cheap luxury (and, O! how much ado I had to get you to consent in those times!) we were used to have a debate two or three days before, and to weigh the for and against, and think what we might spare it out of, and what saving we could hit upon, that should be an equivalent. A thing was worth buying then, when we felt the money that we paid for it.

"Do you remember the brown suit, which you made to hang upon you, till all your friends cried shame upon you, it grew so thread-bare — and all because of that folio Beaumont and Fletcher, which you dragged home late at night from Barker's in Covent-garden? Do you remember how we eyed it for weeks before we could make up our minds to the purchase, and had not come to a determination till it was near ten o'clock of the Saturday night, when you set off from Islington, fearing you should be too late — and when the old bookseller with some grumbling opened his shop, and by the twinkling taper (for he was setting bedwards) lighted out the relic from his dusty treasuries and when you lugged it home, wishing it were twice as cumbersome — and when you presented it to me — and when we were exploring the perfectness of it (collating you called it — and while I was repairing some of the loose leaves with paste, which your impatience would not suffer to be left till day-break — was there no pleasure in being a poor man? or can those neat black clothes which you wear now, and are so careful to keep brushed, since we have become rich and finical, give you half the honest vanity with which you flaunted it about in that over-worn suit — your old corbeau — for four or five weeks longer than you should have done, to pacify your conscience for the mighty sum of fifteen — or sixteen shillings was it? — a great affair we thought it then — which you had lavished on the old folio. Now you can afford to buy any book that pleases you, but I do not see that you ever bring me home any nice old purchases now.

"When you come home with twenty apologies for laying out a less number of shillings upon that print after Lionardo, which we christened the 'Lady Blanch;' when you looked at the purchase, and thought of the money — and thought of the money, and looked again at the picture — was there no pleasure in being a poor man? Now, you have nothing to do but to walk into Colnaghi's, and buy a wilderness of Lionardos. Yet do you?

"Then, do you remember our pleasant walks to Enfield, and Potter's Bar, and Waltham, when we had a holyday — holydays, and all other fun, are gone, now we are rich — and the little hand-basket in which I used to deposit our day's fare of savory cold lamb and salad — and how you would pry about at noon-tide for some decent house, where we might go in, and produce our store — only paying for the ale that you must call for — and speculate upon the looks of the landlady, and whether she was likely to allow us a table-cloth — and wish for such another honest hostess, as Izaak Walton has described many a one on the pleasant banks of the Lea, when he went a fishing — and sometimes they would prove obliging enough, and sometimes they would look grudgingly upon us — but we had cheerful looks still for one another, and would eat our plain food savorily, scarcely grudging Piscator his Trout Hall? Now, when we go out a days pleasuring, which is seldom moreover, we ride part of the way — and go into a fine inn, and order the best of dinners, never debating the expense — which, after all, never has half the relish of those chance country snaps, when we were at the mercy of uncertain usage, and a precarious welcome.

"You are too proud to see a play anywhere now but in the pit. Do you remember where it was we used to sit, when we saw the battle of Hexham, and the surrender of Calais, and Bannister and Mrs. Bland in the Children in the Wood — when we squeezed out our shillings a-piece to sit three or four times in a season in the one-shilling gallery — where you felt all the time that you ought not to have brought me — and more strongly I felt obligation to you for having brought me — and the pleasure was the better for a little shame — and when the curtain drew up, what cared we for our place in the house, or what mattered it where we were sitting, when our thoughts were with Rosalind in Arden, or with Viola at the Court of Illyria. You used to say, that the gallery was the best place of all for enjoying a play socially — that the relish of such exhibitions must be in proportion to the infrequency of going — that the company we met there, not being in general readers of plays, were obliged to attend the more, and did attend, to what was going on, on the stage — because a word lost would have been a chasm, which it was impossible for them to fill up. With such reflections we consoled our pride then — and I appeal to you, whether, as a woman, I met generally with less attention and accommodation, than I have done since in more expensive situations in the house? The getting in indeed, and the crowding up those inconvenient staircases, was bad enough, — but there was still a law of civility to women recognised to quite as great an extent as we ever found in the other passage — and how a little difficulty overcome heightened the snug seat, and the play, afterwards! Now we can only pay our money, and walk in. You cannot see, you say, in the galleries now. I am sure we saw, and heard too, well enough then — but sight, and all, I think, is gone with our poverty.

"There was pleasure in eating strawberries, before they became quite common — in the first dish of peas, while they were yet dear — to have them for a nice supper, a treat. What treat can we have now? If we were to treat ourselves now — that is, to have dainties a little above our means, it would be selfish and wicked. It is the very little more that we allow ourselves beyond what the actual poor can get at, that makes what I call a treat — when two people living together, as we have done, now and then indulge themselves in a cheap luxury, which both like; while each apologises, and is willing to take both halves of the blame to his single share. I see no harm in people making much of themselves in that sense of the word. It may give them a hint how to make much of others. But now — what I mean by the word — we never do make much of ourselves. None but the poor can do it. I do not mean the veriest poor of all, but persons as we were, just above poverty.

"I know what you were going to say, that it is mighty pleasant at the end of the year to make all meet — and much ado we used to have every Thirty-first Night of December to account for our exceedings — many a long face did you make over your puzzled accounts, and in contriving to make it out how we had spent so much — or that we had not spent so much — or that it was impossible we should spend so much next year — and still we found our slender capital decreasing — but then, betwixt ways, and projects, and compromises of one sort or another, and talk of curtailing this charge, and doing without that for the future — and the hope that youth brings, and laughing spirits (in which you were never poor till now,) we pocketed up our loss, and in conclusion, with 'lusty brimmers' (as you used to quote it out of hearty cheerful Mr. Cotton, as you called him), we used to welcome in the 'coming guest.' Now we have no reckoning at all at the end of the old year — no flattering promises about the new year doing better for us."

Bridget is so sparing of her speech on most occasions, that when she gets into a rhetorical vein, I am careful how I interrupt it. I could not help, however, smiling at the phantom of wealth which her dear imagination had conjured up out of a clear income of poor — hundred pounds a year. "It is true we were happier when we were poorer, but we were also younger, my cousin. I am afraid we must put up with the excess, for if we were to shake the superflux into the sea, we should not much mend ourselves. That we had much to struggle with, as we grew up together, we have reason to be most thankful. It strengthened, and knit our compact closer. We could never have been what we have been to each other, if we had always had the sufficiency which you now complain of. The resisting power — those natural dilations of the youthful spirit, which circumstances cannot straiten — with us are long since passed away. Competence to age is supplementary youth; a sorry supplement indeed, but I fear the best that is to be had. We must ride where we formerly walked: live better, and lie softer — and shall be wise to do so — than we had means to do in those good old days you speak of. Yet could those days return — could you and I once more walk our thirty miles a-day — could Bannister and Mrs. Bland again be young, and you and I young to see them — could the good old one shilling gallery days return — they are dreams, my cousin, now — but could you and I at this moment, instead of this quiet argument, by our well-carpeted fire-side, sitting on this luxurious sofa — be once more struggling up those inconvenient stair-cases, pushed about, and squeezed, and elbowed by the poorest rabble of poor gallery scramblers — could I once more hear those anxious shrieks of yours — and the delicious Thank God, we are safe, which always followed when the topmost stair, conquered, let in the first light of the whole cheerful theatre down beneath us — I know not the fathom line that ever touched a descent so deep as I would be willing to bury more wealth in than Croesus had or the great Jew R—— is supposed to have, to purchase it. And now do just look at that merry little Chinese waiter holding an umbrella, big enough for a bed-tester, over the head of that pretty insipid half-Madonna-ish chit of a lady in that very blue summer-house."

Give the best answer or explanation for each of the following questions.

2.19   What does the opening line ("I have an almost feminine partiality for old china") have to do with the speaker's fondness for china?

2.20   Does the speaker describe various pieces of old china objectively or subjectively?

2.21 Why does Bridget wish that the "good old times would come again?"

2.22 How does the speaker (Elia) respond to her long "rhetorical vein?"

2.23 What does the fact that they are older now have to do with his answer?

2.24 Who is more reasonable in thinking, Elia or Bridget, and why do you think so?

2.25 How is Elia's fondness for china related to his discussion with Bridget?

2.26 Why do you think Lamb's style is classified as conversational?

George Gordon, Lord Byron (1788–1824). Charming, witty, childish, daring, eloquent, and morally reckless, George Gordon, Lord Byron was celebrated by his contemporaries. He embodied the Romantic yearnings of his time. However, the Byronic hero that occurs in his work is both a reflection and an exaggeration of that personage. As Bertrand Russell has noted, his "titanic cosmic self-assertion" gave rise to the archrebels of fiction and reality.

At the age of ten, Byron inherited his title and the ancestral estate of Newstead Abbey. His father was known as "Mad Jack." He was a rakish sea captain who had squandered the wealth of his two wives. After the death of his father, Byron's mother, Catherine Gordon of Gight, returned to her native Scotland to raise Byron near the font of Scottish Presbyterianism. The two lived in near-poverty until the death of his great-uncle, the fifth Lord Byron, bestowed worldly honor and a sizable income on Byron.

Byron attended Harrow School and then Trinity College, Cambridge. Determined to overcome the physical, emotional, and social inconveniences of a clubfoot, Byron excelled in boxing and horseback riding and made many close friends. During his time at the university, he began to earn his reputation as a rebel and an exhibitionist. He practiced immoral behavior and struggled to keep himself out of debt. Amid his debauchery, he published his first volume of poetry, *Hours of Idleness,* in 1807. It was unfavorably received by the *Edinburgh Review*. Byron returned the favor in 1809 by writing *English Bards and Scotch Reviewers,* a satire that derided his contemporaries for their Neoclassical style.

After taking his degree, Byron took his seat in the House of Lords, where he advocated many liberal causes. In 1809 he then traveled through Portugal, Spain, Malta, Greece, and the Near East. While in Turkey, he swam the Hellespont, a strait approximately forty miles wide. His adventures spawned *Childe Harold's Pilgrimage* (1812). The poem brought Byron instant fame. When he returned to London he entered the society of the cultured—and often debased—upper class. An exceptionally handsome man, Byron became involved in many scandalous affairs. He finally married Annabella Milbanke, hoping to escape the consequences of his reckless behavior. Aware of his failures, Annabella hoped to change him. However, the marriage lasted only a year. Byron, hopelessly attracted to forbidden sensations, was excluded from high society and forced to leave England.

In 1816 Byron moved to Geneva and was welcomed into the company of Shelley and his wife Mary. He was introduced to Claire Claremont, Shelley's sister-in-law, and soon fathered a daughter by her. Allegra was born in England in January 1817. While staying with the Shelleys, Byron completed the third canto of *Childe Harold's Pilgrimage* and wrote *The Prisoner of Chillon* and two acts of *Manfred*. He then traveled to Venice and Rome. In 1818 he published *Beppo*, a narrative romance poem written in the mock-heroic style. The work was a preview to his masterpiece *Don Juan,* the first two cantos of which he published in 1819. Though well received by romantic writers and thinkers, Don Juan reflects Byron's increasing disillusionment with his worldly escapades. His use of irony seems to convey a sense of emptiness and scorn, yet there is no sign of remorse. The bitter taste of sin has only hardened his heart to the ways of God.

While in Italy, Byron became involved with Teresa Gambas, the wife of Count Guiccioli. He lived in her household and continued to write. He wrote plays and published *The Vision of Judgement* in 1821. While living in Genoa, he became increasingly interested in the political situation in Greece. His earlier tour of the country had endeared him to the people and their culture. Before completing *Don Juan*, Byron sailed for Missolonghi and used the funds that he gained from the sale of *Newstead Abbey* to form the Byron Brigade in the hopes of freeing Greece from Turkish dominance. In April 1824, three months after he arrived, Byron contracted a fever. His doctor prescribed bleeding, but the loss of blood only killed him. To this day, Byron is lauded by Greece as a national hero, although he never even made it to the battlefield.

Byron's work marks a transition from Romanticism to modern literature. As one critic has observed, his heroic figure seemed to function outside of the bounds of good and evil. He is superhuman, able to live and exist according to his own moral standards without any outside restraint. Another writer has noted that Byron's life and poetry inspired writers and philosophers to make the intellectual leap from thinking in terms of moral rebellion to moral relativity. He was one of the most influential writers of the Romantic period.

It is important for the Christian to study Byron to discern that the eventual consequences of a worldview that is not based upon the Word of God are moral and social disintegration.

Fill in each of the following blanks with the correct answer.

2.27 While at Cambridge, Byron published _____, his first volume of poetry.

2.28 Inspired by his adventures in Europe and the Near East, Byron wrote _____, which brought him instant fame as a poet.

2.29 In 1816 Byron, shrouded in shame, was forced to leave _____ never to return.

2.30 Byron lived with the Shelleys while he was in _____.

2.31 Considered Byron's masterpiece, the first two cantos of _____ were first published in 1819.

2.32 In 1824 Byron joined the fight to free _____ from Turkish dominance.

2.33 Byron's heroic figures were influential in shaping modern concepts of moral _____.

What to Look For:

Byron's hero, Don Juan, is characterized as superhuman. His ability to evade the consequences of his sins is intended to be comical. Byron's masterpiece is a satire that is critical of the social conventions of his day. As you read, notice Byron's concept of morality. Does his use of satire affirm traditional standards of morality, or is he arguing that some men are able to function triumphantly outside of these standards?

From: *Don Juan*

This selection from Byron's unfinished epic satire concerns the relationship between the sixteen-year-old Don Juan and Donna Julia. Don Alfonso is Julia's husband, who is much older than she.

From: Canto 1

1

I WANT a hero: an uncommon want,
    When every year and month sends forth a new one,
Till, after cloying the gazettes with cant,
    The age discovers he is not the true one;
Of such as these I should not care to vaunt,
    I'll therefore take our ancient friend Don Juan.
We all have seen him, in the pantomime,
Sent to the devil somewhat ere his time.

63

'Tis a sad thing, I cannot choose but say,
    And all the fault of that indecent sun,
Who cannot leave alone our helpless clay,
    But will keep baking, broiling, burning on,
That howsoever people fast and pray,
    The flesh is frail, and so the soul undone.
What men call gallantry, and gods adultery,
Is much more common where the climate's sultry.

64

Happy the nations of the moral North!
    Where all is virtue, and the winter season
Sends sin, without a rag on, shivering forth
    ('Twas snow that brought St. Anthony to reason);
Where juries cast up what a wife is worth,
    By laying whate'er sum in mulct they please on
The lover, who must pay a handsome price,
Because it is a marketable vice.

133

Man's a phenomenon, one knows not what,
    And wonderful beyond all wondrous measure;
'Tis pity though, in this sublime world, that
    Pleasure's a sin, and sometimes sin's a pleasure;
Few mortals know what end they would be at,
    But whether glory, power, or love, or treasure,
The path is through perplexing ways, and when
The goal is gain'd, we die, you know—and then

134

What then?—I do not know, no more do you
    And so good night.—Return we to our story.
'Twas in November, when fine days are few
    And the far mountains wax a little hoary,
And clap a white cape on their mantles blue;
    And the sea dashes round the promontory,
And the loud breaker boils against the rock,
And sober suns must set at five o'clock.

135

'Twas, as the watchmen say, a cloudy night;

No moon, no stars, the wind was low or loud
By gusts, and many a sparkling hearth was bright
　　With the piled wood, round which the family crowd;
There's something cheerful in that sort of light,
　　Even as a summer sky's without a cloud:
I'm fond of fire, and crickets, and all that,
A lobster salad, and champagne, and chat.

136

'Twas midnight—Donna Julia was in bed,
　　Sleeping, most probably,- when at her door
Arose a clatter might awake the dead,
　　If they had never been awoke before,
And that they have been so we all have read,
　　And are to be so, at the least, once more;
The door was fasten'd, but with voice and fist
First knocks were heard, then 'Madam—Madam—hist!

137

'For God's sake, Madam—Madam—here's my master,
　　With more than half the city at his back
Was ever heard of such a curst disaster!
　　'Tis not my fault—I kept good watch—Alack!
Do pray undo the bolt a little faster
　　They're on the stair just now, and in a crack
Will all be here; perhaps he yet may fly
Surely the window's not so very high!'

138

By this time Don Alfonso was arrived,
　　With torches, friends, and servants in great number;
The major part of them had long been wived,
　　And therefore paused not to disturb the slumber
Of any wicked woman, who contrived
　　By stealth her husband's temples to encumber:
Examples of this kind are so contagious,
Were one not punish'd, all would be outrageous.

139

I can't tell how, or why, or what suspicion
　　Could enter into Don Alfonso's head;
But for a cavalier of his condition
　　It surely was exceedingly ill-bred,
Without a word of previous admonition,
　　To hold a levee round his lady's bed,
And summon lackeys, arm'd with fire and sword,
To prove himself the thing he most abhorr'd.

140

Poor Donna Julia, starting as from sleep
　　(Mind— that I do not say— she had not slept),
Began at once to scream, and yawn, and weep;
　　Her maid Antonia, who was an adept,
Contrived to fling the bed-clothes in a heap,
　　As if she had just now from out them crept:
I can't tell why she should take all this trouble
To prove her mistress had been sleeping double.

141

But Julia mistress, and Antonia maid,
    Appear'd like two poor harmless women, who
Of goblins, but still more of men afraid,
    Had thought one man might be deterr'd by two,
And therefore side by side were gently laid,
    Until the hours of absence should run through,
And truant husband should return, and say,
'My dear, I was the first who came away.'

142

Now Julia found at length a voice, and cried,
    'In heaven's name, Don Alfonso, what d' ye mean?
Has madness seized you? would that I had died
    Ere such a monster's victim I had been!
What may this midnight violence betide,
    A sudden fit of drunkenness or spleen?
Dare you suspect me, whom the thought would kill?
Search, then, the room!'—Alfonso said, 'I will.'

143

He search'd, they search'd, and rummaged everywhere,
    Closet and clothes' press, chest and window-seat,
And found much linen, lace, and several pair
    Of stockings, slippers, brushes, combs, complete,
With other articles of ladies fair,
    To keep them beautiful, or leave them neat:
Arras they prick'd and curtains with their swords,
And wounded several shutters, and some boards.

144

Under the bed they search'd, and there they found
    No matter what— it was not that they sought;
They open'd windows, gazing if the ground
    Had signs or footmarks, but the earth said nought;
And then they stared each other's faces round:
    'Tis odd, not one of all these seekers thought,
And seems to me almost a sort of blunder,
Of looking in the bed as well as under.

145

During this inquisition, Julia's tongue
    Was not asleep—'Yes, search and search,' she cried,
'Insult on insult heap, and wrong on wrong!
    It was for this that I became a bride!
For this in silence I have suffer'd long
    A husband like Alfonso at my side;
But now I'll bear no more, nor here remain,
If there be law or lawyers in all Spain.

146

'Yes, Don Alfonso! husband now no more,
    If ever you indeed deserved the name,
Is't worthy of your years?—you have threescore
    Fifty, or sixty, it is all the same
Is't wise or fitting, causeless to explore

For facts against a virtuous woman's fame?
Ungrateful, perjured, barbarous Don Alfonso,
How dare you think your lady would go on so?

161

But Don Alfonso stood with downcast looks,
    And, truth to say, he made a foolish figure;
When, after searching in five hundred nooks,
    And treating a young wife with so much rigour,
He gain'd no point, except some self-rebukes,
    Added to those his lady with such vigour
Had pour'd upon him for the last half-hour,
Quick, thick, and heavy— as a thunder-shower.

162

At first he tried to hammer an excuse,
    To which the sole reply was tears and sobs,
And indications of hysterics, whose
    Prologue is always certain throes, and throbs,
Gasps, and whatever else the owners choose:
    Alfonso saw his wife, and thought of Job's;
He saw too, in perspective, her relations,
And then he tried to muster all his patience.

163

He stood in act to speak, or rather stammer,
    But sage Antonia cut him short before
The anvil of his speech received the hammer,
    With 'Pray, sir, leave the room, and say no more,
Or madam dies.'—Alfonso mutter'd, 'D--n her,'
    But nothing else, the time of words was o'er;
He cast a rueful look or two, and did,
He knew not wherefore, that which he was bid.

164

With him retired his 'posse comitatus,'
    The attorney last, who linger'd near the door
Reluctantly, still tarrying there as late as
    Antonia let him—not a little sore
At this most strange and unexplain'd 'hiatus'
    In Don Alfonso's facts, which just now wore
An awkward look; as he revolved the case,
The door was fasten'd in his legal face.

165

No sooner was it bolted, than—Oh shame!
    Oh sin! Oh sorrow! and oh womankind!
How can you do such things and keep your fame,
    Unless this world, and t' other too, be blind?
Nothing so dear as an unfilch'd good name!
    But to proceed— for there is more behind:
With much heartfelt reluctance be it said,
Young Juan slipp'd half-smother'd, from the bed.

166

He had been hid— I don't pretend to say
    How, nor can I indeed describe the where

Young, slender, and pack'd easily, he lay,
　　No doubt, in little compass, round or square;
But pity him I neither must nor may
　　His suffocation by that pretty pair;
'Twere better, sure, to die so, than be shut
With maudlin Clarence in his Malmsey butt.*

199

This was Don Juan's earliest scrape; but whether
　　I shall proceed with his adventures is
Dependent on the public altogether;
　　We'll see, however, what they say to this:
Their favour in an author's cap's a feather,
　　And no great mischief's done by their caprice;
And if their approbation we experience,
Perhaps they'll have some more about a year hence.

200

My poem's epic, and is meant to be
　　Divided in twelve books; each book containing,
With love, and war, a heavy gale at sea,
　　A list of ships, and captains, and kings reigning,
New characters; the episodes are three.
　　A panoramic view of hell's in training,
After the style of Virgil and of Homer,
So that my name of Epic's no misnomer.

*pantomime - the legend of Don Juan was a popular one
*butt - wine cask

Fill in each of the following blanks with the correct explanation or answer.

2.34　Considering Byron's own licentious lifestyle, why do you think he chose a man like Don Juan to be the hero of his epic?

2.35　Who or what does Byron fault for Don Juan and Julia's affair? (stanzas 63 and 64)

2.36　In stanza 133, what does Byron say is a pity, and why?

2.37　Why is Don Alphonso's confusion intended to be amusing?

2.38　Where was Don Juan hiding?

2.39　Why does Byron say that he intends to write his epic after the style of the great epic writers, Virgil and Homer?

Percy Bysshe Shelley (1792–1822). A radical nonconformist, Percy Bysshe Shelley viewed the traditional institutions of society as tyrannical. He believed that society could be redeemed only by love. Yet, his personal life was one of self-absorption and self-centeredness. His romantic verses, judged by modern critics as the greatest, are infused with his hatred for royalty, religion, and codified morality.

Born into a family of conservative aristocrats, Shelley was properly educated at Syon House Academy, Eton, and University College, Oxford. The pressures of upper-class society, however, increased Shelley's propensity towards rebellion. Unable to excel in sports, Shelley found in writing an outlet for his frustrations as a much mocked and bullied outcast. With his sister Elizabeth, he privately published a Gothic-horror poem, *Original Poetry by Victor and Cazire,* in 1810. While at Oxford, Shelley read the works of Godwin and Paine. (Godwin would later become his father-in-law.) He discovered in them kindred spirits; they, too, possessed an enthusiasm for the overthrow of oppression in any form, political or religious.

In 1811 Shelley and his friend T. J. Hogg published "The Necessity of Atheism." The pamphlet, which was circulated around Oxford, argued that the existence of God could not be proven. Shelley was quickly expelled from Oxford, bringing shame on his father, who was a conservative member of the House of Lords. Later that year, he eloped with 16-year-old Harriet Westbrook, causing himself further difficulties with his family and society. Harriet was the affectionate daughter of a coffeehouse owner whom the 18-year-old Shelley set himself to "free" from the oppression of her father. Of Harriet's father, Shelley wrote to a friend, he "has persecuted her in a most horrible way by endeavoring to compel her to go to school." In 1812 Shelly published *Address to the Irish People* in the hope of overthrowing the British oppression of poor Irish Catholics.

Living off a small allowance from his family, Shelley traveled with his wife around England, spreading his ideas and forming relationships with prominent leaders of the Romantic Movement. During this time, he corresponded with William Godwin, becoming his devoted disciple. In 1813 he published the long prophetic poem *Queen Mab*.

In 1814 Shelley's relationship with Harriet began to collapse. According to his own standards of morality, he believed that marriage was a degrading institution and that two people should not cohabit unless they were in love. So he abandoned Harriet and traveled to Geneva with Godwin's beautiful daughter, Mary. Claire Clairmont, Mary's stepsister, accompanied them and later became involved with Byron. While on the continent, Mary began to compose her novel *Frankenstein*. In 1815 Shelley returned to London briefly to inherit a vast fortune from his grandfather. He composed *Alastor* during the visit. Its publication in 1816 gained him a measure of fame. Back in Geneva, Shelley invited Harriet to come live with him—but as his sister, not as his wife. In 1816 Harriet, pregnant by an unknown lover, committed suicide in London.

Immediately following Harriet's death, Shelley married Mary in an attempt to gain custody of his two children. But Shelley's reputation as an atheist and an adulterer compelled officials to refuse his request. The children were entrusted to the care of another. Shelley, deeply distressed by the decision, wrote many verse lines expressing his anguish. While living in an estate on the Thames, Shelley wrote *Laon and Cythna*. The poem was published in 1818 as *The Revolt of Islam*. The sonnet "Ozymandias" was published in that same year.

From 1818–1822, Shelley lived with his family in Italy. He met Byron again in Venice and later moved to Rome and Pisa. While in Pisa, he joined the company of romantic thinkers and writers known as the "Pisan Circle" and composed some of his greatest works. "Ode to the West Wind" was published in 1819. "To the Skylark," "The Cloud," and *Prometheus Unbound* were all published in 1820. Shelley also wrote many prose works during this time, including *Essay on the Devil* (1821) and *The Defense of Poetry,* which was not published until 1840. In 1821 after hearing the news of the death of Keats, Shelley wrote the elegy, *Adonais*. Like Byron, Shelley was sympathetic with the Greek war for independence and wrote *Hellas* in 1822.

After moving his household in 1822 to the Bay of Lerici, Shelley began *The Triumph of Life*. But before he could finish it, Shelley and two other men were drowned in a storm that capsized their small sailboat. Ten days later, their bodies washed ashore. After discovering a volume of Keats's poetry in Shelley's pocket, Byron and other friends cremated the men on the beach.

Shelley's works demonstrate an alteration of the romantic spirit. His first works affirm his extreme revolutionary spirit. He believed that man would return to his peaceful existence when traditional institutions were violently removed. Sobered by the trials of life (three of Shelley's children died before they were ten) and the consequences of his own sin (marital difficulties and family strife), Shelley's later works reflect a hardening toward romantic beliefs. He no longer saw the cause of society's problems rooted in institutional defects but in man's own failure to hope and strive for a better existence. Although he maintained a hatred for Christianity all of his life, he later acknowledged the redeeming power of love. His beautiful lyrics undergirded his enduring belief in the power of the imagination to effect a golden age of society. Shelley's variety of lyrics and range of voice mark him duly as one of the greatest of all English poets.

Fill in each of the following blanks with the correct answer.

2.40   As a boy and a man, Shelley rebelled against the conservative ideals of _____ class society.

2.41   In 1811 Shelley was expelled from Oxford for the distribution of _____, which argued that the existence of God could not be proven.

2.42   Shelley published _____ with the intention of starting a revolution in Ireland.

2.43   In 1814 Shelley left his wife and moved to the continent with _____.

2.44   In 1818 Shelley moved with his family to _____, living there until his death.

2.45   While in the company of romantic thinkers and writers known as the _____ Circle, Shelley composed some of his greatest works, including _____, which was published in 1819.

2.46   Shelley's later works reflect a changed disposition toward _____ ideals.

2.47   As a romantic, Shelley believed in the redeeming power of the _____ to effect a golden age of society.

What to Look For:

Many of Shelley's works evidence his rebellion against traditional religious beliefs. Like other Romantics, he exalted the power of Nature to renew the spirit. As you read, notice Shelley's radical religious beliefs. How does he seek to replace the Spirit of God with the West Wind? (For biblical comparison, see John 3:7,8; Acts 2:1–4.)

An ode is an address written as a rhymed lyric intended to evoke exalted feelings. Shelley said that this ode "was conceived and chiefly written in a wood that skirts the Arno, near Florence, and on a day when that tempestuous wind, whose temperature is at once mild and animating, was collecting vapors which pour down autumnal rains. They began, as I foresaw, at sunset with a violent tempest of hail and rain, attended by that magnificent thunder and lightening peculiar to the Cisalpine regions." The ode is divided into five parts, each of which consists of a fourteen-line stanza that is structured in the form of a sonnet with the rhyme scheme: aba bcb cdc ded ee. Each couplet is a passionate cry or question addressed to the West Wind.

Ode to the West Wind

I

O wild west wind, thou breath of autumn's being,
   Thou, from whose unseen presence the leaves dead
Are driven, like ghosts from an enchanter fleeing,

   Yellow, and black, and pale, and hectic red,
Pestilence-stricken multitudes! O thou,   5
   Who chariotest to their dark wintry bed

The wingèd seeds, where they lie cold and low,
   Each like a corpse within its grave, until
Thine azure sister of the spring shall blow

   Her clarion o'er the dreaming earth, and fill   10
(Driving sweet buds like flocks to feed in air)
   With living hues and odours plain and hill:

Wild spirit, which art moving everywhere;
Destroyer and preserver; hear, oh hear!

II

Thou on whose stream, 'mid the steep sky's commotion,   15
   Loose clouds like earth's decaying leaves are shed,
Shook from the tangled boughs of heaven and ocean,

   Angels of rain and lightning! there are spread
On the blue surface of thine airy surge,
   Like the bright hair uplifted from the head   20

Of some fierce Mænad, even from the dim verge
   Of the horizon to the zenith's height,
The locks of the approaching storm. Thou dirge

   Of the dying year, to which this closing night
Will be the dome of a vast sepulchre,   25
   Vaulted with all thy congregated might

Of vapours, from whose solid atmosphere
Black rain, and fire, and hail, will burst: Oh hear!

III

Thou who didst waken from his summer-dreams
   The blue Mediterranean, where he lay,   30
Lull'd by the coil of his crystàlline streams,

   Beside a pumice isle in Baiæ's bay,
And saw in sleep old palaces and towers
   Quivering within the wave's intenser day,

All overgrown with azure moss, and flowers   35
   So sweet, the sense faints picturing them! Thou
For whose path the Atlantic's level powers

Cleave themselves into chasms, while far below
The sea-blooms and the oozy woods which wear
   The sapless foliage of the ocean know   40

Thy voice, and suddenly grow gray with fear
And tremble and despoil themselves: Oh hear!

IV

If I were a dead leaf thou mightest bear;
   If I were a swift cloud to fly with thee;
A wave to pant beneath thy power, and share   45

   The impulse of thy strength, only less free
Than thou, O uncontrollable! If even
   I were as in my boyhood, and could be

The comrade of thy wanderings over heaven,
   As then, when to outstrip thy skyey speed   50
Scarce seem'd a vision; I would ne'er have striven

   As thus with thee in prayer in my sore need.
Oh! lift me as a wave, a leaf, a cloud!
   I fall upon the thorns of life! I bleed!

A heavy weight of hours has chain'd and bow'd   55
One too like thee—tameless, and swift, and proud.

V

Make me thy lyre, even as the forest is:
   What if my leaves are falling like its own?
The tumult of thy mighty harmonies

   Will take from both a deep, autumnal tone,   60
Sweet though in sadness. Be thou, Spirit fierce,
   My spirit! Be thou me, impetuous one!

Drive my dead thoughts over the universe
   Like wither'd leaves to quicken a new birth!
And, by the incantation of this verse,   65

   Scatter, as from an unextinguish'd hearth
Ashes and sparks, my words among mankind!
   Be through my lips to unawaken'd earth

The trumpet of a prophecy! O wind,
If winter comes, can spring be far behind?   70

Circle the letter of the line that best answers each of the following questions.

2.48 What is an ode?

   a. a sonnet
   b. an address written as a rhymed lyric intended to evoke exalted feelings
   c. an unrhymed sonnet written to evoke hatred and grief
   d. an address written as an unrhymed lyric intended to evoke sorrowful feelings

2.49 The five stanzas of the "Ode to the West Wind" are structured into what form?

   a. sonnet
   b. lyric
   c. novel
   d. sermon

2.50 Why is the West Wind called the "Destroyer and preserver?"

   a. It destroys that which is dead and preserves that which has been newly brought to life.
   b. It destroys lies and preserves the truth.
   c. It destroys new life and preserves death.
   d. It destroys newly conceived political ideals.

2.51 At the end of Parts I, II, and III, who does Shelley beg to hear him?

   a. Jesus
   b. the West Wind
   c. his father
   d. the reader

2.52 What three main things found in Parts I, II, and III demonstrate the West Wind's powers as "Destroyer and preserver?"

   a. animal life, leaves, and clouds
   b. leaves, clouds, and planets
   c. leaves, clouds, and waves
   d. clouds, rain, and lightening

2.53 Why does Shelley ask the West Wind to "lift me as a wave, a leaf, a cloud!" in Part IV?

   a. He believes that only the West Wind can bring him new life and preserve it.
   b. He wishes to be happy.
   c. He believes that God Almighty is the Creator and Sustainer of the universe.
   d. He wants to die.

2.54 In Part V, to what does Shelley compare his "dead thoughts?"

   a. the waves of the sea
   b. dead leaves
   c. a lyre
   d. the sound of leaves falling

2.55 What does Shelley ask the West Wind to do for him in Part V?

   a. to make him a forest, to make him one with nature, and to make him a prophet
   b. to grant him repentance and enable him to turn from his sin
   c. to allow him to remain as the dead leaves on the forest floor
   d. to make him a lyre, to be one with his spirit, to give him new life, and to make him a prophet of the West Wind's powers

2.56 What does Shelley prophesy in lines 69 and 70?

   a. The West Wind will bring more death and destruction.
   b. Shelley will never be granted new life.
   c. The West Wind will bring new life after a period of death.
   d. Childhood innocence will be followed by adult experience.

John Keats (1795–1821). John Keats's rapid rise to poetic eminence is incomprehensible to many people. Born the son of a stable owner in London, Keats was not rich in financial or cultural means. He was educated at Clarke's School, Enfield, and after the death of his mother, he was apprenticed to a surgeon-apothecary. In 1815 Keats attended Guy's Hospital as a medical student. The following year, he was licensed as an apothecary. But Keats soon abandoned his promising medical career to pursue his passion for poetry.

While a student at Clarke's School, Keats was introduced to Edmund Spenser. The Renaissance poet's diction greatly influenced Keats's early work. His first poems were published in 1816 by his lifelong friend Leigh Hunt, editor of the radical periodical *The Examiner*. Hunt introduced Keats to Shelley, Lamb, and the painter Richard Haydon, opening for him a new realm of influence. The close friendships that were eventually forged proved essential to Keats's survival as a poet. Although Keats was often unappreciated by contemporary critics for his work, his friends provided him with a much-needed audience. In 1817 Keats published his first volume of poems. Included in the collection was "I stood tip-toe upon a little hill," "Sleep and Poetry," and some of his letters. The works showed the influence of Hunt's romanticism. In the same year, Keats began his work on the long poem *Endymion,* which described his ideal feminine counterpart. It was published in 1818.

The criticism leveled upon *Endymion* was, among other things, savage. *Blackwood's Magazine* categorized him as one of Hunt's "Cockney School of poetry," calling him to give up poetry altogether. Determined to develop his genius, Keats declared, "I will write independently." He then severed himself from all poetic influences.

Along with Charles Armitage Brown, he took a difficult walking tour of the Lake District and Scotland in the summer of 1818. The adventure, though physically grueling, enlivened Keats's spirits and opened his eyes to the inspiring beauty of nature. Later that same year, Keats's younger brother, Tom, contracted tuberculosis, the disease to which their mother had succumbed to when Keats was fourteen. While nursing his brother, Keats himself began to manifest symptoms. A persistent sore throat was an ominous reminder of his own mortality. In December 1818, Tom died. The loss, coupled with the thought of his own death from the disease, did not, however, hamper Keats's creative energy.

In the midst of emotional turmoil, Keats had his "Great Year." From January to September 1819, a succession of masterpieces flowed from his pen. Keats wrote "The Eve of St. Agnes," "La Belle Dame sans Merci," "Ode on a Grecian Urn," "Ode to a Nightingale," and many other odes and sonnets. (The works were published collectively in 1820 in the volume *Lamia, Isabella, The Eve of St. Agnes, and Other Poems.*) As one critic observed, he possessed an "intellectual and spiritual passion" for beauty that rivaled the works of his contemporaries. His language reminded many people of Shakespeare. But his achievement was incomparable. As another critic has observed, at the age of twenty-four and with little experience in writing poetry, Keats had reached a level of poetic maturity that the likes of Chaucer, Milton, or Shakespeare did not attain until much later in life.

By 1819 Keats was engaged to Fanny Bawne. His love for her occupied much of his dwindling energy. He began work on "The Fall of Hyperion" in the fall of 1819, but he never completed the work. After being faced with the inevitable signs of his imminent death, Keats traveled under medical advice to Italy with a friend. His love for Fanny was still strong, and their doomed relationship was exceedingly despairing to Keats. His letters to her reveal some of his most penetrating thoughts on love and suffering.

On February 23, 1821, Keats died in Rome of consumption. His battle with the disease prevented him from visiting Shelley. A year later, when Shelley's body washed up on shore, a volume of Keats's poetry was found in his pocket.

Unlike his Romantic contemporaries, Keats did not envision a golden age of man here on earth. His physical sufferings and poverty probably made this notion seem too fantastical for belief. Instead, Keats imagined a higher existence for man, where the pain and distress of our earthly existence would be no more. Although Keats's understanding of life after death might sound similar to the Christian hope for heaven, his beliefs are rooted in transcendental mysticism. Rejecting the guidance of Scripture, he held an exalted view of art. It alone could elevate one's senses to the spiritual world. In Keats's understanding of reality, truth is relative to one's interpretation of what is beautiful. He saw truth and beauty as two inseparable parts. Christians do not necessarily disagree with the ultimate reality of this conclusion. (That which is beautiful is true, and that which is true is beautiful because God is the Author of Truth, and nothing but goodness and light resides in Him.) However, Christians differ greatly with Keats on what is the standard of truth. Keats interpreted the standard of truth to be the affections of man, which are ever-changing and tainted by sin. Christians, on the other hand, understand it to be the holy and immutable Word of God.

Fill in each of the following blanks with the correct answer.

2.57 To pursue a career as a poet, Keats abandoned a career as a(n) _____ .

2.58 Heavily influential on Keats's earlier works was _____ , a Renaissance poet.

2.59 _____ helped Keats forge some important friendships with other Romantic writers and painters.

2.60 Published in 1818, _____ was unfavorably received by critics.

2.61 _____ is considered Keats's "Great Year" because he produced a rapid succession of masterpieces.

2.62 "The Eve of St. Agnes," "La Belle Dame sans Merci," "Ode on a Grecian Urn," and "Ode to a Nightingale" were published in 1820 in the volume _____ .

2.63 In the fall of 1819, Keats began _____ , but he never completed it.

2.64 Keats was engaged to _____ .

2.65 Keats moved to Italy in the hopes of alleviating the symptoms of _____ .

2.66 Keats's language has been likened to that of _____ .

BRITISH LITERATURE LIFEPAC FOUR TEST

Name _____

Date _____

Score _____

79 / 99

Answer *true* or *false* **for each of the following statements** (each answer, 1 point).

1. _____ After the Napoleonic wars, England experienced an economic depression.

2. _____ The main target of Jane Austen's satire was romantic entanglements of the upper class.

3. _____ In Shelley's "Ode to the West Wind," the West Wind is called the "Destroyer and preserver" because it preserves things that destroy.

4. _____ In *Don Juan*, Byron says that it is a pity that people sin.

5. _____ England experienced dynamic changes in the realms of politics, economics, and religion during the Romantic era.

6. _____ Charles Dickens's novels on societal injustices caused many people to doubt all traditional beliefs about mankind and society.

7. _____ Utilitarians were influential in the abolition of slavery and the enactment of child labor laws.

8. _____ The Oxford Movement emphasized the Word of God as the sole guide to faith and life.

9. _____ The art for art's sake theorists believed that experience was the source of meaning.

10. _____ *Apologia pro Vita Sua* is the autobiographical account of Newman's spiritual quest for certainty, which he eventually found in the traditions and rituals of the Roman Catholic Church.

11. _____ The Romantic Period of literature in England was inaugurated by the publication of *Lyrical Ballads* in 1798.

12. _____ In Wilde's play *The Importance of Being Earnest*, it is important to Gwendolen that the man she marry is named Earnest because it would mean that he would be a faithful husband.

13. _____ In *Alice in Wonderland*, Alice becomes frustrated with the game of croquet because no one is obeying the rules.

14. _____ In *Alice in Wonderland*, the Queen deals with any difficulty that she comes up against by commanding that people's heads be cut off.

15. _____ Coleridge's literary criticism reversed the traditional emphasis of poetry by focusing on poetry's ability to evoke pleasure.

16. _____ The literature of the Victorian period in England is characterized by individualism, mysticism, emotionalism, love of nature, nostalgia, and a fascination with the medieval past.

17. _____ The opening line of *Pride and Prejudice* is ironic because in the story a single man in possession of a good fortune has difficulty finding women willing to become his wife.

Fill in each of the blanks using items from the following word list (each answer, 2 points).

The Pickwick Papers strong leaders elegy
Evolution Sir Walter Scott Alfred, Lord Tennyson
Scenes from Clerical Life *Sartor Resartus* factory
In Memoriam public readings Lewis Carroll

18. In 1833 Thomas Carlyle published a philosophical satire titled _____ outlining his spiritual idealism.

19. Carlyle's histories contend that the basis for strong, stable societies is _____.

20. In 1857 at the encouragement of Lewes, George Eliot published _____ in *Blackwood's Magazine*.

21. Eliot's belief in moral progress was influenced by the theory of _____.

22. As a boy, Charles Dickens was made to work in a _____ when his father was imprisoned for unpaid debts.

23. Published in volume form in 1837, _____ was the first book to make Dickens a celebrity in England and America.

24. In 1867–1868, Dickens traveled for the second time to America to give _____ of his works.

25. Written by Tennyson for his friend Hallam, _____ is considered the greatest _____ in the English language.

26. In 1850 _____ was appointed poet laureate.

27. _____ first told *Alice's Adventures in Wonderland* to the three Liddell daughters.

28. _____ maintained a position as a legal official throughout most of his life.

Fill in each of the blanks with the correct explanation or answer (each answer, 4 points).

29. In the Introduction to *Songs of Experience*, to whom is the reader told to listen for spiritual guidance?
_____

30. In the Preface to *Lyrical Ballads*, how did Wordsworth define "good poetry"?
_____

31. What historical conflict serves as the basis for *Ivanhoe*?
_____

32. In "My Last Duchess," what is our only source of information about the duchess?
_____

33. In *The Pickwick Papers*, what is the stated purpose of the new branch of Pickwickians?
_____

Circle the letter of the line that best answers each of the following questions (each answer, 3 points).

34. William Blake's "two contrary states of the human soul" may be described as:
   a. an insane vision of God versus a sane vision of humanity.
   b. a spiritual state and a fleshly state.
   c. good and evil.
   d. a child-like vision of reality and an adult vision of reality.

35. Because the beliefs of the Tullivers and Dodsons, from *The Mill on the Floss*, are based upon unchanging traditions, their lives are characterized by:

    a. oppressive narrowness.
    b. beauty and truth.
    c. freedom.
    d. greatness and nobility.

36. In *Apologia Pro Vita Sua*, why does John Newman compare the doctrine of transubstantiation to that of the Trinity?

    a. He believes that Roman Catholicism and Protestantism are essentially the same religion.
    b. He thinks that the doctrine of the Trinity is the easiest doctrine to comprehend.
    c. He is trying to establish the point that some religious doctrines cannot be explained intellectually although they are true.
    d. Both doctrines can be proven by philosophical means.

37. What did Carlyle's new faith for a secular society do?

    a. encouraged people to progress morally for the betterment of others.
    b. allowed for a sense of religious awe yet did not dictate a standard of morality
    c. held everyone accountable to a universal standard of right and wrong
    d. trusted in the powers of the Roman Catholic Church to point man to truth

38. In *Sartor Resartus*, why does the professor say that Christianity in the nineteenth century is "lying in ruins, over grown with jungle?"

    a. It is a religion for yesterday, today, and forever.
    b. Christians need to live better lives.
    c. It is teeming with life and vitality.
    d. It is a primitive religion that is not useful to the modern man.

39. In the Prologue of *In Memoriam*, Tennyson explains the differences between:

    a. theory and fact.
    b. Protestantism and Transcendentalism.
    c. faith and knowledge.
    d. innocence and experience.

40. In section 96 of *In Memoriam*, Tennyson excuses his doubt of orthodox Christianity by calling it:

    a. common doubt.
    b. harmless doubt.
    c. honest doubt.
    d. scientific doubt.

41. The style of Charles Lamb, who was known as the prince of English essayists, is:

    a. polished and conversational with a romantic sensibility for the commonplace things and the activities of London.
    b. spontaneous.
    c. polished with a scientific appreciation for nature.
    d. unpolished and emotional.

42. What does Shelley ask the West Wind to do for him in Part V of "Ode to the West Wind?"

    a. to make him a lyre, to be one with his spirit, give him new life, and to make him a prophet of the West Wind's powers.
    b. to grant him all his wishes
    c. to make him poet laureate
    d. to destroy all of the upper class control of England

Underline the correct answer in each of the following statements (each answer, 1 point).

43. Sir Walter Scott is the originator of the (romance, historical, mystery) novel.

44. Coleridge encouraged Wordsworth to espouse (evangelical, traditional, transcendental) beliefs in his poetry.

45. (Tennyson's, Scott's, Byron's) heroic figures were influential in shaping modern concepts of moral relativity.

46. The publication of (*Biographia Literaria*, *Lyrical Ballads*, *The Rime of the Ancient Mariner*) in 1817 established Coleridge's reputation as the father of a new tradition of literary criticism.

47. (Keats, Austen, Tennyson) believed that art alone could elevate one's senses to the spiritual world.

48. (Austen, Scott, Shelley) believed in the redeeming power of the imagination to effect a golden age of society.

49. Intellectually, the Romantic Movement was based on the tenets of the (Enlightenment, Reformation, Roman Catholic Church).

50. The moral lesson of (*The Ring and the Book*, *The Rime of the Ancient Mariner*, *The Importance of Being Earnest*) is that spiritual blessings exist for those who love God's creation.

51. In 1846 (Tennyson, Shelley, Browning) married Elizabeth Barrett and moved with her to Italy.

52. The publication of (*Lyrical Ballads*, *Ivanhoe*, *The Ring and the Book*) in 1868–1869, elevated Browning's reputation as a poet above that of Tennyson.

53. First performed in 1895, (*The Ring and the Book*, *The Importance of Being Earnest*, *Middlemarch*) is considered to be Wilde's masterpiece.

Thinking and Writing:

Choose one activity from the following "Thought and Discussion" topics. Write your answer on a separate piece of paper.

1. Explain the story line of *The Rime of the Ancient Mariner* and the moral lesson that Coleridge is trying to teach. Be sure to mention the Mariner's sin, curse, and method of restoration. Discuss Coleridge's understanding of sin and his answers to the problem of guilt in reference to Psalm 51. Does he understand sin to be an act of rebellion against a holy God? How is the burden of guilt removed?

2. Explain Keats's views on art, beauty, and love. Be sure to mention his concept of beauty and truth as two inseparable realities. Keats believed that art was an eternal standard by which the changing human condition was to be compared. Discuss Keats's elevated view of art in reference to Colossians 1:17 and Revelation 1:8. What is the ultimate standard of truth and goodness? Why is Keats's "eternal standard" subject to change?

3. Explain Carlyle's criticism of Christianity. Be sure to mention that he did not argue against Christian doctrine directly. Rather, his criticism was of the appearance of its followers. Remember that Carlyle described Christianity as the "Worship of Sorrow" and Christians as "doleful." (During the nineteenth century, many people claimed to be Christians, but, in fact, many of them practiced a religion of tradition and ritual rather than a religion rooted in love for God and love for other people (cf. Matthew 22:37–40). As 2 Timothy 3:5 states, they gave an appearance of godliness, but they denied, through word and deed, the God who makes men godly. Read Romans 2:17–24. Discuss how our strict attention to tradition rather than God's Word causes people to curse the name of our Lord unnecessarily? What did Jesus have to say about the legalism of the Pharisees (cf. Matthew 23:23–28)?

2.67 Keats believed that _____ alone could elevate one's senses to the spiritual world.

2.68 Keats understood _____ and _____ to be two inseparable parts.

What to Look For:

As you read, pay attention to Keats's views on art, beauty, and love. To what eternal standard does he compare the changing human condition? Is this biblical? Compare your answer to Colossian 1:17 and Revelation 1:8.

ODE ON A GRECIAN URN

I

Thou still unravished bride of quietness,
Thou foster-child of silence and slow time,
Sylvan historian, who canst thus express
A flowery tale more sweetly than our rhyme:
What leaf-fringed legend haunts about thy shape
Of deities or mortals, or of both,
In Tempe or the dales of Arcady?
What men or gods are these? What maidens loth?
What mad pursuit? What struggle to escape?
What pipes and timbrels? What wild ecstasy?

II

Heard melodies are sweet, but those unheard
Are sweeter; therefore, ye soft pipes, play on;
Not to the sensual ear, but, more endeared,
Pipe to the spirit ditties of no tone:
Fair youth, beneath the trees, thou canst not leave
Thy song, nor ever can those trees be bare;
Bold lover, never, never canst thou kiss,
Though winning near the goal—yet, do not grieve;
She cannot fade, though thou hast not thy bliss,
For ever wilt thou love, and she be fair!

III

Ah, happy, happy boughs! that cannot shed
Your leaves, nor ever bid the spring adieu;
And, happy melodist, unwearied,
For ever piping songs for ever new;
More happy love! more happy, happy love!
For ever warm and still to be enjoyed,
For ever panting, and for ever young;
All breathing human passion far above,
That leaves a heart high-sorrowful and cloyed,
A burning forehead, and a parching tongue.

IV

Who are these coming to the sacrifice?
To what green altar, O mysterious priest,
Lead'st thou that heifer lowing at the skies,
And all her silken flanks with garlands dressed?
What little town by river or sea shore,
Or mountain-built with peaceful citadel,
Is emptied of this folk, this pious morn?
And, little town, thy streets for evermore
Will silent be; and not a soul to tell
Why thou art desolate, can ever return.

V

O Attic shape! Fair attitude! with brede
Of marble men and maidens overwrought,
With forest branches and the trodden weed;
Thou, silent form, dost tease us out of thought
As doth eternity: Cold pastoral!
When old age shall this generation waste,
Thou shalt remain, in midst of other woe
Than ours, a friend to man, to whom thou say'st,
"Beauty is truth, truth beauty,—that is all
Ye know on earth, and all ye need to know."

Give the best answer or explanation for each of the following questions.

2.69 What is the subject of this poem?

2.70 According to stanza 2, explain the poet's meaning of "Heard melodies are sweet, but those unheard/ Are sweeter…"

2.71 Why can the "Bold lover" in stanza 2 never kiss his beloved?

2.72 Does the love and the happiness of the lovers on the urn ever end?

2.73 What does the poet say about the beauty of the women on the urn?

2.74 According to stanza 4, why will the streets of the little town be forever silent?

2.75 How does the urn, as a work of art, tease mortal humans?

2.76 What ultimate reality does the urn convey to humans? Why does Keats say that is "all we need to know?"

Review the material in this section in preparation for the Self Test, which will check your mastery of both this particular section and the previous section.

SELF TEST 2

Underline the correct answer in each of the following statements (each answer, 3 points).

2.01 The Romantic Period of literature in England was inaugurated by the publication of Wordsworth and Coleridge's (*Songs of Experience, The Prelude, Lyrical Ballads*) in 1798.

2.02 Intellectually, the Romantic Movement was based on the tenets of the (Reformation, Enlightenment, Renaissance).

2.03 Sir Walter Scott's first literary success came as a writer of romantic (novels, poems, essays).

2.04 (William Blake's, John Keats's, Samuel Taylor Coleridge's) "two contrary states of the human soul" may be described as a child-like vision of reality and an adult vision of reality.

2.05 According to *The Preface of Lyrical Ballads*, Wordsworth describes "good poetry" as "the (spontaneous, planned, manipulated) overflow of powerful feelings."

2.06 The moral lesson of (*Kubla Khan, The Rime of the Ancient Mariner, Ivanhoe*) is that there are spiritual blessings for those who love God's creation.

Circle the letter of the line that best answers each of the following questions (each answer, 3 points).

2.07 What was the main target of Jane Austen's satire?

a. the unsanitary living conditions of the poor
b. the romantic entanglements of the upper class
c. the religious controversies of the day
d. the romantic entanglements of the lower class

2.08 Austen's reputation as one of the world's greatest novelists is based on the publication of

a. *Sense and Sensibility, Pride and Prejudice, Northanger Abbey, Mansfield Park, Emma,* and *Persuasion.*
b. *Sense and Sensibility, A History of England, Northanger Abbey, Mansfield Park, Emma,* and *Persuasion.*
c. *Love and Friendship, Northanger Abbey, Mansfield Park, Emma,* and *Persuasion.*
d. *A History of England, Love and Friendship,* and *Elinor and Marianne.*

2.09 What is the most pronounced trait that identifies Austen with her Romantic contemporaries?

a. her mystical undertones
b. her fascination with the Middle Ages
c. her focus on the life and circumstances of the lower classes
d. her attention to ordinary things

2.010 From 1821–1823, Charles Lamb published his most famous essays in the *London Magazine*, which were published as a collection titled:

a. *Essays of Moses.*
b. *Essays of Elia.*
c. *The Posthumous Papers of Elia.*
d. *Essays of London and Its People.*

2.011 Known as the prince of English essayists, Lamb's style is:

   a. spontaneous with a romantic sensibility for nature's powers to stir the emotions.
   b. polished with a neoclassical attention to the powers of reason.
   c. polished and conversational with a romantic sensibility for the commonplace things and activities of London.
   d. spontaneous and disorderly.

2.012 In the "Ode to the West Wind," why is the West Wind called the "Destroyer and preserver?"

   a. It destroys that which is dead and preserves that which has been newly brought to life.
   b. It destroys lies and preserves the truth.
   c. It destroys new life and preserves death.
   d. It destroys newly conceived political ideals.

2.013 What three main things found in Parts I, II, and III demonstrate the West Wind's powers as "Destroyer and preserver?"

   a. animal life, leaves, and clouds
   b. leaves, clouds, and planets
   c. leaves, clouds, and waves
   d. clouds, rain, and lightening

2.014 What does Shelley ask the West Wind to do for him in Part V?

   a. to make him a forest, to make him one with nature, and to make him a prophet
   b. to grant him repentance and enable him to turn from his sin
   c. to allow him to remain as the dead leaves on the forest floor
   d. to make him a lyre, to be one with his spirit, to give him new life, and to make him a prophet of the West Wind's powers

2.015 What does Shelley prophesy in lines 69 and 70?

   a. The West Wind will bring more death and destruction.
   b. Shelley will never be granted new life.
   c. The West Wind will bring new life after a period of death.
   d. Childhood innocence will be followed by adult experience.

Answer *true* **or** *false* **for each of the following statements** (each answer, 2 points).

2.016 _____ The opening line of *Pride and Prejudice* is ironic because a single man in possession of a good fortune is never lacking of available women wanting to become his wife.

2.017 _____ Mrs. Bennet is annoyed with Mr. Bennet in Chapter 2 because he has gone to visit Mr. Bingley.

2.018 _____ Mr. Darcy refuses to dance with Elizabeth Bennet because he doesn't think he is worthy of her presence.

2.019 _____ The initial meeting of Elizabeth Bennet, the heroine, and Mr. Darcy, her future husband, differ from other romance stories in that they fall in love with each other at first sight.

2.020 _____ In Lamb's essay "Old China," the speaker describes various pieces of old china subjectively.

2.021 _____ In "Old China," Bridget wishes that the "good old times would come again" so that they could be comfortable and wealthy.

2.022 _____ The speaker responds to Bridget by saying that it is good that they have more money now because they are older and in need of more comfort that only wealth can provide.

2.023 _____ In *Don Juan*, the narrator faults the warm climate for Don Juan and Julia's affair.

2.024 _____ In stanza 133, of *Don Juan* the poet claims that it is a pity that pleasure is a sin and sin is pleasurable.

2.025 _____ Byron says he that intends to write his epic after the style of the great epic writers, Virgil and Homer, so that people will know that it is an epic.

2.026 _____ In the poem "Ode on a Grecian Urn," the love and the happiness of the lovers on the urn never ends.

2.027 _____ The urn, as a work of art, teases mortal humans by making them hope that their happiness will last as long as the happiness of the figures on the urn.

2.028 _____ According to Keats's poem "Ode on a Grecian Urn," the only truth that we need to know on earth is that "Beauty is life, life beauty."

Fill in each of the blanks using items from the following word list (each answer, 2 points).

- tuberculosis
- 1818
- Italy
- Mary Godwin
- imagination
- 1819
- *Ode to the West Wind*
- relativity
- Pisan
- *Childe Harold's Pilgrimage*
- England
- *Don Juan*
- art
- *Lamia, Isabella, The Eve of St. Agnes, and Other Poems*

2.029 Inspired by his adventures in Europe and the Near East, Byron wrote _____ _____, which brought him instant fame as a poet.

2.030 In 1816 Byron, shrouded in shame, was forced to leave _____ never to return.

2.031 Considered Byron's masterpiece, the first two cantos of _____ were first published in 1819.

2.032 Byron's heroic figures were influential in shaping modern concepts of moral _____.

2.033 In 1814 Shelley left his wife and moved to the continent with _____.

2.034 In _____, Shelley moved with his family to _____, living there until his death.

2.035 While in the company of romantic thinkers and writers known as the _____ Circle, Shelley composed some of his greatest works, including _____, which was published in 1819.

2.036 As a romantic, Shelley believed in the redeeming power of the _____ to effect a golden age of society.

2.037 _____ is considered Keats's "Great Year" because he produced a rapid succession of masterpieces.

2.038 "The Eve of St. Agnes," "La Belle Dame sans Merci," "Ode to a Grecian Urn," and "Ode to a Nightingale" were published in 1820 in the volume _____.

2.039 Keats moved to Italy in the hopes of alleviating the symptoms of _____.

2.040 Keats believed that _____ alone could elevate one's senses to the spiritual world.

For Thought and Discussion:

Explain to a parent or a teacher Keats's views on art, beauty, and love. Be sure to mention his concept of beauty and truth as two inseparable realities. Keats believed that art was the eternal standard by which the changing human condition was to be compared. Discuss Keats's elevated view of art in reference to Colossians 1:17 and Revelation 1:8. What is the ultimate standard of truth and goodness? Why is Keats's "eternal standard" subject to change?

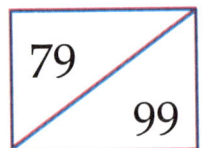

Score _____

Adult Check _____
                Initial   Date

III. THE VICTORIAN ERA

INTRODUCTION

During the long reign of Queen Victoria (1837–1901), England changed in dynamic ways. Voting rights were extended to the middle and lower classes. The growth of industry made it at first "the workhouse of the world" and then "the world's banker." New theories of science and economics caused many people to seek refuge in tradition and others to discover a new faith. Colonization and expansion scattered the British people around the world, creating an empire upon which the sun would always be shining. Although England did not experience a revolution during the nineteenth century, society did experience reform in the realms of politics, economics, and religion.

Reaction and Reform. After the Napoleonic wars, England suffered a depression. High taxes, an influx of soldiers returning to the workforce, and several bad harvests took their toll on the lower classes. Riots frequently occurred but were suppressed in large measure by the Six Acts bill, which was passed in 1819. The Tories, who were in power, feared a revolution that would overturn England's political system which still favored the wealthy and the educated.

Despite the fears of conservatives in Parliament, the Reform Bill was passed in 1832. Riding on the wave of intellectual developments and sentimental feelings for the lower classes, it was the first of many legislative reforms to the political system. It changed the voting districts and voting requirements, allowing for a more equitable representation of the population. Men who paid at least ten pounds per year in rent were allowed to vote. This change provided the middle class with voting rights that they did not have before. Their influence during the Victorian era would prove to be powerful. The lower classes, however, did not benefit from the initial Reform Bill. Seeing the need for further reform, radicals continued to push for a more democratic political system.

During the 1830s, the Chartists presented Parliament with a "People's Charter." Similar to the Magna Carta, the charter advocated an extension of political freedoms. The Chartists presented a program that would allow the working class to vote, giving them equal rights as citizens of the British Empire. Although Pariament initially rejected the reforms advocated by the Chartists, voting rights were eventually extended to all peoples. The Reform Bill of 1884 allowed all working men the right to vote; women, however, were not allowed to vote until 1918.

Concern for the lower classes quickly spread to other areas. During the Industrial Revolution, a laissez-faire approach to economics had allowed working conditions in factories and mines to go unchecked. Leaders in government and industry believed that eventually economic growth would benefit everyone. Unfortunately, this was not the case. Among those who suffered from unsanitary and dangerous working conditions were children. As a cheap source of labor, children were often required to work long hours in factories and mines. They had no time for school. A wave of reforms were instituted after an investigation into the working conditions of children. In 1833 and 1842, laws were passed limiting the number of hours a child could work in a day. In 1881 Parliament passed an act requiring all children from ages five to ten to attend school.

In reaction to the social changes that were occurring, new political parties formed in England. The Conservative Party consisted of Tories who remained faithful to traditional hierarchies. They supported the crown and the Church of England. Its great leader during the Victorian era was Benjamin Disraeli, who served as prime minister in 1868 and from 1874–1880. A novelist of Jewish descent, he supported social reform but remained loyal to the Church of England and the monarchy. He was known to have listened graciously to the suggestions of the queen.

The Liberal party championed the cause of the lower classes and favored religious tolerance toward dissenters. Its foremost leader was William Gladstone, who bettered his rival Disraeli by serving as prime minster from 1868–1874, 1880–1885, 1886, and 1892–1894. Gladstone is most noted for his attempt to grant Ireland home rule after the devastating effects of the potato famine. During his leadership, dissenting Protestants were allowed to attend the universities and serve in government.

Toward the end of the century, another very powerful party emerged. The Labour Party represented more stridently the interests of the common worker. Built upon the socialistic philosophy of Karl Marx, it championed the rights and freedoms of labor unions. Its influence has shaped Britain into a socialistic nation.

Intellectual and Spiritual Currents. In 1833 Charles Lyell published *Principles of Geology*. It contended that the earth was billions of years old. The theory implied that man was older than 6,000 years. Lyell's assertions were disconcerting to many Christians, who believed that the biblical record pointed to a young earth. In 1846, the publication of *The Life of Jesus*, a translation of David Friedrich Strauss's *Higher Criticism*, leveled another blow at traditional beliefs. *Higher Criticism* viewed the Bible as a mere historical record and questioned the miracles of Jesus and mankind's need for a savior.

Charles Darwin

Undoubtedly the most startling publications of the century were Charles Darwin's *Origin of the Species* (1859) and *The Descent of Man* (1871). Aided by the literary talents of Thomas Huxley, Darwin's theory of evolution supported the spirit of progress while calling into doubt all traditional beliefs about mankind and society. Man was seen as just another animal, his life governed by the law of the survival of the fittest.

Alongside these intellectual attempts to diminish the influence of the Scriptures upon society was a vast and powerful movement guided by evangelicals. Founded upon the enthusiastic faith of the eighteenth century Methodists, the evangelical movement consisted of Christians both inside and outside the Church of England. Many evangelicals were middle-class businessmen with the money and political savvy to back their heartfelt causes. In 1807 evangelicals were largely responsible for the abolition of the slave trade, and they finally effected the emancipation of all slaves in 1833. The earnestness of evangelicals to reform the nation on the basis of a more Christ-like attitude toward their fellow man was also manifested in open support of the working class. Child labor laws were of special importance to evangelicals in both the Liberal and the Conservative camps.

The social gospel that developed in the later part of the century was due largely to a dramatic shift in spiritual concerns among Anglicans. The need for the gospel was replaced by the need for social harmony. In groups such as the Salvation Army, the performance of good deeds was equated with the progress of society.

Chief among the evangelical preachers during the Victorian era was the Baptist preacher Charles Haddon Spurgeon. He was known as the "prince of preachers," and his "market language" sermons were heard by more than 5,000 worshippers each week in London's Metropolitan Tabernacle. His sermons have been called the "greatest contribution to the literature of experimental Christianity" in the nineteenth century. Other evidence of the evangelical desire to reform lives was the success of foreign missions alongside the expansion of the British Empire. Among the prominent missionaries were William Carey (1761–1834) in India, David Livingstone (1813–1873) in Africa, and Hudson Taylor (1832–1905) in China. Noted also as an explorer, Livingstone opened the interior of Africa to Europeans. His first concern, however, was to spread the gospel among the African people.

Although many scientists retained their evangelical faith during this season of doubt, many other intellectuals who were unwilling to dismiss the importance of spirituality turned to transcendentalism and other mystical faiths. Unable to reconcile the theories of science and the traditional doctrines of Christianity, men such as Carlyle and Tennyson embraced the faith of their romantic forerunners. Dependent upon intuition, transcendentalism could function without regard to the limitations of reason. Faith was important, they acknowledged, but it had to progress beyond the reaches of traditional religion if it was ever to be useful to the man living in a rapidly changing world.

The Utilitarians also acknowledged society's need for progress in religious matters; their answer, however, called for the eradication of religion. Utilitarians believed in the greatest good for the greatest number of people. The Church of England, as a government institution, did not adhere to this philosophy. Under the scope of human reason, it did not provide an effective cure to society's ills. It was not efficient enough. The utilitarians equated faith with superstition, and therefore considered it an impediment to progress.

In opposition to the conclusions of the Utilitarians and the enthusiasm of the evangelicals stood the leaders of "The Oxford Movement," who found the rituals and traditions of the Church of England to be immensely valuable. Foremost among the leaders of this movement was John Henry Newman, whose conservative tracts on the usefulness of traditional religion led many Anglican priests to Catholicism. Newman himself converted to Roman Catholicism, and he became a priest in 1845.

Imperialism. Bolstered by its economic success and hunger for progress, England expanded its empire. British expansion was largely the result of military conquest. They took India from the French in 1757. They also took the east coast of Africa, including Egypt, from the French, giving the British control over the Suez Canal. They took Hong Kong from the Chinese when port officials in Guang-zhou attempted to stop the opium trade between London and China.

British dominance in these regions continued with the support of military power. Civil service officers ruled the native people with Victorian values and institutions. The British presence in these foreign lands was both positive and negative. Although many colonists tried to improve the lives of the natives, ministering to both their physical and their spiritual needs, other colonists sought to exploit the land and the people. They often treated the natives with contempt because they were less "civilized."

Literature. The literature of Victorian England is both entertaining and full of social criticism. The troubles and triumphs of the times were of great concern to writers. Novels, poems, and essays were written to effect social reform. Religious, social, and economic topics were dealt with in relation to the progress of science and the changes to society caused by the Industrial Revolution. Middle-class standards of right and wrong were characterized, mocked, and catered to.

The most influential Victorian writer was Thomas Carlyle. Although his works are no longer popular today, he was known to his contemporaries as the "Sage of Chelsea." His thoughts on religion, science, politics, and history provided answers to the spiritual and philosophical questions of the day. Like Coleridge before him, Carlyle thought of the poet as a type of prophet. Carlyle pointed to Tennyson, a more popular and able poet than himself, as the prophet of his mixture of transcendentalism and traditional Christianity. Tennyson's *In Memoriam* is reflective of Carlyle's spiritual thought.

Foremost among the novelists, Charles Dickens was among Carlyle's followers. He borrowed many of his storytelling techniques from Carlyle. As one critic has noted, Dickens's brilliant characterization, use of grotesque images, and interpretation of trivial details are all are directly representative of Carlyle's influence.

John Stuart Mill, a key proponent of utilitarianism, was also influenced by Carlyle's ideas on ethics and morals. Mill's most famous essay, *On Liberty* casts doubt on the good of democracy. This attitude was the result of Carlyle's influence as most profoundly stated in his political and historical works *Chartism* and *Past and Present*. Other writers of the era conveyed Carlyle's desire to save society from the destructive powers of materialism that were brought on by the Industrial Revolution. His conviction of duty toward one's fellow man and sense of universal meaning pervaded much of the literature. Summarizing the scope and depth of his influence on Victorian writers, George Eliot once wrote, "There is hardly a superior or active mind of this generation that has not been modified by Carlyle's writings."

Toward the end of the century, the romantic influences evident in Carlyle's work and that of his followers began to lose popularity. Tennyson's medieval legends were replaced by Browning's more intellectual, more realistic verse. Oscar Wilde emerged as a popular proponent of the school of art for art's sake. His plays and the silly stories of Lewis Carroll demonstrate a shift in thought that finds its full manifestation in the next century. Darwin's theories had reduced man to a mere animal. Man's existence suddenly had no divine purpose or meaning. Therefore, the art for art's sake theorists proposed that experience must be the source of meaning. However, as was demonstrated by the results of Wilde's life, this route was only the pathway to greater unhappiness.

Considered the century of the novel, the nineteenth century witnessed the initial publication of many works in periodicals. An inexpensive form of publication, periodicals were popular among the middle class. Many novelists published their works in installments before later publishing them as a collected whole. Periodicals also featured reviews and essays. News reporting was left to the major papers of the time.

Understanding man's relationship to God was of the utmost importance for the middle class in such an age of dynamic change. The novel as a spiritual commentary on the realities of love and marriage, poverty and wealth, and belief and unbelief, gripped the interest of Victorian readers with both delight and instruction. Better than any history book filled with facts and statistics, the Victorian novel represents the attitudes and tastes of the English as they rushed toward the brink of the modern age.

Answer *true* or *false* for each of the following statements.

3.1 _____ England experienced dynamic changes in the realms of politics, economics, and religion during the Victorian era.

3.2 _____ The Reform Bill of 1832 was the first of many legislative reforms to the voting system.

3.3 _____ The working conditions in factories went unchecked by the government because people believed that the factory owners would not obey the law.

3.4 _____ The Conservative Party consisted of Tories who remained faithful to the cause of the lower classes and favored religious tolerance.

3.5 _____ William Gladstone was the foremost leader of the Liberal party.

3.6 _____ Charles Darwin's theory of evolution caused many people to doubt all traditional beliefs about mankind and society.

3.7 _____ *Higher Criticism* questioned the traditional belief in the Bible as a record of history.

3.8 _____ Evangelicals were influential in the abolition of slavery and the enactment of child labor laws.

3.9 _____ The reach of foreign missionaries increased alongside the expansion of the British Empire.

3.10 _____ The Utilitarians' belief in the greatest good for the greatest number of people caused them to support the Church of England.

3.11 _____ The Oxford Movement emphasized the rituals and traditions of the Church of England.

3.12 _____ During the Victorian era, the British Empire controlled lands in Africa, India, and Hong Kong.

3.13 _____ Writers of the period wrote only to entertain their readers.

3.14 _____ Charles Dickens's thoughts on religion, science, politics, and history were immeasurably influential on his contemporaries.

3.15 _____ The art for art's sake theorists believed that experience was the source of meaning.

3.16 _____ Many Victorian novelists published their books first in magazines by monthly installments.

Thomas Carlyle (1795–1881). Thomas Carlyle was one of the most influential writers of the Victorian age. Carlyle was born in Ecclefechan, Scotland, to parents who were members of a dissenting branch of the Presbyterian Church. His father was a hard-working stonemason who affirmed the doctrines of Calvinism. As the eldest son, Carlyle was sent to Annan Academy and the University of Edinburgh in preparation for the ministry. After five years of study, Carlyle abandoned his intentions and left the university without a degree. His reading of Enlightenment writers had led him to become skeptical of Christianity. Remaining in Edinburgh, he taught mathematics at Annan and Kirkcaldy. He studied law briefly in 1818 but then gave himself over to literature. He learned German and studied the works of German romantics. He published a translation of Goethe's novel *Wilhelm Meisters Lehrjahre* in 1824. *The Life of Schiller* was published in book form in 1825. It originally had been published in serial form in the *London Magazine* from 1823 to 1824.

In 1826 Carlyle married Jane Welsh, a spirited woman of more significant social standing than himself. After two years of marriage, Carlyle insisted (for financial reasons) upon moving from Edinburgh to her remote farm at Craigenputtock. Although Carlyle was happy in his literary and scholarly pursuits, his wife was lonely and miserable. While he was on the farm, Carlyle completed *Sartor Resartus (The Tailor Retailored)*, a philosophical satire outlining his spiritual idealism, which was heavily influenced by the German Romantics. It was published in 1833. His criticism of material wealth established him as an influential social critic. Carlyle heavily influenced the philosophy of Ralph Waldo Emerson, who came to visit Carlyle at Craigenputtock.

After eight years of isolation, Carlyle moved to London, where he became known as the "Sage of Chelsea." In 1837 he published *The French Revolution, A History*. The book's success elevated Carlyle's reputation as a philosopher, historian, and writer. In 1840 he delivered a series of lectures in which he communicated his hatred for democracy. One of his lectures was published in 1841 as "On Heroes, Hero-Worship, and the Heroic in History." It contended that strong leaders were the basis for strong, stable societies. In *Chartism* (1839) and *Past and Present* (1843), Carlyle criticized laissez-faire economics and its dangers to society while asserting a need for a form of socialism governed by a new nobility. *Oliver Cromwell's Letters and Speeches, with Elucidations* (1845) and *History of Frederick II of Prussia, Called Frederick the Great* (10 vols., 1858–1865) were histories that emphasized his admiration for powerful leaders and his belief that all of history was "the biography of great men."

When Jane died in 1866, Carlyle's desire to write diminished. He spent the last fifteen years of his life editing his wife's letters, receiving visitors at Cheyne Walk, and reading. In 1874 Bismarck awarded him the Prussian Order of Merit. In the same year, however, he refused to accept a Grand Cross of the Order of the Bath from Prime Minster Disreali. Carlyle died in London on February 4, 1881. He is buried in his family's home of Ecclefechan.

Although Carlyle abandoned his aspiration to be a Christian minister, he continued to preach. He used his writings to broadcast his thoughts on religion and society. Written in his distinctive speech-like prose, *Sartor Resartus* proclaims with much vigor and strength the basis for his rejection of orthodox Christianity. The title, "the tailor retailored," refers to the "clothes philosophy" that was then popular among skeptics. As one writer noted, Carlyle concluded that the "Hebrew Old Clothes" of traditional Christianity were worn out. Man needed to clothe himself in a new philosophy. Frustrated by the authority of Scripture and the guidance of reason, Carlyle pointed to man's heart as the fount of truth. This exaltation of man-made religious experience was of particular importance. Not willing totally to reject the idea of a personal God, Carlyle offered a new faith in which the citizen of secular society could feel a sense of religious awe yet not have to bow to the doctrines of any particular sect. Carlyle was a transcendental mystic who believed that he was free to choose what his heart told him was right despite apparent inconsistencies with facts. The major flaw in Carlyle's beliefs about religion and society is his refusal to acknowledge the sinfulness of man's heart. Believing that he offered the world a new set of beliefs, Carlyle only dressed himself in the tattered clothes of rebellion. The Sage of Chelsea's desire for a more humane world in the midst of growing industrialism and materialism can also be seen in the works of Tennyson, Browning, Eliot, and Dickens.

  Circle the letter of the lines that best answer each of the following questions.

3.17   Carlyle's father sent him to the University of Edinburgh to prepare to be a:

   a. doctor.

   b. minister.

   c. teacher.

   d. poet.

3.18   Carlyle's religious beliefs were heavily influenced by:

   a. Calvinistic Presbyterians.

   b. Roman Catholics.

   c. German Romantics.

   d. Anglicans.

3.19   In 1833 Carlyle published a philosophical satire outlining his spiritual idealism and was titled:

   a. *Wilhelm Meisters Lehrjahre.*

   b. *The French Revolution.*

   c. *On Heroes, Hero-Worship.*

   d. *Sartor Resartus.*

3.20 After living in isolation with his wife at Craigenputtock, Carlyle moved to:
- a. London.
- b. Paris.
- c. New York City.
- d. Germany.

3.21 In 1837 Carlyle's reputation as a philosopher, historian, and writer was elevated with the publication of:
- a. *Past and Present.*
- b. *Oliver Cromwell's Letters and Speeches, with Elucidations.*
- c. *The French Revolution, A History.*
- d. *Sartor Resartus.*

3.22 Carlyle's histories contend that the basis for strong, stable societies is:
- a. strong leaders.
- b. intelligent, informed voters.
- c. a constitution.
- d. God-fearing people.

3.23 Carlyle's desire to write diminished after:
- a. the death of his daughter.
- b. the death of his wife.
- c. Queen Victorian took the throne.
- d. he realized that democracy would help the lower classes.

3.24 What did Carlyle's new faith for a secular society do?
- a. allowed for a sense of religious awe yet did not dictate a standard of morality
- b. called all to repentance according to the Scriptures
- c. held all accountable to a universal standard of right and wrong
- d. trusted in the powers of reason to point man to the truth

3.25 The major flaw in Carlyle's beliefs about religion and society is:
- a. his reliance upon Scripture.
- b. his refusal to acknowledge the sinfulness of man's heart.
- c. his admiration for great leaders.
- d. his hatred for democracy.

3.26 Why was Carlyle known as the "Sage of Chelsea?"
- a. His contemporaries looked to him as a wise philosopher.
- b. He liked to talk to his friends.
- c. People liked to mock his thoughts on politics and religion.
- d. Prime Minister Disraeli awarded him the Grand Cross.

What to Look For:

During the nineteenth century, many people claimed to be Christians; in fact, however, many of them practiced a religion of tradition and ritual rather than a religion rooted in love for God and love for other people (cf. Matthew 22:37–40). As 2 Timothy 3:5 states, they gave an appearance of godliness, but they denied—through word and deed—the God who makes men godly. As you read, pay attention to Carlyle's criticism of Christianity. Notice that he does not argue directly against Christian doctrine. Rather, his criticism is of the appearance of its followers. In one place, he calls Christianity the "Worship of Sorrow." In another place he describes Christians as "doleful." Although, ultimately, it is God's grace that brings someone to Christ, believers are called in love to "be holy as God is holy." If we fail to live according to God's commandments, then we are hypocrites and bring shame on our Lord. According to Romans 2:17–24, how might nineteenth-century Christians be partially responsible for Carlyle's blasphemy? How might our strict attention to tradition rather than God's Word cause people to curse the name of our Lord unnecessarily? What did Jesus have to say about the legalism of the Pharisees (cf. Matthew 23:23–28)?

From: *Sartus Resartus*
From: *'The Everlasting Yea'*

The hero of Sartus Resartus *is Professor Diogenes Teufelsdrôckh. He is an imaginary figure through whom Carlyle conveys his doubts about traditional religion. To add cohesion to the professor's "patchwork" story, an editor's comments are interspersed throughout the work. The following section is from the second part of* Sartus Resartus, *which reads like an autobiographical account of the professor's life. Many of the events and places are similar to that of Carlyle's own life. The chapter titled* "The Everlasting Yea" *tells of the professor's spiritual crisis, in which he rejects traditional religion and embraces a form of transcendentalism.*

"I asked myself: What is this that, ever since earliest years, thou hast been fretting and fuming, and lamenting and self-tormenting, on account of? Say it in a word: is it not because thou art not HAPPY? Because the THOU (sweet gentleman) is not sufficiently honored, nourished, soft-bedded, and lovingly cared for? Foolish soul! What Act of Legislature was there that thou shouldst be Happy? A little while ago thou hadst no right to be at all. What if thou wert born and predestined not to be Happy, but to be Unhappy? Art thou nothing other than a Vulture, then, that fliest through the Universe seeking after somewhat to eat; and shrieking dolefully because carrion enough is not given thee? Close thy Byron; open thy Goethe."*

"*Es leuchtet mir ein*, I see a glimpse of it!" cries he elsewhere: "there is in man a HIGHER than Love of Happiness: he can do without Happiness, and instead thereof find Blessedness! Was it not to preach forth this same HIGHER that sages and martyrs, the Poet and the Priest, in all times, have spoken and suffered; bearing testimony, through life and through death, of the Godlike that is in Man, and how in the Godlike only has he Strength and Freedom? Which God-inspired Doctrine art thou also honored to be taught; O Heavens! and broken with manifold merciful Afflictions, even till thou become contrite and learn it! Oh, thank thy Destiny for these; thankfully bear what yet remain: thou hadst need of them; the Self in thee needed to be annihilated. By benignant fever-paroxysms is Life rooting out the deep-seated chronic Disease, and triumphs over Death. On the roaring billows of Time, thou art not engulfed, but borne aloft into the azure of Eternity. Love not Pleasure; love God. This is the EVERLASTING YEA, wherein all contradiction is solved: wherein who so walks and works, it is well with him."

And again: "Small is it that thou canst trample the Earth with its injuries under thy feet, as old Greek Zeno* trained thee: thou canst love the Earth while it injures thee, and even because it injures thee; for this a Greater than Zeno was needed, and he too was sent. Knowest thou that 'Worship of Sorrow?'* The Temple thereof, founded some eighteen centuries ago, now lies in ruins, overgrown with jungle, the habitation of doleful creatures: nevertheless, venture forward; in a low crypt, arched out of falling fragments, thou findest the Altar still there, and its sacred Lamp perennially burning."

Without pretending to comment on which strange utterances, the Editor will only remark, that there lies beside them much of a still more questionable character; unsuited to the general apprehension; nay wherein he himself does not see his way. Nebulous disquisitions on Religion, yet not without bursts of splendor; on the "perennial continuance of Inspiration"; on Prophecy; that there are "true Priests, as well as Baal-Priests, in our own day:" with more of the like sort. We select some fractions, by way of finish to this farrago.*

"Cease, my much-respected Herr von Voltaire," thus apostrophizes the Professor: "shut thy sweet voice; for the task appointed thee seems finished.

Sufficiently hast thou demonstrated this proposition, considerable or otherwise: That the Mythus* of the Christian Religion looks not in the eighteenth century as it did in the eighth. Alas, were thy six-and-thirty quartos, and the six-and-thirty thousand other quartos and folios, and flying sheets or reams, printed before and since on the same subject, all needed to convince us of so little! But what next? Wilt thou help us to embody the divine Spirit of that Religion in a new Mythus, in a new vehicle and vesture, that our Souls, otherwise too like perishing, may live? What! thou hast no faculty in that kind? Only a torch for burning, no hammer for building? Take our thanks, then, and—thyself away.

"Meanwhile what are antiquated Mythuses to me? Or is the God present, felt in my own heart, a thing which Herr von Voltaire will dispute out of me; or dispute into me? To the 'Worship of Sorrow' ascribe what origin and genesis thou pleasest, has not that Worship originated, and been generated; is it not here? Feel it in thy heart, and then say whether it is of God! This is Belief; all else is Opinion, for which latter who so will, let him worry and be worried."

"Neither," observes he elsewhere, "shall ye tear out one another's eyes, struggling over 'Plenary Inspiration,'* and such like: try rather to get a little even Partial Inspiration, each of you for himself. One BIBLE I know, of whose Plenary Inspiration doubt is not so much as possible; nay with my own eyes I saw the God's-Hand writing it: thereof all other Bibles are but Leaves,—say, in Picture-Writing to assist the weaker faculty."*

farrago - a mixture or collection
Goethe - leading poet of German Romanticism
Zeno - ancient Greek philosopher who struck the earth as if it were responsible for his pain
Worship of Sorrow - Christianity
Mythus - myth
Plenary Inspiration - the doctrine that holds that the Scriptures are God-breathed and therefore infalliable
weaker faculty - the senses or the flesh as opposed to the spirit

 Give the best answer or explanation for each of the following questions.

3.27 What does the professor claim is HIGHER than Love of Happiness?

3.28 Explain what the EVERLASTING YEA is.

3.29 Why does the professor say that Christianity in the nineteenth century is "lying in ruins, over grown with jungle?"

3.30 What comments does the Editor make about the professor and his remarks?

3.31 What observations does the professor make about the history of the Christian church?

3.32 What does the professor claim is the proof of his belief?

3.33 Explain why the professor's Bible cannot be debated on a doctrinal basis. What kind of "bible" is it?

John Henry Cardinal Newman (1801–1890). As a leader of the Oxford Movement, John Henry Newman is noted as a brilliant controversialist. His essays, written in a clear and logical style, display an argumentative power that many opponents found indomitable.

Newman was born in London the son of a banker who was a nominal Anglican. His mother was an evangelical Anglican. After attending school in Ealing, Newman entered Trinity College, Oxford, at the age of fifteen. Following his graduation from Trinity, the prodigious Newman was granted the highest intellectual honor in Oxford, a fellowship at Oriel College. While at Oriel, Newman met and collaborated with some of the most intellectually able men of the time. John Keble and R.H. Froude later joined him in leading the Oxford Movement.

A scholar and a clergyman, Newman became the vicar of St. Mary's Cathedral, the Oxford university church, in 1828. His four o'clock Sunday sermons established his reputation as a powerful and persuasive orator. With his friend and colleague Froude, Newman traveled to the Mediterranean region, visiting, among other places, Rome. He wrote many poems while abroad, including "Lead, Kindly Light" published in the volume *Apostolica* in 1836. During this time, his religious sympathies led him to write of "the wretched perversion of truth" sanctioned by the Roman Catholic Church. Newman was then a High Churchman who objected to the lack of doctrine within the Anglican Church.

Upon returning to England in 1833, Newman heard Keble's sermon "On the National Apostasy." The sermon inaugurated the Oxford Movement, which called for a return to theology and ritual, this in objection to the "liberalism" brought about by the state's control of the church and the rising popularity of dissenting sects. Ready to return the Anglican Church to its catholic heritage, Newman founded *Tracts for the Times*, in which he wrote twenty-nine papers, arguing in favor of the doctrine of apostolic succession, the proper use of the Book of Common Prayer, and a greater appreciation of church history before the Reformation. In *Tract 90*, Newman put forth the assertion that the Thirty-nine Articles of the Church of England did not refute the central doctrines of the Roman Catholic Church. The tract proved to be Newman's final tract written for the Oxford Movement. Anglican dignitaries officially banned him for his Catholic interpretation of the articles.

In 1842 Newman resigned his position at St. Mary's Cathedral. His growing attraction to Rome separated him from his fellow Tractarians, Keble and Pusey. For three years, he isolated himself from his old Oxford life, living with like-minded fellows in the nearby village of Littlemore. Not ready himself to cross over to Roman Catholicism, Newman pleaded with other Anglicans not to convert. But his longing for certainty led him closer and closer to the Roman Catholic Church. Its doctrines, he believed, were the flower and fruit of the ancient teachings of the apostles and the early church fathers. In the face of scientific doubt, cold rationalism, and evangelical dissent, the Roman Catholic Church offered Newman an authoritative system of beliefs that was safe from "liberalism." In 1846 he was ordained a priest and returned to England to establish the Oratory in Birmingham.

From 1854 to 1858, Newman served as rector of the Catholic University in Dublin and published his lectures and essays on university education under the title *The Idea of a University Defined and Illustrated* in 1873. Newman declared that the purpose of the university was to train the mind to think rather than to function as a mere vocational institution, teaching the student only practical information.

In 1864 Newman published his rebuttal to Charles Kingsley's accusation that Newman, and Roman Catholicism, ultimately did not care about the pursuit of truth.

Apologia pro Vita Sua was first published serially in *Macmillan's Magazine* and later in volume form. An account of Newman's spiritual quest for certainty, the religious autobiography is written in a masterful style. It is considered Newman's masterpiece and a classic of English prose. Many Catholics compared its power and influence to that of Augustine's *Confessions*. In 1870 Newman published *An Essay in Aid of a Grammar of Assent,* which propounded the inferior abilities of logic in matters of faith. As one critic has noted, he argued that faith is not based upon logic but is intuitively perceived.

Newman also wrote fiction and poetry. His two novels *Loss and Gain* (1848) and *Callista* (1876) were published anonymously. His long visionary poem *The Dream of Gerontius* was published in book form in 1866. Elgar set it to music as an oratorio. In 1874 Newman published *Verses on Various Occasions*.

Newman's full embrace of the Roman Catholic Church led him to defend the doctrines of papal infallibility, devotion to the saints, and Mary's perfect nature. His writings helped to achieve greater respectability for Catholics. In 1879 Pope Leo XIII appointed Newman a cardinal.

Newman's work as a clergyman, priest, and writer did much to combat the influence of secularism within Victorian society. However, "his excellent chain of reasoning" led many people to base their faith on the traditions and rituals of an institution—the Anglican Church or the Roman Catholic Church—instead of the Word of God. His answers to society's problems would not effect a complete cure. As the Reformers had pointed out in the sixteenth century, religious tradition is not a sure foundation for faith; like the scientific rationalism that Newman opposed, it is subject to the faulty reasoning of man.

Answer *true* **or** *false* **for each of the following statements.**

3.34 _____ Newman's parents were both staunch Roman Catholics.

3.35 _____ Newman's four o'clock sermons at St. Mary's Cathedral in Oxford distinguished him as a powerful and persuasive orator.

3.36 _____ In opposition to the Oxford Movement, Newman established *Tracts for the Times*.

3.37 _____ The Oxford Movement sought to return the Church of England to its catholic heritage and remove the influence of dissenting sects.

3.38 _____ In *Tract 90*, Newman asserted that the Thirty-nine Articles of the Church of England did not refute the central doctrines of the Reformation.

3.39 _____ In 1846 Newman was ordained a priest in the Roman Catholic Church.

3.40 _____ Newman's lectures and essays on university education were written while he served as rector of the Catholic University in Dublin.

3.41 _____ *Apologia pro Vita Sua* is the autobiographical account of Newman's spiritual quest for certainty, which he eventually found in the traditions and rituals of the Church of England.

3.42 _____ In 1879 Pope Leo XIII appointed Newman a cardinal.

3.43 _____ Newman's liberal ideas encouraged the spread of secularism in Victorian society.

What to Look For:

As you read, notice how Newman, after his conversion to Roman Catholicism, deals with doubt. How does he answer perplexing questions about the doctrine of transubstantiation and the Trinity? Are his answers sufficient? Were critics correct in saying that Newman's religion eventually leads to superstition and hypocrisy? Why have Protestants emphasized that the Bible alone must be the Christians' sole guide in faith and life?

From: *Apologia Pro Vita Sua*
From: Chapter 5

This section originally appeared under the title "General Answer to Mr. Kingsley." Apologia *is Newman's rebuttal to Reverend Kingsley's accusation that Catholic priests were not being intellectually honest about their beliefs.*

PART VII: POSITION OF MY MIND SINCE 1845

From the time that I became a Catholic, of course, I have no further history of my religious opinions to narrate. In saying this, I do not mean to say that my mind has been idle, or that I have given up thinking on theological subjects; but that I have had no changes to record, and have had no anxiety of heart whatever. I have been in perfect peace and contentment. I never have had one doubt. I was not conscious, on my conversion, of any inward difference of thought or of temper from what I had before. I was not conscious of firmer faith in the fundamental truths of revelation, or of more self-command; I had not more fervour; but it was like coming into port after a rough sea; and my happiness on that score remains to this day without interruption.

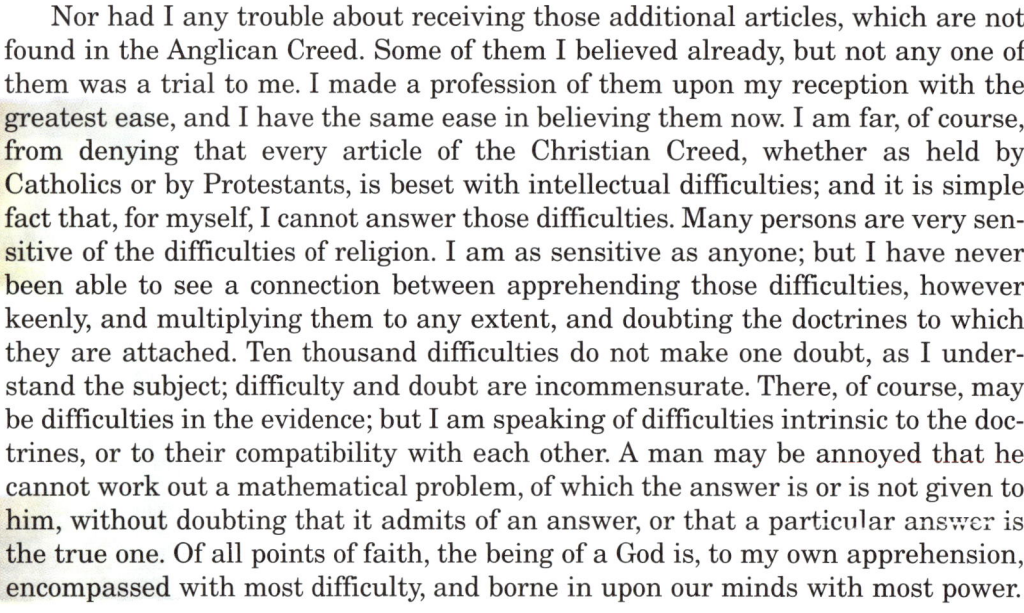

Nor had I any trouble about receiving those additional articles, which are not found in the Anglican Creed. Some of them I believed already, but not any one of them was a trial to me. I made a profession of them upon my reception with the greatest ease, and I have the same ease in believing them now. I am far, of course, from denying that every article of the Christian Creed, whether as held by Catholics or by Protestants, is beset with intellectual difficulties; and it is simple fact that, for myself, I cannot answer those difficulties. Many persons are very sensitive of the difficulties of religion. I am as sensitive as anyone; but I have never been able to see a connection between apprehending those difficulties, however keenly, and multiplying them to any extent, and doubting the doctrines to which they are attached. Ten thousand difficulties do not make one doubt, as I understand the subject; difficulty and doubt are incommensurate. There, of course, may be difficulties in the evidence; but I am speaking of difficulties intrinsic to the doctrines, or to their compatibility with each other. A man may be annoyed that he cannot work out a mathematical problem, of which the answer is or is not given to him, without doubting that it admits of an answer, or that a particular answer is the true one. Of all points of faith, the being of a God is, to my own apprehension, encompassed with most difficulty, and borne in upon our minds with most power.

People say that the doctrine of transubstantiation* is difficult to believe; I did not believe the doctrine till I was a Catholic. I had no difficulty in believing it as soon as I believed that the Catholic Roman Church was the oracle of God, and that she had declared this doctrine to be part of the original revelation. It is difficult, impossible to imagine, I grant—but how is it difficult to believe? Yet Macaulay thought it so difficult to believe, that he had need of a believer in it of talents as eminent as Sir Thomas More, before he could bring himself to conceive that the Catholics of an enlightened age could resist "the overwhelming force of the argument against it." "Sir Thomas More," he says, "...is one of the choice specimens of wisdom and virtue; and the doctrine of transubstantiation is a kind of proof charge. A faith which stands that test, will stand any test." But for myself, I cannot indeed prove it, I cannot tell how it is; but I say, "Why should not it be? What's to hinder it? What do I know of substance or matter? just as much as the greatest philosophers, and that is nothing at all; –so much is this the case, that there is a rising school of philosophy now, which considers phenomena to constitute the whole of our knowledge in physics. The Catholic doctrine leaves phenomena alone. It does not say that the phenomena go; on the contrary, it says that they remain: nor does it say that the same phenomena are in several places at once. It deals with what no one on earth knows anything about, the material substances themselves. And, in like manner, of that majestic Article of the Anglican as well as of the Catholic Creed –the doctrine of the Trinity in Unity. What do I know of the Essence of the Divine Being? I know that my abstract idea of three is simply incompatible with my idea of one; but when I come to the question of concrete fact, I have no means of proving that there is not a sense in which one and three can equally be predicated of the Incommunicable God.

But I am going to take upon myself the responsibility of more than the mere Creed of the Church; as the parties accusing me are determined I shall do. They say, that now, in that I am a Catholic, though I may not have offences of my own against honesty to answer for, yet, at least, I am answerable for the offences of others, of my co-religionists, of my brother priests, of the Church herself. I am quite willing to accept the responsibility; and, as I have been able, as I trust, by means of a few words, to dissipate, in the minds of all those who do not begin with disbelieving me, the suspicion with which so many Protestants start, in forming their judgment of Catholics, viz., that our Creed is actually set up in inevitable superstition and hypocrisy, as the original sin of Catholicism; so now I will go on, as before, identifying myself with the Church and vindicating it—not, of course, denying the enormous mass of sin and ignorance which exists of necessity in that world-wide multiform Communion—but going to the proof of this one point, that its system is in no sense dishonest, and that therefore the upholders and teachers of that system, as such, have a claim to be acquitted in their own persons of that odious imputation.

Transubstantiation - the doctrine that teaches the alleged conversion of the bread and wine into the actual body and blood of Christ during the sacrament of the Eucharist (Holy Communion); however, the bread and the wine retain their physical form.

Circle the letter of the line that best answers each of the following questions.

3.44 After his conversion to Roman Catholicism, Newman states that he has:

a. been troubled with doubt.

b. not had one doubt.

c. doubted every doctrine of the Catholic Church.

d. searched the Scriptures and found the doctrines of the Church of England to be false.

3.45 If a doctrine of religion is beset with intellectual difficulties, Newman sees no reason to:

a. believe the doctrine.

b. include it in the creeds of the church.

c. doubt the doctrine.

d. doubt the motives of those who disbelieve.

3.46 Which doctrine did Newman not believe until he was a Catholic?

a. Transubstantiation

b. The Trinity

c. Predestination

d. Communion

3.47 Why did he not experience any difficulty in believing the Catholic doctrine of Transubstantiation?

- a. Because the Word of God affirms this doctrine.
- b. Because the Roman Catholic Church said it was true.
- c. Because he had really believed it all along.
- d. Because in his heart he knew it to be true.

3.48 Newman compares the doctrine of transubstantiation to that of the Trinity because:

- a. He is trying to establish the point that some religious doctrines cannot be explained intellectually although they are true.
- b. He believes that Thomas More invented both doctrines.
- c. He thinks that the doctrine of the Trinity is intellectually removed from doubt.
- d. Both doctrines can be proven by philosophical means.

3.49 Who is Newman attempting to defend against the accusation of superstition and hypocrisy?

- a. Protestants
- b. The Roman Catholic Church
- c. Evangelicals
- d. The Church of England

Alfred, Lord Tennyson (1809–1892). Much admired as a lyrical genius during his own day and in ours, Alfred, Lord Tennyson was one of the most popular, if not one of the most gifted, poets of the nineteenth century. His concern for the major crises of the age and his mastery of idyllic poetry elevated him to the position of poet laureate.

Tennyson was born in Sombersby, Lincolnshire, a remote part of the country. His father, Reverend Dr. George Tennyson, was the rector of the parish. His mother was a kind woman, the daughter of a clergyman. As a result of his father's disinheritance, Tennyson grew up in an unstable environment. His father had become a clergyman out of necessity and grew to hate his profession. The hypocrisy and dissatisfaction that ensued fostered abnormal and violent behavior among the Tennyson family members. Tennyson's father was prone to fits of drunken violence. Several of the children were plagued by mental illness. Tennyson himself admitted "more than once Alfred, scared by his father's fits of despondency, went out through the black night, and threw himself on a grave in the churchyard, praying to be beneath the sod himself." Turning to friends and poetry for comfort, Tennyson later rejected the evangelical faith of his mother. As a boy, he greatly admired Byron and sorely lamented his death.

Despite his troubled family life, Tennyson was partly educated by his father and published with one of his brothers a collection of poems titled *Poems by Two Brothers* (1827). He attended Trinity College, Cambridge, and in 1829 was awarded the Chancellor's Medal for his poem "Timbuctoo." He joined the Apostles—a group of undergraduates who were intently interested in politics, literature, and philosophy— and became friends with Arthur Hallam. In 1830 Tennyson published *Poems, Chiefly Lyrical*; however, the volume received unfavorable reviews. Tennyson endured the painful criticism with the help of his friend Hallam. In the summer of 1830, Tennyson and Hallam joined a revolutionary army in Spain, but they did not engage in any combat.

In 1831 Tennyson was forced to leave Cambridge when his father died. He dedicated himself to his poetry and published a second volume, *Poems*, in 1832. Many of his famous works are included in this collection, namely, "The Lady of Shalott" and "The Lotus-Eaters." Again, Tennyson received fierce criticism for his poems. In 1832 Tennyson and Hallam toured the Continent. While they were abroad, Hallam died. The anguish of this loss coupled with the rejection of his poetic works, caused Tennyson to sink into a deep depression. He vowed not to publish any poetry for ten years. Instead, Tennyson studied the works of other poets and rewrote many of his earlier works, hoping to perfect his craft. As one critic has noted, the fact that he was not born a great poet but developed into one is evidenced by his sense of meter in the much-revised edition of *Poems*, published in 1842. Tennyson had added such poems as "Le Morte d'Arthur," "Locksley Hall," and "Ulysses." The volume made him immensely popular, and in 1845, he was granted a civilian pension of £200 per year.

During his time of silence, Tennyson also worked intermittently on the long elegy for his dear friend, Hallam. Published in 1850, *In Memoriam A.H.H.* reflects Tennyson's transcendental beliefs. It is considered the greatest elegy ever written in the English language. Also in 1850, Tennyson succeeded Wordsworth as poet laureate. He published "Death of the Duke of Wellington" and in 1852 "The Charge of the Light Brigade" in 1854.

As the sales of his poems rose, Tennyson increased in wealth and station. In 1850 he married Emily Sellwood, whom he had been prevented from marrying because of his poverty and unorthodox religious beliefs. The two had been engaged since 1836. In 1854 he moved to the Isle of Wight and rented Farringford, a large country estate. A few years later, Tennyson bought Farringford. Prince Albert and other figures of grand importance visited him there.

In 1859 Tennyson began publishing installments of *Idylls of the King*. The narrative poems on the subject of Arthurian legend secured his popularity. The last installment was published in 1885. During the 1880s, Tennyson also published historical dramas and poems. In 1884 he was made the first Baron Tennyson of Farringford, taking his seat in the House of Lords. At his death, he was honored as a "Poet of the People" and the "prophet...of a Spiritual Universe." He was buried in Westminster Abbey.

Although some critics do not consider Tennyson's poems to possess much intellectual and spiritual depth, the poems are some of the best representations of Victorian culture. He wrote in a classical style much like that of Milton and Shakespeare. Polished and technically superb, his verses could be found in almost every English household during the later part of the nineteenth century. He was, as T. S. Eliot described him, "the great master of metric"; and, as W. H. Auden stated, he possessed "the finest ear, perhaps, of any English poet."

Tennyson's works, although masterfully crafted, were not solidly biblical. He struggled, like many other writers of his time, to reconcile faith and science without much reliance upon Scripture. His understanding of man's relationship to God was confused by recent scientific theories on the age of the earth and the origin of man. As one critic has noted, although *In Memoriam* is written in traditional religious language, it is a proclamation of transcendental beliefs. Many conservative readers, however, did not perceive what he was doing and lauded his work as Christian. This, of course, confused the distinctions between orthodox and unorthodox Christian beliefs, thus allowing romantic views of man to take a greater hold on the culture.

Underline the correct answer in each of the following statements.

3.50 Tennyson's father was a (farmer, clergyman, politician).

3.51 In 1830 Tennyson published (*Poems, Chiefly Lyrical*, *Poems by Two Brothers*, *In Memoriam*), which received unfavorable reviews.

3.52 After the death of (Arthur Hallam, Tennyson's father, Tennyson's wife) in 1832, Tennyson vowed not to publish any poetry for (ten, eight, two) years.

3.53 The publication of (*In Memoriam*, "Timbuctoo," *Poems*) in 1842 made him immensely popular among Victorian readers.

3.54 Written for his friend Hallam, (*Poems*, *In Memoriam*, "Le Morte d'Arthur") is considered the greatest (elegy, novel, sonnet) in the English language.

3.55 In 1850 Tennyson was appointed (a baron, poet laureate, a clergyman).

3.56 Tennyson published his popular narrative poems ("Le Morte d'Arthur," *Poems of Arthur*, *Idylls of the King*) in installments from 1859 through 1885.

3.57 Tennyson wrote in a (classical, modern, romantic) style.

3.58 Tennyson tried to reconcile faith and science in his own heart and mind by turning to (Christianity, transcendentalism, Roman Catholicism).

What to Look For:

One of the reactions to the theory of evolution was to separate religion and science. Transcendentalists believed that spiritual truths were "deeper" truths that transcended the realm of science. At first, this view appears to be an easy solution to the problem. However, as J. Gresham Machen has pointed out, for religion to be true, it must be connected to fact. Science and religion cannot be separated. (Science is not to be equated with the pseudoscience of evolution, or as 1 Timothy 6:20 calls it, "science falsely so called".) As you read, notice Tennyson's contrasting views of faith and knowledge. Compare his views with Hebrews 11:1–3. According to the Bible, is knowledge an essential element of faith? How important is the historical fact of Christ's resurrection to the truthfulness of Christianity (cf. 1 Corinthians 15:17)? How does Tennyson's faith differ from the Christian faith?

From: *In Memoriam A.H.H.*

In Memoriam was written over a period of seventeen years for Tennyson's close friend, Arthur Hallam. In varying moods of lament, its 132 sections search out the meaning of faith in a world of rationalistic and evolutionary doubt. Tennyson's references to Christ and His coming millennial reign might lead one to consider the work Christian. Many people including Queen Victoria, have so mistaken it. Queen Victoria stated after the death of her husband, "Next to the Bible, In Memoriam is my comfort." However, upon closer inspection, one is bound to agree with T. S. Eliot's assessment that it is a poem of doubt more than of faith and more of despair than of hope. As a transcendentalist, Tennyson considered Christianity to be an incomplete revelation of God. Deeper truths were needed that only "A warmth within the breast" could supply.

In Memorium—Alfred, Lord Tennyson

Strong Son of God, immortal Love,
    Whom we, that have not seen thy face,
    By faith, and faith alone, embrace,
Believing where we cannot prove;

Thine are these orbs of light and shade;
    Thou madest Life in man and brute;
    Thou madest Death; and lo, thy foot
Is on the skull which thou hast made.

Thou wilt not leave us in the dust:
    Thou madest man, he knows not why,
    He thinks he was not made to die;
And thou hast made him: thou art just.

Thou seemest human and divine,
    The highest, holiest manhood, thou.
    Our wills are ours, we know not how;
Our wills are ours, to make them thine.

Our little systems have their day;
    They have their day and cease to be;
    They are but broken lights of thee,
And thou, O Lord, art more than they.

We have but faith: we cannot know,
    For knowledge is of things we see;
    And yet we trust it comes from thee,
A beam in darkness: let it grow.

Let knowledge grow from from more to more,
    But more of reverence in us dwell;
    That mind and soul, according well,
May make one music as before,

But vaster. We are fools and slight;
    We mock thee when we do not fear,
    But help thy foolish ones to bear;
Help thy vain worlds to bear thy light.

Forgive what seemed my sin in me,
    What seemed my worth since I began;
    For merit lives from man to man,
And not from man, O LORD, to thee.

Forgive my grief for one removed,
    Thy creature, whom I found so fair.
    I trust he lives in thee, and there
I find him worthier to be loved.

Forgive these wild and wandering cries,
    Confusion of a wasted youth;
    Forgive them where they fail in truth,
And in thy wisdom make me wise.

LIV

O, yet we trust that somehow good
    Will be the final goal of ill,
    To pangs of nature, sins of will,
Defects of doubt, and taints of blood;

That nothing walks with aimless feet;
    That not one life shall be destroy'd,
    Or cast as rubbish to the void,
When God hath made the pile complete;

That not a worm is cloven in vain;
    That not a moth with vain desire
    Is shrivell'd in a fruitless fire,
Or but subserves another's gain.

Behold, we know not anything;
    I can but trust that good shall fall
    At last—far off—at last, to all,
And every winter change to spring.

So runs my dream: but what am I?
    An infant crying in the night;
    An infant crying for the light,
And with no language but a cry.

LV

The wish, that of the living whole
    No life may fail beyond the grave,
    Derives it not from what we have
The likest God within the soul?

Are God and Nature then at strife,
    That Nature lends such evil dreams?
    So careful of the type she seems,
So careless of the single life,

That I, considering everywhere
    Her secret meaning in her deeds,
    And finding that of fifty seeds
She often brings but one to bear,

I falter where I firmly trod,
    And falling with my weight of cares
    Upon the great world's altar-stairs
That slope thro' darkness up to God,

I stretch lame hands of faith, and grope,
    And gather dust and chaff, and call
    To what I feel is Lord of all,
And faintly trust the larger hope.

XCV

By night we linger'd on the lawn,
    For underfoot the herb was dry;
    And genial warmth; and o'er the sky
The silvery haze of summer drawn;

And calm that let the tapers burn
    Unwavering: not a cricket chirr'd;
    The brook alone far-off was heard,
And on the board the fluttering urn:

And bats went round in fragrant skies,
    And wheel'd or lit the filmy shapes
    That haunt the dusk, with ermine capes
And woolly breasts and beaded eyes;

While now we sang old songs that peal'd
    From knoll to knoll, where, couch'd at ease,
    The white kine glimmer'd, and the trees
Laid their dark arms about the field.

But when those others, one by one,
    Withdrew themselves from me and night,
    And in the house light after light
Went out, and I was all alone,

A hunger seized my heart; I read
    Of that glad year which once had been,
    In those fall'n leaves which kept their green,
The noble letters of the dead.

And strangely on the silence broke
    The silent-speaking words, and strange
    Was love's dumb cry defying change
To test his worth; and strangely spoke

The faith, the vigour, bold to dwell
    On doubts that drive the coward back,
    And keen thro' wordy snares to track
Suggestion to her inmost cell.

So word by word, and line by line,
    The dead man touch'd me from the past,
    And all at once it seem'd at last
The living soul was flash'd on mine,

And mine in his was wound, and whirl'd
    About empyreal heights of thought,
    And came on that which is, and caught
The deep pulsations of the world,

Æonian music measuring out
    The steps of Time—the shocks of chance—
    The blows of death. At length my trance
Was cancell'd, stricken thro' with doubt.

Vague words! but ah, how hard to frame
    In matter-moulded forms of speech,
    Or ev'n for intellect to reach
Thro' memory that which I became;

Till now the doubtful dusk reveal'd
    The knolls once more where, couch'd at ease,
    The white kine glimmer'd, and the trees
Laid their dark arms about the field;

And suck'd from out the distant gloom
    A breeze began to tremble o'er
    The large leaves of the sycamore,
And fluctuate all the still perfume,

And gathering freshlier overhead,
    Rock'd the full-foliaged elms, and swung
    The heavy-folded rose, and flung
The lilies to and fro, and said,

"The dawn, the dawn," and died away;
    And East and West, without a breath,
    Mixt their dim lights, like life and death,
To broaden into boundless day.

XCVI

You say, but with no touch of scorn,
    Sweet-hearted, you, whose light-blue eyes
    Are tender over drowning flies,
You tell me, doubt is devil-born.

I know not. One indeed I knew
    In many a subtle question versed,
    Who touch'd a jarring lyre at first,
But ever strove to make it true;

Perplext in faith, but pure in deeds,
    At last he beat his music out.
    There lives more faith in honest doubt,
Believe me, than in half the creeds.

He fought his doubts, and gather'd strength,
    He would not make his judgment blind,
    He faced the spectres of the mind
And laid them; thus he came at length

To find a stronger faith his own,
    And power was with him in the night,
    Which makes the darkness and the light,
And dwells not in the light alone,

But in the darkness and the cloud,
    As over Sinaï's peaks of old,
    While Israel made their gods of gold,
Altho' the trumpet blew so loud.

CXXIV

That which we dare invoke to bless;
    Our dearest faith; our ghastliest doubt;
    He, they, one, all; within, without;
The Power in darkness whom we guess—

I found him not in world or sun,
    Or eagle's wing, or insect's eye,
    Nor thro' the questions men may try,
The petty cobwebs we have spun.

If e'er when faith had fall'n asleep,
    I heard a voice, "believe no more,"
    And heard an ever-breaking shore
That tumbled in the Godless deep,

A warmth within the breast would melt
    The freezing reason's colder part,
    And like a man in wrath the heart
Stood up and answer'd, "I have felt."

No, like a child in doubt and fear:
    But that blind clamour made me wise;
    Then was I as a child that cries,
But, crying, knows his father near;

And what I am beheld again
    What is, and no man understands;
    And out of darkness came the hands
That reach thro' nature, moulding men.

CXXIX

Dear friend, far off, my lost desire,
    So far, so near in woe and weal;
    O loved the most, when most I feel
There is a lower and a higher;

Known and unknown; human, divine;
    Sweet human hand and lips and eye;
    Dear heavenly friend that canst not die,
Mine, mine, for ever, ever mine;

Strange friend, past, present, and to be;
    Loved deeplier, darklier understood;
    Behold, I dream a dream of good,
And mingle all the world with thee.

CXXX

Thy voice is on the rolling air;
    I hear thee where the waters run;
    Thou standest in the rising sun,
And in the setting thou art fair.

What art thou then? I cannot guess;
    But tho' I seem in star and flower
    To feel thee some diffusive power,
I do not therefore love thee less.

My love involves the love before;
    My love is vaster passion now;
    Tho' mix'd with God and Nature thou,
I seem to love thee more and more.

Far off thou art, but ever nigh;
    I have thee still, and I rejoice;
    I prosper, circled with thy voice;
I shall not lose thee tho' I die.

CXXXI

O living will that shalt endure
    When all that seems shall suffer shock,
    Rise in the spiritual rock,
Flow thro' our deeds and make them pure,

That we may lift from out of dust
    A voice as unto him that hears,
    A cry above the conquer'd years
To one that with us works, and trust,

With faith that comes of self-control,
    The truths that never can be proved
    Until we close with all we loved,
And all we flow from, soul in soul.

Fill in each of the following blanks with the correct explanation or answer.

3.59 From the Prologue, explain Tennyson's contrasting views of faith and knowledge.

3.60 Why does Tennyson compare himself with an infant in section 54?

3.61 Explain how Tennyson contrasts Nature (science) with faith in section 55.

3.62 According to section 95, how does "the dead man touch [Tennyson] from the past?"

3.63 What cancels Tennyson's trance?

3.64 In section 96, how does Tennyson excuse his doubting of orthodox Christianity?

3.65 In section 124, on what does Tennyson rely to answer the questions of doubt that plague him?

3.66 According to sections 129 and 130, explain why Tennyson's "dear heavenly friend" cannot die.

3.67 To what truths is Tennyson referring in the last stanza of section 131?

Charles John Huffman Dickens (1812–1870). Considered one of the best storytellers to have ever lived, Charles Dickens is the quintessential Victorian novelist. His power to capture the imagination lies in his narrative skill and acute perception of human nature.

Like his books, Dickens's early life was full of sensationalism and melodrama. His father was a clerk in the Naval Pay Office. A flamboyant man who did not manage money well, John Dickens was thrown into the Marshalsea prison for debts that he could not pay. Although the rest of the family lived with him in prison, Charles was sent to work at a boot-blacking factory. For the young Dickens, who aspired to be a gentleman and a scholar, the experience was quite traumatic. His sense "of being utterly neglected and hopeless; of the shame I felt in my position; of the misery it was to my young heart" is much expressed in the novel *David Copperfield* (1849–1850).

After his father was released from prison, Dickens attended school from 1824–1827. At the age of fifteen, he went to work in London as an office boy for an attorney. He taught himself shorthand at night and soon put his new skills to work as a reporter for the *Morning Chronicle.* In 1830 he met and fell in love with Maria Beadnell. However, Maria's parents discouraged the relationship, and it soon ended. Maria's father was a banker and aspired to marry his daughter to someone of greater importance than a mere newspaper reporter.

Ironically, people soon recognized, Dickens's ability to write interesting descriptions of people and places. In 1833 he began writing a series of articles on London life for the *Monthly Magazine.* A collection of the articles was later published as *Sketches by 'Boz', Illustrative of Every Day Life and Every-Day People* (1836–1837). Dickens's descriptive articles, accompanied by the illustrations of George Cruikshank, were well received. In 1834 his father again was thrown into debtors' prison. Dickens paid his debts and had him released. His father was a burden that the wealthy Dickens had to bear the rest of his life.

In 1835 Dickens became engaged to Catherine Hogarth, the daughter of a fellow writer. Soon after the publication of the first series of *Sketches by Boz,* Dickens was approached by Chapman and Hall to publish a series of monthly episodes in collaboration with Robert Seymour, a popular artist. Initially, Dickens's work was to conform to Seymour's; however, the strongminded and ambitious Dickens would not stand for the arrangement. No one would dictate *how* or *what* he would write. The illustrator, Dickens thought, came after the writer in such creative decisions. As a result of previous emotional problems, Seymour committed suicide. H. K. Brown (a.k.a. "Phiz") took his place, remaining Dickens's illustrator for many years. The two men complemented each other well, making *The Posthumous Papers of the Pickwick Club* an enormous hit. Dickens became a literary celebrity in both England and America when he was only in his twenties. The complete volume of *The Pickwick Papers* was published in 1837.

In 1836 Dickens married Catherine Hogarth and became the first editor of *Bentley's Miscellany.* During that same year, Dickens became a friend of John Forster, who would later become his biographer. Despite his other duties as an editor and a journalist, Dickens embarked on a career as a novelist. In 1837 he began work on *Oliver Twist,* publishing it in monthly installments. In 1838 he began *Nicholas Nickleby.* Both novels were published monthly until 1839. After resigning his position as editor of *Bentley's Miscellany,* Dickens began editing the weekly *Master Humphrey's Clock* in 1840. *The Curiosity Shop* and *Barnaby Rudge* were published in installments in *Master Humphrey.* Both works were completed before 1842, when Dickens and his wife traveled to America and Canada to advocate international copyright laws and the abolition of slavery. The publication of the travel book *American Notes* and the novel *Martin Chuzzlewit* (1843–44) followed the tour. The books were ill received by Americans, who found the characterizations distasteful.

In 1844 Dickens published his first of a series of Christmas books, which he described as "a whimsical sort of masque intended to awaken loving and forebearing thoughts." The children's story *A Christmas Carol* was followed by *The Chimes, The Cricket on the Hearth,* and *The Haunted Man.* In the same year that *Pictures from Italy* was published (1846), Dickens traveled to Switzerland and wrote *Dombey and Son* (1848).

Even as a young boy, Dickens dreamed of being involved in the theater; however, Dickens showed more talent for writing than for acting. In 1845 Dickens began an amateur theatrical company for which he wrote many plays. While he was involved with the theater, he forged a close friendship with a young actress, Ellen Ternan. The questionable nature of the relationship caused further division between Dickens and his wife. The two were separated in 1858 but never divorced. The couple had ten children.

Always fearful of falling into debt like his father, Dickens continued to take on writing assignments and editorial positions with undying enthusiasm. In 1843 he served as editor for the *Daily News* and took on *Household Words* in 1850. In 1859 *Household Words* became *All the Year Round,* of which Dickens remained the editor until his death. The first installment of *A Tale of Two Cities* appeared in the first edition of that publication. *A Child's History of England, The Christmas Stories, David Copperfield* (1849–1850), and *Bleak House* (1852–1853) were all published in *All the Year Round. Hard Times* was published weekly in *Household Words* in 1854. While he was in Europe in 1855, Dickens began work on *Little Dorrit,* and he completed the series in June 1857. Great Expectations (1860–1861) and *Our Mutual Friend* (1864–1865) were also published in *All the Year Round.*

During the latter part of his life, Dickens gave public readings of his works, acting out various characters with much dramatic enthusiasm. The readings were exhilarating for Dickens, but, as his daughter has commented, they led to his death. In (1867–1868), he traveled again to America to give a series of public readings. On June 9, 1870, he suffered a stroke and died, leaving *The Mystery of Edwin Drood* unfinished. He is buried in Westminster Abbey.

In an attempt to summarize the work of Charles Dickens, Peter Ackroyd has observed, "He was brazenly optimistic and as anxiously doubtful as any of his contemporaries; he shared with them the same violence and the same energy, and in his earnestness as well as in his sentimentality, in his enthusiasm and in his theatricality, in his sense of duty and in his sense of the ridiculous, we see the Victorian era as it truly was…in his novels there is to be found the soul of the English people."

 Underline the correct answer in each of the following statements.

3.68 As a boy, Charles Dickens was made to work in a (factory, mine, lawyer's office) when his father was imprisoned for (stealing, unpaid debts, murder).

3.69 Dickens's first job as a writer was as a (novelist, essayist, reporter) for the *Morning Chronicle*.

3.70 Published in 1833, (*The Pickwick Papers, Sketches by Boz, David Copperfield*) was Dickens's first series of articles on the people and places of London.

3.71 Published in volume form in 1837, (*The Pickwick Papers, Sketches by Boz, David Copperfield*) made Dickens a celebrity in England and America.

3.72 In 1836 Dickens married (Catherine Hogarth, Maria Beadnell, Ellen Ternan).

3.73 In 1842 Dickens traveled with his wife to (America, Paris, Greece) to advocate international copyright laws and the (abolition of slavery, return of British rule, women's suffrage movement).

3.74 The first of Dickens's (political essays, Christmas books, religious books) was published in 1844.

3.75 In 1845 Dickens began an amateur (theatrical company, writers club, athletic club), fulfilling his life-long desire to be involved in the (theater, education of other writers, training of young athletes).

3.76 Dickens initially published many of his novels in the magazines for which he served as (illustrator, editor, owner).

3.77 Many of Dickens's later novels were published in the monthly magazine (*Westminster Review, All the Year Round, Bentley's Miscellany*).

3.78 In (1867–1868), Dickens traveled again to America to give (public readings of his works, speeches on slavery, free lectures on social issues).

What to Look For:

C. S. Lewis once wrote, "The Christian…has no objection to comedies that merely amuse and tales that merely refresh.…We can play, as we can eat, to the glory of God." As you read, notice the warmth and humor of the characters. Although the story is more delightful than educational, how can reading comical literature such as *The Pickwick Papers* prove valuable to the Christian? How can reading be enjoyed as a form of rest?

From: *The Pickwick Papers*—Chapter 1: The Pickwickians

The first ray of light which illumines the gloom, and converts into a dazzling brilliancy that obscurity in which the earlier history of the public career of the immortal Pickwick would appear to be involved, is derived from the perusal of the following entry in the Transactions of the Pickwick Club, which the editor of these papers feels the highest pleasure in laying before his readers, as a proof of the careful attention, indefatigable assiduity, and nice discrimination, with which his search among the multifarious documents confided to him has been conducted.

'May 12, 1827. Joseph Smiggers, Esq., P.V.P.M.P.C. [Perpetual Vice-President—Member Pickwick Club], presiding. The following resolutions unanimously agreed to:—

'That this Association has heard read, with feelings of unmingled satisfaction, and unqualified approval, the paper communicated by Samuel Pickwick, Esq., G.C.M.P.C. [General Chairman—Member Pickwick Club], entitled "Speculations on the Source of the Hampstead Ponds, with some Observations on the Theory of Tittlebats;" and that this Association does hereby return its warmest thanks to the said Samuel Pickwick, Esq., G.C.M.P.C., for the same.

'That while this Association is deeply sensible of the advantages which must accrue to the cause of science, from the production to which they have just adverted—no less than from the unwearied researches of Samuel Pickwick, Esq., G.C.M.P.C., in Hornsey, Highgate, Brixton, and Camberwell—they cannot but entertain a lively sense of the inestimable benefits which must inevitably result from carrying the speculations of that learned man into a wider field, from extending his travels, and, consequently, enlarging his sphere of observation, to the advancement of knowledge, and the diffusion of learning.

'That, with the view just mentioned, this Association has taken into its serious consideration a proposal, emanating from the aforesaid, Samuel Pickwick, Esq., G.C.M.P.C., and three other Pickwickians hereinafter named, for forming a new branch of United Pickwickians, under the title of The Corresponding Society of the Pickwick Club.

'That the said proposal has received the sanction and approval of this Association.

'That the Corresponding Society of the Pickwick Club is therefore hereby constituted; and that Samuel Pickwick, Esq., G.C.M.P.C., Tracy Tupman, Esq., M.P.C., Augustus Snodgrass, Esq., M.P.C., and Nathaniel Winkle, Esq., M.P.C., are hereby nominated and appointed members of the same; and that they be requested to forward, from time to time, authenticated accounts of their journeys and investigations, of their observations of character and manners, and of the whole of their adventures, together with all tales and papers to which local scenery or associations may give rise, to the Pickwick Club, stationed in London.

'That this Association cordially recognises the principle of every member of the Corresponding Society defraying his own travelling expenses; and that it sees no objection whatever to the members of the said society pursuing their inquiries for any length of time they please, upon the same terms.

'That the members of the aforesaid Corresponding Society be, and are hereby informed, that their proposal to pay the postage of their letters, and the carriage of their parcels, has been deliberated upon by this Association: that this Association considers such proposal worthy of the great minds from which it emanated, and that it hereby signifies its perfect acquiescence therein.'

A casual observer, adds the secretary, to whose notes we are indebted for the following account—a casual observer might possibly have remarked nothing extraordinary in the bald head, and circular spectacles, which were intently turned towards his (the secretary's) face, during the reading of the above resolutions: to those who knew that the gigantic brain of Pickwick was working beneath that forehead, and that the beaming eyes of Pickwick were twinkling behind those glasses, the sight was indeed an interesting one. There sat the man who had traced to their source the mighty ponds of Hampstead, and agitated the scientific world with his Theory of Tittlebats, as calm and unmoved as the deep waters of the one on a frosty day, or as a solitary specimen of the other in the inmost recesses of an earthen jar. And how much more interesting did the spectacle become, when, starting into full life and animation, as a simultaneous call for 'Pickwick' burst from his followers, that illustrious man slowly mounted into the Windsor chair, on which he had been previously seated, and addressed the club himself had founded. What a study for an artist did that exciting scene present! The eloquent Pickwick, with one hand gracefully concealed behind his coat tails, and the other waving in air to assist his glowing declamation; his elevated position revealing those tights and gaiters, which, had they clothed an ordinary man, might have passed without observation, but which, when Pickwick clothed them—if we may use the expression—inspired involuntary awe and respect; surrounded by the men who had volunteered to share the perils of his travels, and who were destined to participate in the glories of his discoveries. On his right sat Mr. Tracy Tupman—the too susceptible Tupman, who to the wisdom and experience of maturer years superadded the enthusiasm and ardour of a boy in the most interesting and pardonable of human weaknesses—love. Time and feeding had expanded that once romantic form; the black silk waistcoat had become more and more developed; inch by inch had the gold watch-chain beneath it disappeared from within the range of Tupman's vision; and gradually had the capacious chin encroached upon the borders of the white cravat: but the soul of Tupman had known no change—admiration of the fair sex was still its ruling passion. On the left of his great leader sat the poetic Snodgrass, and near him again the sporting Winkle; the former poetically enveloped in a mysterious blue cloak with a canine-skin collar, and the latter communicating additional lustre to a new green shooting-coat, plaid neckerchief, and closely-fitted drabs.

Mr. Pickwick's oration upon this occasion, together with the debate thereon, I entered on the Transactions of the Club. Both bear a strong affinity to the discussions of other celebrated bodies; and, as it is always interesting to trace a resemblance between the proceedings of great men, we transfer the entry to these pages.

'Mr. Pickwick observed (says the secretary) that fame was dear to the heart of every man. Poetic fame was dear to the heart of his friend Snodgrass; the fame of conquest was equally dear to his friend Tupman; and the desire of earning fame in the sports of the field, the air, and the water was uppermost in the breast of his friend Winkle. He (Mr. Pickwick) would not deny that he was influenced by human passions and human feelings (cheers)—possibly by human weaknesses (loud cries of "No"); but this he would say, that if ever the fire of self-importance broke out in his bosom, the desire to benefit the human race in preference effectually quenched it. The praise of mankind was his swing; philanthropy was his insurance office. (Vehement cheering.) He had felt some pride—he acknowledged it freely, and let his enemies make the most of it—he had felt some pride when he presented his Tittlebatian Theory to the world; it might be celebrated or it might not. (A cry of "It is," and great cheering.) He would take the assertion of that honourable Pickwickian whose voice he had just heard—it was celebrated; but if the fame of that treatise were to extend to the farthest confines of the known world, the pride with which he should reflect on the authorship of that production would be as nothing compared with the pride with which he looked around him, on this, the proudest moment of his existence. (Cheers.) He was a humble individual. ("No, no.") Still he could not but feel that they had selected him for a service of great honour, and of some danger. Travelling was in a troubled state, and the minds of coachmen were unsettled. Let them look abroad and contemplate the scenes which were enacting around them. Stage-coaches were upsetting in all directions, horses were bolting, boats were overturning, and boilers were bursting. (Cheers—a voice "No.") No! (Cheers.) Let that honourable Pickwickian who cried "No" so loudly come forward and deny it, if he could. (Cheers.) Who was it that cried "No"? (Enthusiastic cheering.) Was it some vain and disappointed man—he would not say haberdasher (loud cheers)—who, jealous of the praise which had been—perhaps undeservedly—bestowed on his (Mr. Pickwick's) researches, and smarting under the censure which had been heaped upon his own feeble attempts at rivalry, now took this vile and calumnious mode of—

'Mr. BLOTTON (of Aldgate) rose to order. Did the honourable Pickwickian allude to him? (Cries of "Order," "Chair," "Yes," "No," "Go on," "Leave off," etc.)

'Mr. PICKWICK would not put up to be put down by clamour. He had alluded to the honourable gentleman. (Great excitement.)

'Mr. BLOTTON would only say then, that he repelled the hon. gent.'s false and scurrilous accusation, with profound contempt.

(Great cheering.) The hon. gent. was a humbug. (Immense confusion, and loud cries of "Chair," and "Order.")

'Mr. A. SNODGRASS rose to order. He threw himself upon the chair. (Hear.) He wished to know whether this disgraceful contest between two members of that club should be allowed to continue. (Hear, hear.)

'The CHAIRMAN was quite sure the hon. Pickwickian would withdraw the expression he had just made use of.

'Mr. BLOTTON, with all possible respect for the chair, was quite sure he would not.

'The CHAIRMAN felt it his imperative duty to demand of the honourable gentleman, whether he had used the expression which had just escaped him in a common sense.

'Mr. BLOTTON had no hesitation in saying that he had not—he had used the word in its Pickwickian sense. (Hear, hear.) He was bound to acknowledge that, personally, he entertained the highest regard and esteem for the honourable gentleman; he had merely considered him a humbug in a Pickwickian point of view. (Hear, hear.)

'Mr. PICKWICK felt much gratified by the fair, candid, and full explanation of his honourable friend. He begged it to be at once understood, that his own observations had been merely intended to bear a Pickwickian construction. (Cheers.)'

Here the entry terminates, as we have no doubt the debate did also, after arriving at such a highly satisfactory and intelligible point. We have no official statement of the facts which the reader will find recorded in the next chapter, but they have been carefully collated from letters and other MS. authorities, so unquestionably genuine as to justify their narration in a connected form.

Chapter XII: Descriptive of a very important Proceeding on the Part of Mr. Pickwick; no less an Epoch in his Life, than in this History

Mr. Pickwick's apartments in Goswell Street, although on a limited scale, were not only of a very neat and comfortable description, but peculiarly adapted for the residence of a man of his genius and observation. His sitting-room was the first-floor front, his bedroom the second-floor front; and thus, whether he were sitting at his desk in his parlour, or standing before the dressing-glass in his dormitory, he had an equal opportunity of contemplating human nature in all the numerous phases it exhibits, in that not more populous than popular thoroughfare. His landlady, Mrs. Bardell—the relict and sole executrix of a deceased custom-house officer—was a comely woman of bustling manners and agreeable appearance, with a natural genius for cooking, improved by study and long practice, into an exquisite talent. There were no children, no servants, no fowls. The only other inmates of the house were a large man and a small boy; the first a lodger, the second a production of Mrs. Bardell's. The large man was always home precisely at ten o'clock at night, at which hour he regularly condensed himself into the limits of a dwarfish French bedstead in the back parlour; and the infantine sports and gymnastic exercises of Master Bardell were exclusively confined to the neighbouring pavements and gutters. Cleanliness and quiet reigned throughout the house; and in it Mr. Pickwick's will was law.

To anyone acquainted with these points of the domestic economy of the establishment, and conversant with the admirable regulation of Mr. Pickwick's mind, his appearance and behaviour on the morning previous to that which had been fixed upon for the journey to Eatanswill would have been most mysterious and unaccountable. He paced the room to and fro with hurried steps, popped his head out of the window at intervals of about three minutes each, constantly referred to his watch, and exhibited many other manifestations of impatience very unusual with him. It was evident that something of great importance was in contemplation, but what that something was, not even Mrs. Bardell had been enabled to discover.

'Mrs. Bardell,' said Mr. Pickwick, at last, as that amiable female approached the termination of a prolonged dusting of the apartment.

'Sir,' said Mrs. Bardell.

'Your little boy is a very long time gone.'

'Why it's a good long way to the Borough, sir,' remonstrated Mrs. Bardell.

'Ah,' said Mr. Pickwick, 'very true; so it is.' Mr. Pickwick relapsed into silence, and Mrs. Bardell resumed her dusting.

'Mrs. Bardell,' said Mr. Pickwick, at the expiration of a few minutes.'Sir,' said Mrs. Bardell again.

'Do you think it a much greater expense to keep two people, than to keep one?

'La, Mr. Pickwick,' said Mrs. Bardell, colouring up to the very border of her cap, as she fancied she observed a species of matrimonial twinkle in the eyes of her lodger; 'La, Mr. Pickwick, what a question!'

'Well, but do you?' inquired Mr. Pickwick.

'That depends,' said Mrs. Bardell, approaching the duster very near to Mr. Pickwick's elbow which was planted on the table. 'that depends a good deal upon the person, you know, Mr. Pickwick; and whether it's a saving and careful person, sir.' 'That's very true,' said Mr. Pickwick, 'but the person I have in my eye (here he looked very hard at Mrs. Bardell) I think possesses these qualities; and has, moreover, a considerable knowledge of the world, and a great deal of sharpness, Mrs. Bardell, which may be of material use to me.'

'La, Mr. Pickwick,' said Mrs. Bardell, the crimson rising to her cap-border again.

'I do,' said Mr. Pickwick, growing energetic, as was his wont in speaking of a subject which interested him— 'I do, indeed; and to tell you the truth, Mrs. Bardell, I have made up my mind.'

'Dear me, sir,' exclaimed Mrs. Bardell.

'You'll think it very strange now,' said the amiable Mr. Pickwick, with a good-humoured glance at his companion, 'that I never consulted you about this matter, and never even mentioned it, till I sent your little boy out this morning—eh?'

Mrs. Bardell could only reply by a look. She had long worshipped Mr. Pickwick at a distance, but here she was, all at once, raised to a pinnacle to which her wildest and most extravagant hopes had never dared to aspire. Mr. Pickwick was going to propose—a deliberate plan, too—sent her little boy to the Borough, to get him out of the way—how thoughtful—how considerate!

'Well,' said Mr. Pickwick, 'what do you think?'

'Oh, Mr. Pickwick,' said Mrs. Bardell, trembling with agitation, 'you're very kind, sir.'

'It'll save you a good deal of trouble, won't it?' said Mr. Pickwick. 'Oh, I never thought anything of the trouble, sir,' replied Mrs. Bardell; 'and, of course, I should take more trouble to please you then, than ever; but it is so kind of you, Mr. Pickwick, to have so much consideration for my loneliness.'

'Ah, to be sure,' said Mr. Pickwick; 'I never thought of that. When I am in town, you'll always have somebody to sit with you. To be sure, so you will.'

'I am sure I ought to be a very happy woman,' said Mrs. Bardell.

'And your little boy—' said Mr. Pickwick.

'Bless his heart!' interposed Mrs. Bardell, with a maternal sob. 'He, too, will have a companion,' resumed Mr. Pickwick, 'a lively one, who'll teach him, I'll be bound, more tricks in a week than he would ever learn in a year.' And Mr. Pickwick smiled placidly.

'Oh, you dear—' said Mrs. Bardell.

Mr. Pickwick started.

'Oh, you kind, good, playful dear,' said Mrs. Bardell; and without more ado, she rose from her chair, and flung her arms round Mr. Pickwick's neck, with a cataract of tears and a chorus of sobs.

'Bless my soul,' cried the astonished Mr. Pickwick; 'Mrs. Bardell, my good woman—dear me, what a situation—pray consider. —Mrs. Bardell, don't—if anybody should come—'

'Oh, let them come,' exclaimed Mrs. Bardell frantically; 'I'll never leave you—dear, kind, good soul;' and, with these words, Mrs. Bardell clung the tighter.

'Mercy upon me,' said Mr. Pickwick, struggling violently, 'I hear somebody coming up the stairs. Don't, don't, there's a good creature, don't.' But entreaty and remonstrance were alike unavailing; for Mrs. Bardell had fainted in Mr. Pickwick's arms; and before he could gain time to deposit her on a chair, Master Bardell entered the room, ushering in Mr. Tupman, Mr. Winkle, and Mr. Snodgrass.

Mr. Pickwick was struck motionless and speechless. He stood with his lovely burden in his arms, gazing vacantly on the countenances of his friends, without the slightest attempt at recognition or explanation. They, in their turn, stared at him; and Master Bardell, in his turn, stared at everybody.

The astonishment of the Pickwickians was so absorbing, and the perplexity of Mr. Pickwick was so extreme, that they might have remained in exactly the same relative situations until the suspended animation of the lady was restored, had it not been for a most beautiful and touching expression of filial affection on the part of her youthful son. Clad in a tight suit of corduroy, spangled with brass buttons of a very considerable size, he at first stood at the door astounded and uncertain; but by degrees, the impression that his mother must have suffered some personal damage pervaded his partially developed mind, and considering Mr. Pickwick as the aggressor, he set up an appalling and semiearthly kind of howling, and butting forward with his head, commenced assailing that immortal gentleman about the back and legs, with such blows and pinches as the strength of his arm, and the violence of his excitement, allowed.

'Take this little villain away,' said the agonised Mr. Pickwick, 'he's mad.'

'What is the matter?' said the three tongue-tied Pickwickians.

'I don't know,' replied Mr. Pickwick pettishly. 'Take away the boy.' (Here Mr. Winkle carried the interesting boy, screaming and struggling, to the farther end of the apartment.) 'Now help me, lead this woman downstairs.'

'Oh, I am better now,' said Mrs. Bardell faintly.

'Let me lead you downstairs,' said the ever-gallant Mr. Tupman.

'Thank you, sir—thank you;' exclaimed Mrs. Bardell hysterically. And downstairs she was led accordingly, accompanied by her affectionate son.

'I cannot conceive,' said Mr. Pickwick when his friend returned—'I cannot conceive what has been the matter with that woman. I had merely announced to her my intention of keeping a man-servant, when she fell into the extraordinary paroxysm in which you found her. Very extraordinary thing.'

'Very,' said his three friends.

'Placed me in such an extremely awkward situation,' continued Mr. Pickwick.

'Very,' was the reply of his followers, as they coughed slightly, and looked dubiously at each other.

This behaviour was not lost upon Mr. Pickwick. He remarked their incredulity. They evidently suspected him.

'There is a man in the passage now,' said Mr. Tupman.

'It's the man I spoke to you about,' said Mr. Pickwick; 'I sent for him to the Borough this morning. Have the goodness to call him up, Snodgrass.'

Mr. Snodgrass did as he was desired; and Mr. Samuel Weller forthwith presented himself.

'Oh—you remember me, I suppose?' said Mr. Pickwick. 'I should think so,' replied Sam, with a patronising wink. 'Queer start that 'ere, but he was one too many for you, warn't he? Up to snuff and a pinch or two over—eh?'

'Never mind that matter now,' said Mr. Pickwick hastily; 'I want to speak to you about something else. Sit down.'

'Thank'ee, sir,' said Sam. And down he sat without further bidding, having previously deposited his old white hat on the landing outside the door. ''Tain't a wery good 'un to look at,' said Sam, 'but it's an astonishin' 'un to wear; and afore the brim went, it was a wery handsome tile. Hows'ever it's lighter without it, that's one thing, and every hole lets in some air, that's another—wentilation gossamer I calls it.' On the delivery of this sentiment, Mr. Weller smiled agreeably upon the assembled Pickwickians.

'Now with regard to the matter on which I, with the concurrence of these gentlemen, sent for you,' said Mr. Pickwick.

'That's the pint, sir,' interposed Sam; 'out vith it, as the father said to his child, when he swallowed a farden.'

'We want to know, in the first place,' said Mr. Pickwick, 'whether you have any reason to be discontented with your present situation.'

'Afore I answers that 'ere question, gen'l'm'n,' replied Mr. Weller, 'I should like to know, in the first place, whether you're a-goin' to purwide me with a better?'

A sunbeam of placid benevolence played on Mr. Pickwick's features as he said, 'I have half made up my mind to engage you myself.'

'Have you, though?' said Sam.

Mr. Pickwick nodded in the affirmative.

'Wages?' inquired Sam.

'Twelve pounds a year,' replied Mr. Pickwick.

'Clothes?'

'Two suits.'

'Work?'

'To attend upon me; and travel about with me and these gentlemen here.' 'Take the bill down,' said Sam emphatically. 'I'm let to a single gentleman, and the terms is agreed upon.'

'You accept the situation?' inquired Mr. Pickwick. 'Cert'nly,' replied Sam. 'If the clothes fits me half as well as the place, they'll do.'

'You can get a character of course?' said Mr. Pickwick.

'Ask the landlady o' the White Hart about that, Sir,' replied Sam. 'Can you come this evening?'

'I'll get into the clothes this minute, if they're here,' said Sam, with great alacrity. 'Call at eight this evening,' said Mr. Pickwick; 'and if the inquiries are satisfactory, they shall be provided.'

With the single exception of one amiable indiscretion, in which an assistant housemaid had equally participated, the history of Mr. Weller's conduct was so very blameless, that Mr. Pickwick felt fully justified in closing the engagement that very evening. With the promptness and energy which characterised not only the public proceedings, but all the private actions of this extraordinary man, he at once led his new attendant to one of those convenient emporiums where gentlemen's new and second-hand clothes are provided, and the troublesome and inconvenient formality of measurement dispensed with; and before night had closed in, Mr. Weller was furnished with a grey coat with the P. C. button, a black hat with a cockade to it, a pink striped waistcoat, light breeches and gaiters, and a variety of other necessaries, too numerous to recapitulate.

'Well,' said that suddenly transformed individual, as he took his seat on the outside of the Eatanswill coach next morning; 'I wonder whether I'm meant to be a footman, or a groom, or a gamekeeper, or a seedsman. I looks like a sort of compo of every one on 'em. Never mind; there's a change of air, plenty to see, and little to do; and all this suits my complaint uncommon; so long life to the Pickvicks, says I!'

✱ **Fill in each of the following blanks with the correct explanation or answer.**

3.79 What is the stated purpose of the new branch of United Pickwickians?

___

3.80 Briefly, describe Mr. Pickwick.

___

3.81 Why does Mrs. Bardell live in the same house as Mr. Pickwick?

___

3.82 When Mr. Pickwick begins to speak to Mrs. Bardell privately, what does she assume Mr. Pickwick has asked her to do?

___

3.83 Why is Mr. Pickwick worried that someone will see Mrs. Bardell hugging him?

___

3.84 How does Master Bardell react to his mother's being unconscious in the arms of Mr. Pickwick?

___

3.85 Who is Mr. Sam Weller, and why has he been brought to Mr. Pickwick?

___

Robert Browning (1812–1889). Browning was born to middle class parents in Camberwell, a suburb of London. His father was a cultured, wealthy clerk for the Bank of England. His mother was of German-Scottish descent, a kind woman strong in her evangelical faith. Up until Browning was thirty-four, he remained close to home. Disliking the normative classroom setting, he was educated by tutors. He read voraciously in his father's library of more than six thousand volumes and enjoyed frequent trips to the Dulwich Picture Gallery.

As he read about a variety of subjects, Browning discovered a particular fondness for the Romantics. His interest in Shelley led him to dramatically reject his mother's biblical influence. At the age of fourteen, he announced that he was an atheist. However, Browning later forsook his childlike foolishness and advocated a form of biblical theism. (Although he refuted the historical criticism of the Bible, he continued to resist the doctrine of the atonement. Christ's death was nothing more to him than a demonstration of love; it did not effect our forgiveness.)

In 1828 Browning attended the University of London for a short time. Five years later, he anonymously published his first poem, "Pauline." In 1835 he published "Paracelsus" and received much critical acclaim. The poem's success allowed him to become acquainted with Tennyson and Dickens. In 1837, he wrote his first of several unsuccessful plays. However, he demonstrated a talent for dramatic monologue, which he later published as dramatic poems in several volumes. *Dramatic Lyrics* was the first published in 1842.

After traveling first to St. Petersburg in 1834 and then to Italy in 1838, Browning began to publish a series of poems titled *Bells and Pomegranates*. The last poem of the series was published in 1846. Included in the collection are some of Browning's most loved works, including "My Last Duchess" and "The Bishop Orders His Tomb."

In 1845 Browning returned from his second trip to Italy and began a lively correspondence with Elizabeth Barrett. The thirty-three-year-old poet was six years his senior, a semiinvalid, and jealously guarded by her father. But Browning loved both her and her poetry. In romantic fashion, Browning rescued Elizabeth from her father's domestic tyranny by eloping with her to Italy in 1846. The warm Mediterranean climate cured Barrett's health, and the two lived in seeming marital bliss. In 1855 Browning published *Men and Women*. The collection contains several poems that are studies of Renaissance artists.

After the death of Elizabeth in 1861, Browning returned to London with their son, Robert Wiedemann Barrett Browning. With the publication of *The Ring and the Book* in 1868–1869, Browning's reputation soared to unexpected heights. He was awarded an honorary degree from Oxford, and the Browning Society was formed in 1881. Before returning to Italy in 1878, his popularity surpassed that of Tennyson.

Browning died in Venice on December 12, 1889. He is buried in Westminster Abbey.

Although Browning and Tennyson both enjoyed the admiration of Victorian readers, their poetry is not similar. As one critic has observed, Browning's often obscure yet psychologically insightful works demonstrate a likeness to the metaphysical poet John Donne. Another critic noted that Browning used a discordant, colloquial style similar to the romantics. His development of the dramatic monologue has heavily influenced the form of modern poetry.

     Fill in each of the following blanks with the correct answer.

3.86 Browning rejected his mother's evangelical faith for a form of biblical _____.

3.87 Browning was educated at home by _____ and read voraciously in his father's library.

3.88 The publication of _____ in 1835 brought Browning much critical acclaim.

3.89 Published in 1842, _____ contained a collection of Browning's dramatic monologues.

3.90 In 1846 Browning married _____ and moved with her to Italy.

3.91 In 1855 Browning published _____, which contained studies of various Renaissance artists.

3.92 Elizabeth Barrett Browning died in Italy in _____.

3.93 The publication of _____ in 1868–1869 elevated Browning's reputation as a poet above that of Tennyson.

3.94 In _____, Browning was awarded an honorary degree from _____ and the Browning Society was formed.

3.95 Browning's work favors the discordant, colloquial style of the _____.

What to Look For:

Browning is credited with the creation of the poetic dramatic monologue. The genre affords a limited point of view that leads to psychological insights that might not otherwise be revealed. As you read, pay attention to the duke's manner of speech. Does it command your attention and allegiance? Are you sympathetic toward his judgment of the last duchess? Does his monologue contain anything that would make you suspect foul play? Do you believe that he is giving a true representation of the character of the last duchess?

A speech given by Alfonso II, duke of Ferrara after the death of his young wife.

MY LAST DUCHESS—FERRARA

That's my last Duchess painted on the wall,
Looking as if she were alive. I call
That piece a wonder, now; Fra Pandolf's* hand *fictional artist*
Worked busily a day, and there she stands.
Will't please you sit and look at her? I said 5
"Fra Pandolf" by design, for never read
Strangers like you that pictured countenance,
The depth and passion of its earnest glance,
But to myself they turned (since none puts by
The curtain I have drawn for you, but I) 10
And seemed as they would ask me, if they durst,
How such a glance came there; so, not the first
Are you to turn and ask thus. Sir, 'twas not
Her husband's presence only, called that spot
Of joy into the Duchess' cheek: perhaps 15
Fra Pandolf chanced to say, "Her mantle laps
Over my lady's wrist too much," or "Paint
Must never hope to reproduce the faint
Half-flush that dies along her throat"; such stuff
Was courtesy, she thought, and cause enough 20
For calling up that spot of joy. She had
A heart—how shall I say?—too soon made glad,
Too easily impressed: she liked whate'er
She looked on, and her looks went everywhere.
Sir, 'twas all one! My favor at her breast, 25
The dropping of the daylight in the west,
The bough of cherries some officious fool
Broke in the orchard for her, the white mule
She rode with round the terrace—all and each
Would draw from her alike the approving speech, 30
Or blush, at least. She thanked men,—good! but thanked
Somehow- I know not how- as if she ranked
My gift of a nine-hundred-years-old name
With anybody's gift. Who'd stoop to blame
This sort of trifling? Even had you skill 35
In speech—which I have not—to make your will
Quite clear to such an one, and say, "Just this
Or that in you disgusts me; here you miss,
Or there exceed the mark"—and if she let
Herself be lessoned so, nor plainly set 40
Her wits to yours, forsooth, and made excuse,
—E'en then would be some stooping; and I choose
Never to stoop. Oh sir, she smiled, no doubt,
Whene'er I passed her; but who passed without
Much the same smile? This grew; I gave commands; 45
Then all smiles stopped together. There she stands
As if alive. Will't please you rise? We'll meet
The company below, then. I repeat,

> The count your master's known munificence
> Is ample warrant that no just pretence 50
> Of mine for dowry will be disallowed;
> Though his fair daughter's self, as I avowed
> At starting, is my object. Nay, we'll go
> Together down, sir! Notice Neptune, though,
> Taming a sea-horse, thought a rarity, 55
> Which Claus of Innsbruck* cast in bronze for me! *fictional sculptor*

✉ **Fill in each of the following blanks with the correct explanation or answer.**

3.96   Describe the person of the duke briefly.
_____

3.97   At what does the duke ask the listener to sit and look?
_____

3.98   Who, other than himself, does the duke claim "called that spot of joy into the Duchess's cheek?"
_____

3.99   According to lines 22–45, why was the duke so disgusted with the last duchess?
_____

3.100 What do you think stopped the duchess's smiles altogether?
_____

3.101 What is our only source of information about the duchess?
_____

3.102 In the first line and the last ten lines, whom does the duke address directly?
_____

3.103 When do you discover that the duke is addressing someone other than "you," the reader?
_____

3.104 According to lines 49–56, why has the count's servant come to the duke?
_____

George Eliot (Mary Ann Evans) (1819–1880). Born Mary Ann Evans in Warwickshire, England, Eliot was the daughter of an estate agent. Her father, although a servant, was considered a Tory of Tories. He loved the Church of England and held firm to the class system of society and politics. To receive a proper education for a girl of her social standing, Eliot was sent to Mrs. Wallington's School at Neneaton, where she met Miss Lewis. Although she was a member of the Church of England, like Eliot's father, Miss Lewis was different. Her religion was based on doctrines that evoked personal conviction and appealed to the emotions. Because Miss Lewis's evangelical faith acknowledged the Bible as its ultimate authority, it called into question the hierarchy of the Church of England and, consequently, the whole order of traditional society. This leveling of class distinctions had an enduring appeal for Eliot. It opened the door in her thinking for the rejection of all traditional structures of authority. Her father, for example, could not force her to live the restricted and uneventful life of a middle-class woman in Victorian England. As an intelligent and strong-willed woman, Eliot wanted opportunities that were normally reserved only for men.

Although for a time Eliot seemed to embrace the evangelical faith, she soon proved that she never possessed a saving knowledge of Christ. After her mother died, Eliot, then 17, was called home to care for her father. The two moved to Coventry, where Eliot met Charles Bray, a religious free thinker who was married to the sister of Charles Hennel, the author of *An Inquiry Concerning the Origin of Christianity*. Conversations with her new friends and the reading of rationalist thinkers fed her desire to doubt the evangelical faith. Although she maintained a sense of Christian love and duty, Eliot remained an agnostic for the rest of her life. Her rationalistic convictions led her to translate Strauss's *The Life of Jesus* (1846) and Feuerbach's *Essence of Christianity* (1854). The books affirmed the principles of higher criticism. Emphasizing Jesus' humanity while denying His miracles, these books placed man at the center of religion as both the basis for moral values and the object of worship.

In 1851 Eliot began contributing to the *Westminster Review* and soon became its assistant editor. Her influence led to the publication of articles on evolution, which influenced her understanding of moral progress. While she was with the *Review,* she met many literary figures. During this time, she met George Henry Lewes and fell in love with him, but they could not get married. Lewes's wife, although she had two children by another man, would not give him a divorce. Eliot and Lewes lived together as husband and wife until Lewes's death in 1878.

After many years of writing articles and reviews and dabbling in poetry, Lewes encouraged Eliot to write fiction. In 1857 the first installment of *Scenes from Clerical Life* was published in *Blackwood's Magazine.* "The Sad Fortunes of the Reverend Amos Barton" and its following tales were signed by George Eliot. Not until an imposter tried to claim the authorship of one of her books did Eliot reveal her true identity. *Scenes from Clerical Life* was published in book form in 1858.

The works that followed were also published in installments in the *Cornhill Magazine. Adam Bede* was published in 1859, *The Mill on the Floss* in 1860, *Silas Marner* in 1861, *Romola* from 1862–1863, *Felix Holt, the Radical* in 1866, *Middlemarch* from 1871–1877, and *Daniel Deronda* from 1874–1876. A collection of essays was published in 1879 with the title *The Impressions of Theophrastus Such*. Some of her poems, (for example,"O May I join the choir invisible" [1867]) were well-known during her lifetime. After the death of Lewes, Eliot never wrote again. He had supported her work and protected her from harsh criticism. In 1880 she married John Cross, an American banker twenty years her junior; Eliot was sixty, and Cross was forty. She died six months later.

A sensitive woman of high intellect, Eliot was drawn to an elaborate system of thinking that allowed people to be, as one writer put it, good without God. Her books portray the consequences of human actions with "traditional moral sensibility." Drawn from her own life, her characters and settings are depicted realistically. The humor and pathos felt by the heart are essential elements of Eliot's storytelling and ethics. Like some of the romantics before her, she understood that a connection exists between art and morals. She once wrote, "My own experience and development deepen every day my conviction that our moral progress may be measured by the degree in which we sympathize with individual suffering and individual joy." Eliot believed that literature, realistically written, could aid us in our moral progression by evoking sympathy for our fellow man. Although Christians can agree that ethics or morals are based on a love for our fellow man, however, we affirm that the reason for that love must be rooted in a love for God. ("'You shall love the LORD your God with all your heart, with all your soul, and with all your mind.' This is the first and great commandment. And the second is like it: 'You shall love your neighbor as yourself.' On these two commandments hang all the Law and the Prophets" [Matthew 22:37–40].) Dependent upon the will and emotions of man, Eliot's brand of ethics is the proven pathway to moral chaos.

✳ **Circle the letter of the line that best answers each of the following questions.**

3.105 Eliot was attracted to evangelicalism mainly because:

    a. it emphasized the Bible.

    b. it called into question the whole system of traditional society.

    c. it affirmed the hierarchical system of the Church of England.

    d. it affirmed class distinctions.

3.106 Eliot's agnostic convictions led her to translate books that affirmed:

    a. the principles of higher criticism.

    b. the doctrines of the Reformation.

    c. the miracles of Jesus.

    d. God-centered worship.

3.107 In 1851 Eliot began contributing regularly to:

    a. the *Morning Chronicle*.

    b. the *Westminster Review*.

    c. *Blackwood's Magazine*.

    d. *Cornhill Magazine*.

3.108 While working as editor for the *Review*, Eliot met and fell in love with:

    a. Oscar Wilde.

    b. Robert Browning.

    c. John Cross.

    d. George Henry Lewes.

3.109 In 1857 at the encouragement of Lewes, Eliot published her first fictional piece in *Blackwood's Magazine*, a novel titled:

    a. *Middlemarch*.

    b. *Silas Marner*.

    c. *Scenes from Clerical Life*.

    d. *The Mill on the Floss*.

3.110 Eliot was forced to reveal her true identity when:

    a. Lewes's wife offered him a divorce.

    b. someone tried to claim the authorship of *Scenes from Clerical Life*.

    c. someone tried to claim the authorship of *Middlemarch*.

    d. someone tried to claim the authorship of *Silas Marner*.

3.111 Eliot believed that literature, if written realistically, could:

    a. help humans progress morally by evoking sympathy for their fellow man.

    b. scare people into behaving properly.

    c. cause people to mistreat others.

    d. help us to acknowledge that God was the basis of morality.

3.112 Eliot's belief in moral progress was influenced by which prominent scientific theory?

    a. Higher criticism   c. Utilitarianism

    b. Evolution   d. Neo-orthodoxy

What to Look For:

Eliot acknowledged the fact that the moral and religious principles of a community will shape its culture and social conventions. As you read, notice the narrator's comments about religion and morality. By what standard are vices and virtues formed? Why is this standard so limiting? How does this standard affect adversely the lives of the characters? Why is it important to have the Bible as the standard for morality and religion rather than tradition and customs? By what standard did the Reformation judge customs and traditions to be oppressive?

From: *The Mill on the Floss*

The novel is about the two children, Tom and Maggie, of a simple miller, Mr. Tulliver. Maggie is an intelligent girl whom desires emotional companionship. Tom is Maggie's older brother, who tries to curb her rebellious behavior. The contrasting personalities lead to much frustration for both characters. The story is set in the countryside.

Book 4, Chapter 1: **A Variation of Protestantism Unknown to Bossuet**

JOURNEYING down the Rhône on a summer's day, you have perhaps felt the sunshine made dreary by those ruined villages which stud the banks in certain parts of its course, telling how the swift river once rose, like an angry, destroying god sweeping down the feeble generations whose breath is in their nostrils and making their dwellings a desolation. Strange contrast, you may have thought, between the effect produced on us by these dismal remnants of commonplace houses, which in their best days were but the sign of a **sordid*** life, belonging in all its details to our own vulgar era—and the effect produced by those ruins on the castled Rhine which have crumbled and mellowed into such harmony with the green and rocky steeps, that they seem to have a natural fitness, like the mountain pine: nay, even in the day when they were built they must have had this fitness, as if they had been raised by an earth-born race who had inherited from their mighty parent a sublime instinct of form. And that was a day of romance! If those robber barons were somewhat grim and drunken ogres, they had a certain grandeur of the wild beast in them—they were forest boars with tusks tearing and rending, not the ordinary domestic grunter: they represented the demon forces for ever in collision with beauty, virtue, and the gentle uses of life: they made a fine contrast in the picture with the wandering minstrel, the soft-lipped princess, the pious recluse and the timid Israelite. That was a time of colour when the sunlight fell on glancing steel and floating banners: a time of adventure and fierce struggle—nay, of living, religious art and religious enthusiasm; for were not cathedrals built in those days and did not great emperors leave their western palaces to die before the infidel strongholds in the sacred east? Therefore it is that these Rhine castles thrill me with a sense of poetry: they belong to the grand historic life of humanity, and raise up for me the vision of an epoch. But these dead-tinted, hollow-eyed, angular skeletons of villages on the Rhône, oppress me with the feeling that human life—very much of it—is a narrow, ugly, grovelling existence, which even calamity does not elevate, but rather tends to exhibit in all its bare vulgarity of conception; and I have a cruel conviction that the lives these ruins are the traces of were part of a gross sum of obscure vitality, that will be swept into the same oblivion with the generations of ants and beavers. Perhaps something akin to this oppressive feeling may have weighed upon you in watching this old-fashioned family life on the banks of the Floss, which even sorrow hardly suffices to lift above the level of the tragi-comic. It is a sordid life, you say, this of the Tullivers and Dodsons—irradiated by no sublime principles, no romantic visions, no active, self-renouncing faith—moved by none of those wild, uncontrollable passions which create the dark shadows of misery and crime—without that primitive rough simplicity of wants, that hard submissive ill-paid toil, that child-like spelling-out of what nature has written, which gives its poetry to peasant life. Here, one has conventional worldly notions and habits without instruction and without polish—surely the most prosaic form of human life: proud respectability in a gig of unfashionable build: worldliness without side-dishes. Observing these people narrowly, even when the iron hand of misfortune has shaken them from their unquestioning hold on the world, one sees little trace of religion, still less of a distinctively Christian creed. Their belief in the unseen, so far as it manifests itself at all, seems to be rather of a pagan kind: their moral notions, though held with strong tenacity, seem to have no standard beyond hereditary custom. You could not live among such people; you are stifled for want of an outlet towards something beautiful, great, or noble: you are irritated with these dull men and women, as a kind of population out of keeping with the earth on which they live—with this rich plain where the great river flows for ever onward and links the small pulse of the old English town with the beatings of the world's mighty heart. A vigorous superstition that lashes its gods or lashes its own back, seems to be more congruous with the mystery of the human lot, than the mental condition of these emmet-like Dodsons and Tullivers.

I share with you this sense of oppressive narrowness; but it is necessary that we should feel it, if we care to understand how it acted on the lives of Tom and Maggie—how it has acted on young natures in many generations, that in the onward tendency of human things have risen above the mental level of the generation before them, to which they have been nevertheless tied by the strongest fibres of their hearts. The suffering, whether of martyr or victim, which belongs to every historical advance of mankind, is represented in this way in every town and by hundreds of obscure hearths: and we need not shrink from this comparison of small things with great; for does not science tell us that its highest striving is after the ascertainment of a unity which shall bind the smallest things with the greatest? In natural science, I have understood, there is nothing petty to the mind that has a large vision of relations, and to which every single object suggests a vast sum of conditions. It is surely the same with the observation of human life.

Certainly, the religious and moral ideas of the Dodsons and Tullivers were of too specific a kind to be arrived at deductively, from the statement that they were part of the Protestant population of Great Britain. Their theory of life had its core of soundness, as all theories must have on which decent and prosperous families have been reared and have flourished; but it had the very slightest tincture of theology. If, in the maiden days of the Dodson sisters, their Bibles opened more easily at some parts than others, it was because of dried tulip petals, which had been distributed quite impartially, without preference for the historical, devotional, or doctrinal. Their religion was of a simple, semipagan kind, but there was no heresy in it, if heresy properly means choice, for they didn't know there was any other religion, except that of chapel-goers, which appeared to run in families, like asthma. How *should* they know? The vicar of their pleasant rural parish was not a controversialist, but a good hand at whist, and one who had a joke always ready for a blooming female parishioner. The religion of the Dodsons consisted in revering whatever was customary and respectable: it was necessary to be baptised, else one could not be buried in the churchyard, and to take the sacrament before death as a security against more dimly understood perils; but it was of equal necessity to have the proper pallbearers and well-cured hams at one's funeral, and to leave an unimpeachable will. A Dodson would not be taxed with the omission of anything that was becoming, or that belonged to that eternal fitness of things which was plainly indicated in the practice of the most substantial parishioners, and in the family traditions—such as obedience to parents, faithfulness to kindred, industry, rigid honesty, thrift, the thorough scouring of wooden and copper utensils, the hoarding of coins likely to disappear from the currency, the production of first-rate commodities for the market, and the general preference for whatever was homemade. The Dodsons were a very proud race, and their pride lay in the utter frustration of all desire to tax them with a breach of traditional duty or propriety. A wholesome pride in many respects; since it identified honour with perfect integrity, thoroughness of work, and faithfulness to admitted rules; and society owes some worthy qualities in many of her members to mothers of the Dodson class, who made their butter and their fromenty well and would have felt disgraced to make it otherwise. To be honest and poor was never a Dodson motto, still less, to seem rich though being poor; rather, the family badge was to be honest and rich, and not only rich, but richer than was supposed. To live respected and have the proper bearers at your funeral was an achievement of the ends of existence that would be entirely nullified if on the reading of your Will, you sank in the opinion of your fellowmen either by turning out to be poorer than they expected or by leaving your money in a capricious manner without strict regard to degrees of kin. The right thing must always be done towards kindred: the right thing was to correct them severely, if they were other than a credit to the family, but still not to alienate from them the smallest rightful share in the family shoe-buckles and other property. A conspicuous quality in the Dodson character was its genuineness: its vices and virtues alike were phrases of a proud, honest egoism which had a hearty dislike to whatever made against its own credit and interest, and would be frankly hard of speech to inconvenient "kin" but would never forsake or ignore them—would not let them want bread, but only require them to eat it with bitter herbs.

The same sort of traditional belief ran in the Tulliver veins, but it was carried in richer blood, having elements of generous imprudence, warm affection and hot-tempered rashness. Mr. Tulliver's grandfather had been heard to say that he was descended from one Ralph Tulliver, a wonderfully clever fellow who had ruined himself.—It is likely enough that the clever Ralph was a high liver, rode spirited horses, and was very decidedly of his own opinion. On the other hand, nobody had ever heard of a Dodson who had ruined himself; it was not the way of that family.

If such were the views of life on which the Dodsons and Tullivers had been reared in the praiseworthy past of Pitt and high prices, you will infer from what you already know concerning the state of society in St. Ogg's that there had been no highly modifying influence to act on them in their maturer life. It was still possible, even in that later time of anti-Catholic preaching, for people to hold many pagan ideas and believe themselves good church people notwithstanding: so we need hardly feel any surprise at the fact that Mr. Tulliver, though a regular church-goer, recorded his vindictiveness on the fly-leaf of his Bible. It was not that any harm could be said concerning the vicar of that charming rural parish to which Dorlcote Mill belonged: he was a man of excellent family, an irreproachable bachelor, of elegant pursuits, had taken honours, and held a fellowship: Mr. Tulliver regarded him with dutiful respect, as he did everything else belonging to the church-service; but he considered that church was one thing and common sense another, and he wanted nobody to tell *him* what common sense was. Certain seeds which are required to find a nidus for themselves under unfavourable circumstances have been supplied by nature with an apparatus of hooks, so that they will get a hold on very unreceptive surfaces. The spiritual seed which had been scattered over Mr. Tulliver had apparently been destitute of any corresponding provision, and had slipped off to the winds again from a total absence of hooks.

That was a painful thought to Maggie, and she wished much that the subsequent history of the young man had not been left a blank.

Circle the letter of the line that best answers each of the following questions.

3.113 How does the narrator describe the life of the Tullivers and Dodsons?
   a. sordid
   b. dignified
   c. reverent
   d. morally strict

3.114 How does the narrator describe their religious beliefs?
   a. Christian
   b. Roman Catholic
   c. pagan
   d. sincere

3.115 What is the basis of their morality?
   a. custom passed down from one generation to the next
   b. the Word of God
   c. church creeds
   d. individual desires

3.116 Because of their beliefs, the lives of the Tullivers and Dodsons are characterized by:
   a. freedom.
   b. beauty and truth.
   c. oppressive narrowness.
   d. greatness and nobility.

3.117 Why did the Bibles of the Dodson sisters open more easily in some parts than others?
   a. their particular devotion to those passages
   b. the placement of dried flowers
   c. the family frequently disputed the doctrines in those passages
   d. their pastor frequently preached out of those passages

3.118 What was the proper end to a respectable life for the Dodsons?
   a. a funeral with the proper pallbearers and a will that properly distributed their money
   b. death in the line of duty
   c. reception of the last sacrament
   d. a private family funeral

3.119 In what way did Mr. Tulliver's regular church attendance affect his life?
   a. He incorporated the Word of God into every aspect of his life.
   b. He believed that common sense and church were the same things
   c. It didn't affect his life at all.
   d. It brought him closer to God.

Oscar Wilde (1854–1900). Oscar Wilde was an aesthete in both art and life. "I have given my genius to my life," he said, "to my work only my talent." As a poet, playwright, novelist, and literary critic, Wilde was a leading advocate of the Aesthetic movement, which was based on the school of "art for art's sake."

Wilde was born in Dublin and educated at Trinity College. His father, Sir William Wilde, was an Irish surgeon. His mother, Jane

Francesca Elgee, was a writer. Wilde continued his studies of the classics at Magdalen College, Oxford, and distinguished himself as a poet, winning the university Newdigate Prize for his poem "Ravenna" in 1878. While at Oxford, Wilde became the disciple of Walter Pater, incorporating his aesthetic theories into his art and life. Wilde wore his hair long and dressed in flamboyant clothes. He collected blue china and peacock feathers. Eccentric and brilliantly witty, Wilde seemed to thrive off attention. He won many friends and admirers.

In 1881 Wilde traveled to America to lecture on the aesthetic movement and offer commentary on Gilbert and Sullivan's comic opera, *Patience,* which mocked the Aesthetic movement. That same year, Wilde published his first volume of poetry, *Poems.* In 1883 Wilde's first play, *Vera, or the Nihilists,* was performed in New York City, but it was not as successful as his lecture series.

In 1884 Wilde married Constance Lloyd, a wealthy Irish woman. The couple moved to London and within two years were the parents of Cyril and Vyvyan, two boys. *The Happy Prince,* a collection of children's stories originally written for his sons, was published in 1888.

Settled as a father and a husband, Wilde gave himself to his writing, creating works at a rapid rate. As a critic, he published *Decay of Lying* in 1889 and *The Soul of Man Under Socialism* in 1891. A group of short stories, *Lord Arthur Savile's Crime;* a second collection of fairy tales, *A House of Pomegranates;* his second play, *The Duchess of Padua;* and his only novel, *The Picture of Dorian Gray,* were also published in 1891.

Although he was a talented poet and novelist, Wilde is particularly noted for his comic plays *Lady Windermere's Fan* (1892), *A Woman of No Importance* (1893), *An Ideal Husband* (1895), and his masterpiece, *The Importance of Being Earnest* (1895). All of these works display Wilde's clever wit and talent for farce. In 1894 Lord Alfred Douglas published *Salomè* in an English translation. The serious play about uncontrollable passion was written in French and refused a performance license in London. It was first performed in Paris in 1896.

Desirous of new experiences and new sensations, Wilde became entangled in a web of perversity and scandal. When it was all over, Wilde was given a certificate of divorce, declared bankrupt, and convicted on charges of sodomy. While he was in jail for two years, he composed the poem "The Ballad of Reading Gaol" (1898), and a confessional work, *De Profundis* (1905). Humiliated and disgraced, Wilde lived the last three years of his life in France under the assumed name Sebastian Melmoth. He is said to have converted to Roman Catholicism before dying in a hotel in Paris.

In the morally strict culture of Victorian England, Wilde and the aesthetes struck a Bohemian cord that would continue to resound into the next century. The school of art for art's sake was based on the philosophy that the experience of art was the only thing that could offer meaning to life. Art itself could not do this because as Wilde claimed, "There is no such thing as a moral or an immoral book. Books are well written or badly written. That is all." As a devoted follower of Pater, Wilde was led to treat "art as the supreme reality." He searched for meaning in *experience,* often in its extreme form.

But his exile from society made him see the folly of the art for art's sake movement. Wilde's *De Profundis* reads like the confession of the prodigal son in the pig's pen. Acknowledging his shameful way of life, he wrote:

"I had a genius, a distinguished name, high social position, brilliancy, intellectual daring....But I let myself be lured into long spells of senseless and sensual ease....Tired of being on the heights, I deliberately went to the depths in the search for new sensation....I ended in horrible disgrace. There is only one thing for me now, absolute humility."

Fill in each of the following blanks with the correct answer.

3.120 Oscar Wilde was a leading advocate of the _____ movement, which was based on the school of art _____.

3.121 While at Oxford, Wilde incorporated the aesthetic theories of _____ into his art and life.

3.122 In 1881 Wilde traveled to _____ to give a series of lectures on the comic play *Patience*.

3.123 In 1883 _____ was performed in New York City. It was his first play.

3.124 In 1884 Wilde married _____, a wealthy Irish woman, and moved to London, where the couple had two boys.

3.125 *The Picture of Dorian Gray*, Wilde's only novel, was published in _____.

3.126 First performed in 1895, _____ is considered to be Wilde's masterpiece.

3.127 The school of art for art's sake was based on the philosophy that the _____ of art was the only thing that could offer meaning to life.

3.128 Written while he was imprisoned for sodomy, _____ expresses Wilde's deep remorse and shame for his perverse lifestyle.

3.129 Wilde converted to _____ before his death.

What to Look For:

Wilde was noted for his brilliant wit and exceptional ability in conversation. As you read, pay attention to the two essential elements of the play: wordplay and farce. How do these tools make the *experience* of the play so delightful? Why is it important to be "earnest" and/or "Earnest?" In their attempts to be earnest, are the characters actually being absurd?

From: *The Importance of Being Earnest*

THE PERSONS OF THE PLAY

JOHN WORTHING, J.P.

ALGERNON MONCRIEFF

REV. CANON CHASUBLE, D.D.

MERRIMAN, Butler

LANE, Manservant

LADY BRACKNELL

HON. GWENDOLEN FAIRFAX

CECILY CARDEW

MISS PRISM, Governess

CR80

From: ACT I: Algernon Moncrieff's Flat in Half-Moon Street, W.

Scene - Morning-room in Algernon's flat in Half-Moon Street. The room is luxuriously and artistically furnished. The sound of a piano is heard in the adjoining room.

[*Lane, the manservant, has been arranging afternoon tea on the table for his master, Algernon.*]
[*Enter Lane.*]

LANE: Mr. Ernest Worthing.

[*Enter Jack.*]

[*Lane goes out.*]

ALG: How are you, my dear Ernest? What brings you up to town?

JACK: Oh, pleasure, pleasure! What else should bring one anywhere? Eating as usual, I see, Algy!

ALG: [*Stiffly.*] I believe it is customary in good society to take some slight refreshment at five o'clock. Where have you been since last Thursday?

JACK: [*Sitting down on the sofa.*] In the country.

ALG: What on earth do you do there?

JACK: [*Pulling off his gloves.*] When one is in town one amuses oneself. When one is in the country one amuses other people. It is excessively boring.

ALG: And who are the people you amuse?

JACK: [Airily.] Oh, neighbours, neighbours.

ALG: Got nice neighbours in your part of Shropshire?

JACK: Perfectly horrid! Never speak to one of them.

ALG: How immensely you must amuse them! [*Goes over and takes sandwich.*] By the way, Shropshire is your county, is it not?

JACK: Eh? Shropshire? Yes, of course. Hallo! Why all these cups? Why cucumber sandwiches? Why such reckless extravagance in one so young? Who is coming to tea?

ALG: Oh! merely Aunt Augusta and Gwendolen.

JACK: How perfectly delightful!

ALG: Yes, that is all very well; but I am afraid Aunt Augusta won't quite approve of your being here.

JACK: May I ask way?

ALG: My dear fellow, the way you flirt with Gwendolen is perfectly disgraceful. It is almost as bad as the way Gwendolen flirts with you.

JACK: I am in love with Gwendolen. I have come up to town expressly to propose to her.

ALG: I thought you had come up for pleasure?… I call that business.

JACK: How utterly unromantic you are!

ALG: I really don't see anything romantic in proposing. It is very romantic to be in love. But there is nothing romantic about a definite proposal. Why, one may be accepted. One usually is, I believe. Then the excitement is all over. The very essence of romance is uncertainty. If ever I get married, I'll certainly try to forget the fact.

JACK: I have no doubt about that, dear Algy. The Divorce Court was specially invented for people whose memories are so curiously constituted.

ALG: Oh! there is no use speculating on that subject. Divorces are made in Heaven— [*Jack puts out his hand to take a sandwich. Algernon at once* *interferes.*] Please don't touch the cucumber sandwiches. They are ordered specially for Aunt Augusta. [*Takes one and eats it.*]

JACK: Well, you have been eating them all the time.

ALG: That is quite a different matter. She is my aunt. [*Takes plate from below.*] Have some bread and butter. The bread and butter is for Gwendolen. Gwendolen is devoted to bread and butter.

JACK: [*Advancing to table and helping himself.*] And very good bread and butter it is too.

ALG: Well, my dear fellow, you need not eat as if you were going to eat it all. You behave as if you were married to her already. You are not married to her already, and I don't think you ever will be.

JACK: Why, on earth do you say that?

ALG: Well, in the first place girls never marry the men they flirt with. Girls don't think it right.

JACK: Oh, that is nonsense!

ALG: It isn't. It is a great truth. It accounts for the extraordinary number of bachelors that one sees all over the place. In the second place, I don't give my consent.

JACK: Your consent!

ALG: My dear fellow, Gwendolen is my first cousin. And before I allow you to marry her, you will have to clear up the whole question of Cecily. [*Rings bell.*]

JACK: Cecily! What on earth do you mean? What do you mean, Algy, by Cecily? I don't know anyone of the name of Cecily.

[*Enter Lane.*]

ALG: Bring me that cigarette case Mr. Worthing left in the smokingroom the last time he dined here.

LANE: Yes, sir.

[*Lane goes out.*]

JACK: Do you mean to say you have had my cigarette case all this time? I wish to goodness you had let me know. I have been writing frantic letters to Scotland Yard about it. I was very nearly offering a large reward.

ALG: Well, I wish you would offer one. I happen to be more than usually hard up.

JACK: There is no good offering a large reward now that the thing is found.

[*Enter Lane with the cigarette case on a salver. Algernon takes it at once. Lane goes out.*]

ALG: I think that is rather mean of you, Ernest, I must say. [*Opens case and examines it.*] However, it makes no matter, for, now that I look at the inscription inside, I find that the thing isn't yours after all.

JACK: Of course it's mine. [*Moving to him.*] You have seen me with it a hundred times, and you have no right whatsoever to read what is written inside. It is a very ungentlemanly thing to read a private cigarette case.

ALG: Oh! it is absurd to have a hard-and-fast rule about what one should read and what one shouldn't. More than half of modern culture depends on what one shouldn't read.

JACK: I am quite aware of the fact, and I don't propose to discuss modern culture. It isn't the sort of thing one should talk of in private. I simply want my cigarette case back.

ALG: Yes; but this isn't your cigarette case. This cigarette case is a present from someone of the name of Cecily, and you said you didn't know anyone of that name.

JACK: Well, if you want to know, Cecily happens to be my aunt.

ALG: Your aunt!

JACK: Yes. Charming old lady she is, too. Lives at Tunbridge Wells. Just give it back to me, Algy.

ALG: [*Retreating to back of sofa.*] But why does she call herself Cecily if she is your aunt and lives at Tunbridge Wells? [*Reading.*] "From little Cecily with her fondest love."

JACK: [*Moving to sofa and kneeling upon it.*] My dear fellow, what on earth is there in that? Some aunts are tall, some aunts are not tall. That is a matter that surely an aunt may be allowed to decide for herself. You seem to think that every aunt should be exactly like your aunt! That is absurd! For Heaven's sake give me back my cigarette case. [*Follows Algy round the room.*]

ALG: Yes. But why does your aunt call you her uncle? "From little Cecily, with her fondest love to her dear Uncle Jack." There is no objection, I admit, to an aunt being a small aunt, but why an aunt, no matter what her size may be, should call her own nephew her uncle, I can't quite make out. Besides, your name isn't Jack at all; it is Ernest.

JACK: It isn't Ernest; it's Jack.

ALG: You have always told me it was Ernest. I have introduced you to everyone as Ernest. You answer to the name of Ernest. You look as if your name was Ernest. You are the most earnest looking person I ever saw in my life. It is perfectly absurd your saying that your name isn't Ernest. It's on your cards. Here is one of them. [*Taking it from case.*] "Mr. Ernest Worthing, B. 4, The Albany." I'll keep this as a proof that your name is Ernest if ever you attempt to deny it to me, or to Gwendolen, or to anyone else. [*Puts the card in his pocket.*]

JACK: Well, my name is Ernest in town and Jack in the country, and the cigarette case was given to me in the country.

ALG: Yes, but that does not account for the fact that your small Aunt Cecily, who lives at Tunbridge Wells, calls you her dear uncle. Come, old boy, you had much better have the thing out at once.

JACK: My dear Algy, you talk exactly as if you were a dentist. It is very vulgar to talk like a dentist when one isn't a dentist. It produces a false impression.

ALG: Well, that is exactly what dentists always do. Now, go on! Tell me the whole thing. I may mention that I have always suspected you of being a confirmed and secret Bunburyist; and I am quite sure of it now.

JACK: Bunburyist! What on earth do you mean by a Bunburyist?

ALG: I'll reveal to you the meaning of that incomparable expression as soon as you are kind enough to inform me why you are Ernest in town and Jack in the country.

JACK: Well, produce my cigarette case first.

ALG: Here it is. [*Hands cigarette case.*] Now produce your explanation, and pray make it improbable. [*Sits on sofa.*]

JACK: My dear fellow, there is nothing improbable about my explanation at all. In fact, it's perfectly ordinary. Old Mr. Thomas Cardew, who adopted me when I was a little boy, made me in his will guardian to his granddaughter, Miss Cecily Cardew. Cecily, who addresses me as her uncle from motives of respect that you could not possibly appreciate, lives at my place in the country under the charge of her admirable governess, Miss Prism.

ALG: Where is that place in the country, by the way?

JACK: That is nothing to you, dear boy. You are not going to be invited. I may tell you candidly that the place is not in Shropshire.

ALG: I suspected that, my dear fellow! I have Bunburyed all over Shropshire on two separate occasions. Now go on. Why are you Ernest in town and Jack in the country?

JACK: My dear Algy, I don't know whether you will be able to understand my real motives. You are hardly serious enough. When one is placed in the position of guardian, one has to adopt a very high moral tone on all subjects. It's one's duty to do so. And as a high moral tone can hardly be said to conduce very much to either one's health or one's happiness, in order to get up to town I have always pretended to have a younger brother of the name of Ernest, who lives in the Albany, and gets into the most dreadful scrapes. That, my dear Algy, is the whole truth pure and simple.

ALG: The truth is rarely pure and never simple. Modern life would be very tedious if it were either, and modern literature a complete impossibility!

JACK: That wouldn't be at all a bad thing.

ALG: Literary criticism is not your forte, my dear fellow. Don't try it. You should leave that to people who haven't been at a university. They do it so well in the daily papers. What you really are is a Bunburyist. I was quite right in saying you were a Bunburyist. You are one of the most advanced Bunburyists I know.

JACK: What on earth do you mean?

ALG: You have invented a very useful young brother called Ernest in order that you may be able to come up to town as often as you like. I have invented an invaluable permanent invalid called Bunbury in order that I may be able to go down into the country whenever I choose. Bunbury is perfectly invaluable. If it wasn't for Bunbury's extraordinary bad health, for instance, I wouldn't be able to dine with you at Willis's to-night, for I have been really engaged to Aunt Augusta for more than a week.

JACK: I haven't asked you to dine with me anywhere to-night.

ALG: I know. You are absurdly careless about sending out invitations. It is very foolish of you. Nothing annoys people so much as not receiving invitations.

JACK: You had much better dine with your Aunt Augusta.

ALG: I haven't the smallest intention of doing anything of the kind. To begin with, I dined there on Monday, and once a week is quite enough to dine with one's own relations. In the second place, whenever I do dine there I am always treated as a member of the family, and sent down with either no woman at all, or two. In the third place, I know perfectly well whom she will place me next to to-night. She will place me next to Mary Farquhar, who always flirts with her own husband across the dinner-table. That is not very pleasant. Indeed, it is not even decent… and that sort of thing is enormously on the increase. The amount of women in London who flirt with their own husbands is perfectly scandalous. It looks so bad. It is simply washing one's clean linen in public. Besides, now that I know you to be a confirmed Bunburyist, I naturally want to talk to you about Bunburying. I want to tell you the rules.

JACK: I'm not a Bunburyist at all. If Gwendolen accepts me, I am going to kill my brother, indeed I think I'll kill him in any case. Cecily is a little too much interested in him. It is rather a bore. So I am going to get rid of Ernest. And I strongly advise you to do the same with Mr.… with your invalid friend who has the absurd name.

ALG: Nothing will induce me to part with Bunbury, and if you ever get married, which seems to me extremely problematic, you will be very glad to know Bunbury. A man who marries without knowing Bunbury has a very tedious time of it.

JACK:	That is nonsense. If I marry a charming girl like Gwendolen, and she is the only girl I ever saw in my life that I would marry, I certainly won't want to know Bunbury.
ALG:	Then your wife will. You don't seem to realize, that in married life three is company and two is none.
JACK:	[*Sententiously.*] That, my dear young friend, is the theory that the corrupt French Drama has been propounding for the last fifty years.
ALG:	Yes; and that the happy English home has proved in half the time.
JACK:	For Heaven's sake, don't try to be cynical. It's perfectly easy to be cynical.
ALG:	My dear fellow, it isn't easy to be anything now-a-days. There's such a lot of beastly competition about. [*The sound of an electric bell is heard.*] Ah! that must be Aunt Augusta. Only relatives, or creditors, ever ring in that Wagnerian manner. Now, if I get her out of the way for ten minutes, so that you can have an opportunity for proposing to Gwendolen, may I dine with you to-night at Willis's?
JACK:	I suppose so, if you want to.
ALG:	Yes, but you must be serious about it. I hate people who are not serious about meals. It is so shallow of them.

[*Enter Lane.*]

LANE:	Lady Bracknell and Miss Fairfax.

[*Algernon goes forward to meet them. Enter Lady Bracknell and Gwendolen.*]

[*Lady Bracknell and Algernon go into the music-room, Gwendolen remains behind.*]

JACK:	Charming day it has been, Miss Fairfax.
GWEN:	Pray don't talk to me about the weather, Mr. Worthing. Whenever people talk to me about the weather, I always feel quite certain that they mean something else. And that makes me so nervous.
JACK:	I do mean something else.
GWEN:	I thought so. In fact, I am never wrong.
JACK:	And I would like to be allowed to take advantage of Lady Bracknell's temporary absence…
GWEN:	I would certainly advise you to do so. Mamma has a way of coming back suddenly into a room that I have often had to speak to her about.
JACK:	[*Nervously.*] Miss Fairfax, ever since I met you I have admired you more than any girl… I have ever met since… I met you.
GWEN:	Yes, I am quite aware of the fact. And I often wish that in public, at any rate, you had been more demonstrative. For me you have always had an irresistible fascination. Even before I met you I was far from indifferent to you. [*Jack looks at her in amazement.*] We live, as I hope you know, Mr. Worthing, in an age of ideals. The fact is constantly mentioned in the more expensive monthly magazines, and has reached the provincial pulpits I am told: and my ideal has always been to love some one of the name of Ernest. There is something in that name that inspires absolute confidence. The moment Algernon first mentioned to me that he had a friend called Ernest, I knew I was destined to love you.
JACK:	You really love me, Gwendolen?
GWEN:	Passionately!
JACK:	Darling! You don't know how happy you've made me.
GWEN:	My own Ernest!

JACK:	But you don't really mean to say that you couldn't love me if my name wasn't Ernest?
GWEN:	But your name is Ernest.
JACK:	Yes, I know it is. But supposing it was something else? Do you mean to say you couldn't love me then?
GWEN:	[*Glibly.*] Ah! that is clearly a metaphysical speculation, and like most metaphysical speculations has very little reference at all to the actual facts of real life, as we know them.
JACK:	Personally, darling, to speak quite candidly, I don't much care about the name of Ernest... I don't think the name suits me at all.
GWEN:	It suits you perfectly. It is a divine name. It has a music of its own. It produces vibrations.
JACK:	Well, really, Gwendolen, I must say that I think there are lots of other much nicer names. I think Jack, for instance, a charming name.
GWEN:	Jack?... No, there is very little music in the name Jack, if any at all, indeed. It does not thrill. It produces absolutely no vibrations.... I have known several Jacks, and they all, without exception, were more than usually plain. Besides, Jack is a **notorious*** domesticity for John! And I pity any woman who is married to a man called John. She would probably never be allowed to know the entrancing pleasure of a single moment's solitude. The only really safe name is Ernest.
JACK:	Gwendolen, I must get christened at once—I mean we must get married at once. There is no time to be lost.
GWEN:	Married, Mr. Worthing?
JACK:	[*Astounded.*] Well... surely. You know that I love you, and you led me to believe, Miss Fairfax, that you were not absolutely indifferent to me.
GWEN:	I adore you. But you haven't proposed to me yet. Nothing has been said at all about marriage. The subject has not even been touched on.
JACK:	Well... may I propose to you now?
GWEN:	I think it would be an admirable opportunity. And to spare you any possible disappointment, Mr. Worthing, I think it only fair to tell you quite frankly beforehand that I am fully determined to accept you.
JACK:	Gwendolen!
GWEN:	Yes, Mr. Worthing, what have you got to say to me?
JACK:	You know what I have got to say to you.
GWEN:	Yes, but you don't say it.
JACK:	Gwendolen, will you marry me? [*Goes on his knees.*]
GWEN:	Of course I will, darling. How long you have been about it! I am afraid you have had very little experience in how to propose.
JACK:	My own one, I have never loved anyone in the world but you.
GWEN:	Yes, but men often propose for practice. I know my brother Gerald does. All my girl-friends tell me so. What wonderfully blue eyes you have, Ernest! They are quite, quite blue. I hope you will always look at me just like that, especially when there are other people present.

➤ **Give the best answer or explanation for each of the following questions.**

3.130 Who is Algernon expecting for afternoon tea?
_____

3.131 Why does Algernon think it is not a good idea that Jack stay for tea?
_____

3.132 Why does Algernon think that proposing is unromantic?
_____

3.133 Why is Algernon so concerned about Jack's relationship to Cecily?
_____

3.134 How does Jack at first try to explain his relationship to Cecily?
_____

3.135 Why does Jack call himself Jack in the country and Ernest in the city?
_____

3.136 Why does Algernon call Jack a Bunburyist?
_____

3.137 Who is Ernest?
_____

3.138 Why is it important to Gwendolen that the man she marry is named Ernest?
_____

3.139 Why is important that Jack reveal his true identity?
_____

3.140 The dictionary defines *earnest* as "serious in intention, purpose, or effort." Explain how neither Jack nor Gwendolen is serious in their intentions toward one another.
_____

Lewis Carroll (Charles Lutwidge Dodgson) (1832–1898). Best known for his book *Alice's Adventures in Wonderland*, Lewis Carroll created children's stories that transport the reader into a world of fantasy and nonsense.

Carroll was born the first of eleven children. His father, Dr. Dodgson, was a clergyman who later became the Archdeacon of Richmond. Like his father, Carroll served in the church (he was ordained a deacon in 1887) and held a particular interest in mathematics. He was educated at Rugby and Christ Church, Oxford, where he was a lecturer in mathematics for more than twenty years. A noted logician, he was the author of several treatises on symbolic logic.

His most famous work, *Alice's Adventures in Wonderland*, originated as an impromptu story while he was on a boat trip with the young daughters of H. G. Liddell, the dean of Christ Church College. It was published in 1865 under his pseudonym.

A shy bachelor, Carroll liked to entertain children. He wrote them colorful letters, invented educational games and puzzles, and photographed them in costumes. He even preached to them on occasions. In 1871 Carroll followed Alice's adventures with a sequel, *Through the Looking-Glass and What Alice Found There*. Illustrated by Sir John

Tenniell, both books were immediately popular. One critic has noted that the success of the zany tales among Victorian readers was that they didn't teach a moral. However, upon deeper inspection, it is evident that Carroll is offering a commentary on the chaos within society during the end of the Victorian era. Using his mathematical skill and flair for fantasy, Carroll created a brilliant mix of parody, foolishness, and logic that delighted both children and adults. The lasting appeal of the lighthearted works is evidenced even to this day by the familiarity of children with characters such as the Mad Hatter, the Cheshire Cat, and Tweedledee and Tweedledumb.

Underline the correct answer in each of the following statements.

3.141 Carroll's father was a (clergyman, policeman, professor) who had a particular interest in mathematics.

3.142 After graduating from Christ Church College, Carroll became a lecturer in (religion, mathematics, biology).

3.143 In addition to his children's stories, Carroll was a noted author of several treatises on (children's ministries, English literature, symbolic logic).

3.144 *Alice's Adventures in Wonderland* was first told to (three women friends, the three Liddell daughters, two boys).

3.145 *Alice in Wonderland* was followed by the sequel (*Through the Looking Glass*, *Sylvie and Bruno*, *Humpty Dumpty*).

What to Look For:

During the end of the Victorian era, society struggled to find meaning in life. Many artists and writers, namely, the art for art's sake school, looked for significance in experience. As a religious man and a mathematician, Carroll understood that the universe was built upon order. The chaotic state of society was a natural result of its rejection of reality: God created the world with purpose and meaning. As you read, notice Alice's anxiety as she struggles to find order in Wonderland. What might Carroll be trying to illustrate with Alice's frustrations? How does the Bible characterize those who are unwilling to acknowledge that God created the world and the order that exists because of Him? (See Romans 1:20–25.)

From: *Alice in Wonderland.*
CHAPTER VIII THE QUEEN'S CROQUET GROUND.

A large rose-tree stood near the entrance of the garden; the roses growing on it were white, but there were three gardeners at it, busily painting them red.

Alice thought this a very curious thing, and she went nearer to watch them, and, just as she came up to them, she heard one of them say, "Look out now, Five! Don't go splashing paint over me like that!" "I couldn't help it," said Five, in a sulky tone. "Seven jogged my elbow." On which Seven looked up and said "That's right, Five! Always lay the blame on others!" "You'd better not talk!" said Five. "I heard the Queen say only yesterday you deserved to be beheaded." "What for?" said the one who had spoken first.

"That's none of your business, Two!" said Seven.

"Yes, it is his business!" said Five. "And I'll tell him—it was for bringing the cook tulip-roots instead of onions." Seven flung down his brush and had just begun "Well, of all the unjust things" when his eye chanced to fall upon Alice, as she stood watching them, and he checked himself suddenly; the others looked round also, and all of them bowed low.

"Would you tell me, please," said Alice, a little timidly, "why you are painting those roses?" Five and Seven said nothing, but looked at Two. Two began, in a low voice, "Why, the fact is, you see, Miss, this here ought to have been a red rose-tree, and we put a white one in by mistake; and, if the Queen was to find it out, we should all have our heads cut off, you know. So you see, Miss, we're doing our best, afore she comes, to—" At this moment, Five, who had been anxiously looking across the garden, called out, "The Queen! The Queen!" and the three gardeners instantly threw themselves flat upon their faces. There was a sound of many footsteps, and Alice looked round, eager to see the Queen.

First came ten soldiers carrying clubs; these were all shaped like the three gardeners, oblong and flat, with their hands and feet at the corners: next the ten courtiers: these were ornamented all over with diamonds, and walked two and two, as the soldiers did. After these came the royal children: there were ten of them, and the little dears came jumping merrily along, hand in hand, in couples: they were all ornamented with hearts. Next came the guests, mostly Kings and Queens, and among them Alice recognized the White Rabbit: it was talking in a hurried nervous manner, smiling at everything that was said, and went by without noticing her. Then followed the Knave of Hearts, carrying the King's crown on a crimson velvet cushion; and, last of all this grand procession, came THE KING AND THE QUEEN OF HEARTS.

Alice was rather doubtful whether she ought not to lie down on her face like the three gardeners, but she could not remember ever having heard of such a rule at processions; "and besides, what would be the use of a procession," thought she, "if people had all to lie down on their faces, so that they couldn't see it?" So she stood where she was, and waited.

When the procession came opposite to Alice, they all stopped and looked at her, and the Queen said, severely, "Who is this?" She said it to the Knave of Hearts, who only bowed and smiled in reply.

"Idiot!" said the Queen, tossing her head impatiently; and, turning to Alice, she went on: "What's your name, child?" "My name is Alice, so please your Majesty," said Alice very politely; but she added, to herself, "Why, they're only a pack of cards, after all. I needn't be afraid of them!" "And who are these!" said the Queen, pointing to the three gardeners who were lying round the rose-tree; for, you see, as they were lying on their faces, and the pattern on their backs was the same as the rest of the pack, she could not tell whether they were gardeners, or soldiers, or courtiers, or three of her own children.

"How should I know?" said Alice, surprised at her own courage. "It's no business of mine." The Queen turned crimson with fury, and, after glaring at her for a moment like a wild beast, began screaming, "Off with her head! Off with—" "Nonsense!" said Alice, very loudly and decidedly, and the Queen was silent.

The King laid his hand upon her arm, and timidly said, "Consider, my dear:

she is only a child!" The Queen turned angrily away from him and said to the Knave, "Turn them over!" The Knave did so, very carefully, with one foot.

"Get up!" said the Queen in a shrill, loud voice, and the three gardeners instantly jumped up and began bowing to the King, the Queen, the royal children, and everybody else.

"Leave off that!" screamed the Queen. "You make me giddy." And then, turning to the rose-tree, she went on, "What have you been doing here?" "May it please your Majesty," said Two, in a very humble tone, going down on one knee as he spoke, "we were trying—" "I see!" said the Queen, who had meanwhile been examining the roses. "Off with their heads!" And the procession moved on, three of the soldiers remaining behind to execute the unfortunate gardeners, who ran to Alice for protection.

"You sha'n't be beheaded!" said Alice, and she put them into a large flowerpot that stood near. The three soldiers wandered about for a minute or two, looking for them, and then quietly marched off after the others.

"Are their heads off?" shouted the Queen.

"Their heads are gone, if it please your Majesty!" the soldiers shouted in reply.

"That's right!" shouted the Queen. "Can you play croquet?" The soldiers were silent and looked at Alice, as the question was evidently meant for her.

"Yes!" shouted Alice.

"Come on, then!" roared the Queen, and Alice joined the procession, wondering very much what would happen next.

"It's— it's a very fine day!" said a timid voice at her side. She was walking by the White Rabbit, who was peeping anxiously into her face.

"Very," said Alice. "Where's the Duchess?" "Hush! Hush!" said the Rabbit in a low, hurried tone. He looked anxiously over his shoulder as he spoke, and then raised himself upon tiptoe, put his mouth close to her ear, and whispered "She's under sentence of execution." "What for?" said Alice.

"Did you say 'What a pity!'?" the Rabbit asked.

"No, I didn't," said Alice. "I don't think it's at all a pity. I said 'What for?'"

"She boxed the Queen's ears—" the Rabbit began. Alice gave a little scream of laughter. "Oh, hush!" the Rabbit whispered in a frightened tone. "The Queen will hear you! You see she came rather late, and the Queen said—" "Get to your places!" shouted the Queen in a voice of thunder, and people began running about in all directions, tumbling up against each other; however, they got settled down in a minute or two, and the game began.

Alice thought she had never seen such a curious croquet-ground in her life; it was all ridges and furrows: the croquet balls were live hedgehogs, and the mallets live flamingoes, and the soldiers had to double themselves up and stand on their hands and feet, to make the arches.

The chief difficulty Alice found at first was in managing her flamingo: she succeeded in getting its body tucked away, comfortably enough, under her arm, with its legs hanging down, but generally, just as she had got its neck nicely straightened out, and was going to give the hedgehog a blow with its head, it would twist itself round and look up in her face, with such a puzzled expression that she could not help bursting out laughing; and, when she had got its head down, and was going to begin again, it was very provoking to find that the hedgehog had unrolled itself, and was in the act of crawling away: besides all this, there was generally a ridge or a furrow in the way wherever she wanted to send the hedgehog to, and, as the doubled-up soldiers were always getting up and walking off to other parts of the ground, Alice soon came to the conclusion that it was a very difficult game indeed.

The players all played at once, without waiting for turns, quarreling all the while, and fighting for the hedgehogs; and in a very short time the Queen was in a furious passion, and went stamping about, and shouting "Off with his head!" or "Off with her head!" about once in a minute.

Alice began to feel very uneasy: to be sure, she had not as yet had any dispute with the Queen, but she knew that it might happen any minute, "and then," thought she, "what would become of me? They're dreadfully fond of beheading people here: the great wonder is, that there's anyone left alive!" She was looking about for some way of escape, and wondering whether she could get away without being seen, when she noticed a curious appearance in the air: it puzzled her very much at first, but after watching it a minute or two she made it out to be a grin, and she said to herself "It's the Cheshire-Cat: now I shall have somebody to talk to." "How are you getting on?" said the Cat, as soon as there was mouth enough for it to speak with.

Alice waited till the eyes appeared, and then nodded. "It's no use speaking to it," she thought, "till its ears have come, or at least one of them." In another minute the whole head appeared, and then Alice put down her flamingo, and began an account of the game, feeling very glad she had someone to listen to her. The Cat seemed to think that there was enough of it now in sight, and no more of it appeared.

"I don't think they play at all fairly," Alice began, in rather a complaining tone, "and they all quarrel so dreadfully one can't hear oneself speak— and they don't seem to have any rules in particular: at least, if there are, nobody attends to them— and you've no idea how confusing it is all the things being alive: for instance, there's the arch I've got to go through next walking about at the other end of the ground— and I should have croqueted the Queen's hedgehog just now, only it ran away when it saw mine coming!" "How do you like the Queen?" said the Cat in a low voice.

"Not at all," said Alice: "she's so extremely—" Just then she noticed that the Queen was close behind her, listening: so she went on "—likely to win, that it's hardly worthwhile finishing the game." The Queen smiled and passed on.

"Who are you talking to?" said the King, coming up to Alice, and looking at the Cat's head with great curiosity.

"It's a friend of mine— a Cheshire-Cat," said Alice: "allow me to introduce it." "I don't like the look of it at all," said the King: "however, it may kiss my hand, if it likes." "I'd rather not," the Cat remarked.

"Don't be impertinent," said the King, "and don't look at me like that!" He got behind Alice as he spoke.

"A cat may look at a king," said Alice. "I've read that in some book, but I don't remember where." "Well, it must be removed," said the King very decidedly; and he called to the Queen, who was passing at the moment, "My dear! I wish you would have this Cat removed!" The Queen had only one way of settling all difficulties, great or small. "Off with his head!" she said without even looking around.

"I'll fetch the executioner myself," said the King eagerly, and he hurried off.

Alice thought she might as well go back and see how the game was going on, as she heard the Queen's voice in the distance, screaming with passion. She had already heard her sentence three of the players to be executed for having missed their turns, and she did not like the look of things at all, as the game was in such confusion that she never knew whether it was her turn or not. So she went off in search of her hedgehog.

The hedgehog was engaged in a fight with another hedgehog, which seemed to Alice an excellent opportunity for croqueting one of them with the other: the only difficulty was, that her flamingo was gone across the other side of the garden, where Alice could see it trying in a helpless sort of way to fly up into a tree.

By the time she had caught the flamingo and brought it back, the fight was over, and both the hedgehogs were out of sight: "but it doesn't matter much," thought Alice, "as all the arches are gone from this side of the ground." So she tucked it away under her arm, that it might not escape again, and went back to have a little more conversation with her friend.

When she got back to the Cheshire-Cat, she was surprised to find quite a large crowd collected round it; there was a dispute going on between the executioner, the King, and the Queen, who were all talking at once, while all the rest were quite silent, and looked very uncomfortable.

The moment Alice appeared, she was appealed to by all three to settle the question, and they repeated their arguments to her, though, as they all spoke at once, she found it very hard to make out exactly what they said.

The executioner's argument was that you couldn't cut off a head unless there was a body to cut it off from: that he had never had to do such a thing before, and he wasn't going to begin at his time of life.

The King's argument was that anything that had a head could be beheaded, and that you were not to talk nonsense.

The Queen's argument was that if something wasn't done about it in less than no time, she'd have everybody executed, all round. (It was this last remark that had made the whole party look so grave and anxious.) Alice could think of nothing else to say but "It belongs to the Duchess: you'd better ask her about it." "She's in prison," the Queen said to the executioner: "fetch her here." And the executioner went off like an arrow.

The Cat's head began fading away the moment he was gone, and, by the time he had come back with the Duchess, it had entirely disappeared: so the King and the executioner ran wildly up and down, looking for it, while the rest of the party went back to the game.

Give the best answer or explanation for each of the following the questions.

3.146 What are the gardeners painting and why?
_____

3.147 How are the Queen's soldiers shaped?
_____

3.148 What game does the Queen ask Alice to play?
_____

3.149 What is different about the croquet-ground?
_____

3.150 Why is Alice afraid of the Queen?
_____

3.151 To whom does Alice talk in the air?
_____

3.152 Why does Alice become frustrated with the game?
_____

3.153 How does the Queen deal with any difficulties that she comes up against?
_____

Before you take this last Self Test, you might want to do one or more of the following self checks.

1. _____ Read the objectives. Determine if you can do them.

2. _____ Restudy the material related to any objectives that you cannot do.

3. _____ Use the **SQ3R** study procedure to review the material:

   a. **S**can the sections.
   b. **Q**uestion yourself again (review the questions you wrote initially).
   c. **R**ead to answer your questions.
   d. **R**ecite the answers to yourself.
   e. **R**eview areas you didn't understand.

4. _____ Review all vocabulary, activities, and Self Tests, writing a correct answer for each answer that you got wrong.

SELF TEST 3

Answer *true* **or** *false* **for each of the following statements** (each answer, 1 point).

3.01 _____ The main target of Jane Austen's satire was the religious controversies of the day.

3.02 _____ In Shelley's "Ode to the West Wind," the West Wind is called the "Destroyer and preserver" because it destroys that which is dead and preserves new life.

3.03 _____ In *Don Juan*, Byron says that it is a pity that pleasure is a sin and sin is pleasurable.

3.04 _____ According to Keats's poem "Ode on a Grecian Urn," the only thing that we need to know is that "Beauty is truth, truth beauty."

3.05 _____ England experienced dynamic changes in the realms of politics, economics, and religion during the Victorian era.

3.06 _____ Charles Darwin's theory of evolution caused many people to doubt all traditional beliefs about mankind and society.

3.07 _____ Evangelicals were influential in the abolition of slavery and the enactment of child labor laws.

3.08 _____ The Oxford Movement emphasized the rituals and traditions of the Church of England.

3.09 _____ Writers of the Victorian period wrote only to entertain their readers.

3.010 _____ Charles Dickens's thoughts on religion, science, politics, and history were immeasurably influential on his contemporaries.

3.011 _____ The art for art's sake theorists believed that experience was the source of meaning.

3.012 _____ In opposition to the Oxford Movement, Newman published *Tracts for the Times*.

3.013 _____ *Apologia pro Vita Sua* is the autobiographical account of Newman's spiritual quest for certainty, which he eventually found in the traditions and rituals of the Church of England.

3.014 _____ Newman's liberal ideas encouraged the spread of secularism in Victorian society.

Underline the correct answer in each of the following statements (each answer, 4 points).

3.015 In 1833 Thomas Carlyle published a philosophical satire titled (*The French Revolution*, *On Heroes, Hero-Worship*, *Sartor Resartus*) outlining his spiritual idealism.

3.016 Carlyle's histories contend that the basis for strong, stable societies is (strong leaders, intelligent voters, God-fearing people).

3.017 Carlyle was known to his contemporaries as the ("Sage of Chelsea," "Vicar of London," "Dictator of Westminster").

3.018 In 1857 at the encouragement of Lewes, George Eliot published (*Middlemarch*, *Silas Marner*, *Scenes from Clerical Life*) in *Blackwood's Magazine*.

3.019 Eliot's belief in moral progress was influenced by (higher criticism, evolution, Utilitarianism, evangelicalism).

Circle the letter of the line that best answers each of the following questions (each answer, 1 point).

3.020 In Eliot's novel *The Mill on the Floss*, what is the basis of the community's moral standards?

    a. custom passed down from one generation to the next
    b. the Word of God
    c. church creeds
    d. individual desires

3.021 Because of their beliefs, the lives of the Tullivers and Dodsons, from *The Mill on the Floss*, are characterized by:

    a. freedom.
    b. beauty and truth.
    c. oppressive narrowness.
    d. greatness and nobility.

3.022 According to *Apologia Pro Vita Sua*, why did John Newman not experience any difficulty in believing the Catholic doctrine of transubstantiation?

    a. The Word of God affirms this doctrine.
    b. The Roman Catholic Church said it was true.
    c. He had really believed it all along.
    d. In his heart he knew it to be true.

3.023 Newman compares the doctrine of transubstantiation to that of the Trinity because:

    a. he is trying to establish the point that some religious doctrines cannot be explained intellectually although they are true.
    b. he believes that Thomas More invented both doctrines.
    c. he thinks that the doctrine of the Trinity is intellectually removed from doubt.
    d. both doctrines can be proven by philosophical means.

3.024 Who is Newman attempting to defend against the accusation of superstition and hypocrisy?

    a. Protestants
    b. the Roman Catholic Church
    c. evangelicals
    d. the Church of England

3.025 What did Carlyle's new faith for a secular society do?

    a. allowed for a sense of religious awe yet did not dictate a standard of morality
    b. called everyone to repentance according to the Scriptures
    c. held everyone accountable to a universal standard of right and wrong
    d. trusted in the powers of reason to point man to the truth

3.026 Carlyle's EVERLASTING YEA may be defined as:

    a. the God-like that is in Man.
    b. selfishness and conceit.
    c. hatred of all other beings.
    d. love of pleasure.

3.027 In *Sartor Resartus*, why does the professor say that Christianity in the nineteenth century is "lying in ruins, over grown with jungle?"

    a. It is the religion best suited for the modern man.
    b. It is useless now and needs to be replaced.
    c. It is teeming with life and vitality.
    d. It needs to be rebuilt.

3.028 The infalliability of the professor's Bible cannot be debated because:

    a. God speaks to him directly.
    b. everyone has agreed that it is correct.
    c. scholars have proven that his version is the most accurate.
    d. it is written in the original languages.

3.029 In the Prologue of *In Memoriam*, Tennyson explains the differences between:

    a. faith and knowledge.
    b. Protestantism and Roman Catholicism.
    c. happiness and grief.
    d. men and women.

3.030 In section 96 of *In Memoriam*, Tennyson excuses his doubt of orthodox Christianity by calling it:

    a. deceiving doubt.
    b. honest doubt.
    c. hurried doubt.
    d. rational doubt.

3.031 What is the stated purpose of the new branch of the United Pickwickians?

    a. to conduct scientific experiements
    b. to move to America and record accounts of its society
    c. to discuss relevant political matters
    d. to share accounts of their journeys and adventures

3.032 When Mr. Pickwick begins to speak to Mrs. Bardell privately, what does she assume Mr. Pickwick has asked her to do?

    a. marry his brother
    b. move out
    c. marry him
    d. find another job

3.033 According to lines 22–45 of "My Last Duchess," why was the duke so disgusted with the last duchess?

    a. She loved him more than anything else.
    b. She was shy.
    c. She rarely smiled at anyone.
    d. She did not value the good name that he had given her above anything else that she loved.

3.034 What is our only source of information about the duchess?

    a. the duchess herself

    b. the painting

    c. the duke

    d. the Count's messenger

3.035 According to lines 49–56, why has the count's servant come to the duke?

    a. To arrange another marriage

    b. To buy the painting of the duchess

    c. To purchase a sculptor

    d. To tell the duke of the duchess's whereabouts

Answer *true* **or** *false* **for each of the following statements** (each answer, 3 points).

3.036 _____ The Romantic Period of literature in England was inaugurated by the publication of *Songs of Experience* in 1798.

3.037 _____ In Wilde's play *The Importance of Being Earnest*, Algernon calls Jack a Bunburyist because he has invented an imaginary young brother called Earnest so that he may come into town when he likes.

3.038 _____ It is important to Gwendolen that the man she marry is named Earnest because the sound of the name produces just the right vibrations.

3.039 _____ In *Alice in Wonderland*, the croquet-ground is made up of living things that never seem to stay still.

3.040 _____ Alice becomes frustrated with the game because nobody will let her bend the rules to win.

3.041 _____ The Queen deals with any difficulty that she comes up against by crying.

Underline the correct answer in each of the following statements (each answer, 1 point).

3.042 As a boy, Charles Dickens was made to work in a (factory, mine, lawyer's office) when his father was imprisoned for (stealing, unpaid debts, murder).

3.043 Published in volume form in 1837, (*The Pickwick Papers, Sketches by Boz, David Copperfield*) was the first book to make Dickens a celebrity in England and America.

3.044 Dickens initially published many of his novels in the magazines in which he served as (illustrator, editor, owner).

3.045 In 1867–1868, Dickens traveled again to America to give (public readings of his works, speeches on slavery, free lectures on social issues).

3.046 After the death of (Arthur Hallam, Tennyson's father, Tennyson's wife) in 1832, Tennyson vowed not to publish any poetry for (ten, eight, two) years.

3.047 Written by Tennyson for his friend Hallam, (*Poems, In Memoriam, Le Morte d' Arthur*) is considered the greatest (elegy, novel, sonnet) in the English language.

3.048 In 1850 (Dickens, Shelley, Tennyson) was appointed poet laureate.

3.049 In addition to his children's stories, Carroll was a noted author of several treatises on (children's ministries, English literature, symbolic logic).

3.050 *Alice's Adventures in Wonderland* was first told to (three women friends, the three Liddell daughters, two boys).

Fill in each of the blanks using items from the following word list (each answer, 2 points).

Elizabeth Barrett	imagination	Aesthetic
The Importance of Being Earnest	Romantics	relativity
The Rime of the Ancient Mariner	Enlightenment	art
The Ring and the Book		

3.051 Byron's heroic figures were influential in shaping modern concepts of moral _____.

3.052 John Keats believed that _____ alone could elevate one's senses to the spiritual world.

3.053 Shelley believed in the redeeming power of the _____ to effect a golden age of society.

3.054 Intellectually, the Romantic Movement was based on the tenets of the _____.

3.055 The moral lesson of _____ is that spiritual blessings exist for those who love God's creation.

3.056 In 1846 Browning married _____ and moved with her to Italy.

3.057 The publication of _____ in 1868–1869, elevated Browning's reputation as a poet above that of Tennyson.

3.058 Browning's work favors the discordant, colloquial style of the _____.

3.059 Oscar Wilde was a leading advocate of the _____ movement, which was based on the school of art for art's sake.

3.060 First performed in 1895, _____ is considered Wilde's masterpiece.

For Thought and Discussion:

Explain to a parent or teacher Carlyle's criticism of Christianity. Be sure to mention that he did not argue against Christian doctrine directly. Rather, his criticism was of the appearance of its followers. Remember that Carlyle described Christianity as the "Worship of Sorrow" and Christians as "doleful." (During the nineteenth century, many people claimed to be Christians, but, in fact, many of them practiced a religion of tradition and ritual rather than a religion rooted in love for God and love for other people (cf. Matthew 22:37–40). As 2 Timothy 3:5 states, they gave an appearance of godliness, but they denied, through word and deed, the God who makes men godly.) Read Romans 2:17–24. Discuss how strict attention to tradition rather than God's Word causes people to curse the name of our Lord unnecessarily? What did Jesus have to say about the legalism of the Pharisees (cf. Matthew 23:23–28)?

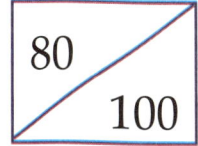

Score _____

Adult Check _____

Initial   Date

Before taking the LIFEPAC Test, you might want to do one or more of the following self checks.

1. _____ Read the objectives. Check to see if you can do them.

2. _____ Restudy the material related to any objectives that you cannot do.

3. _____ Use the **SQ3R** study procedure to review the material.

4. _____ Review activities, Self Tests, and LIFEPAC vocabulary words.

5. _____ Restudy areas of weakness indicated by the last Self Test.